Sophie de Grouchy self-portrait (circa 1786). © J.A. collection particulière.

Letters on Sympathy
(1798)

A Critical Edition

TRANSACTIONS
of the
AMERICAN PHILOSOPHICAL SOCIETY
Held at Philadelphia
For Promoting Useful Knowledge
Volume 98, Part 4

Sophie de Grouchy
Letters on Sympathy
(1798)

A Critical Edition

Karin Brown
James E. McClellan III

AMERICAN PHILOSOPHICAL SOCIETY
Philadelphia 2008

Copyright © 2008 by the American Philosophical Society for its *Transactions* series, Volume 98. All rights reserved.

ISBN-13: 978-1-60618-984-9

US ISSN: 0065-9746

Library of Congress Cataloging-in-Publication Data

Condorcet, Marie-Louise-Sophie de Grouchy, marquise de, 1764–1822.
  [Lettres sur la sympathie. English]
  Letters on sympathy (1798) : a critical edition / Sophie de Grouchy ; edited by Karen Brown ; letters translated by James E. McClellan III.
     p. cm. -- (Transactions of the American Philosophical Society held at Philadelphia for promoting useful knowledge ; v. 98, pt. 4)
  Includes bibliographical references and index.
  ISBN 978-1-60618-984-9
 1. Condorcet, Marie-Louise-Sophie de Grouchy, marquise de, 1764–1822--Correspondence. 2. Condorcet, Jean-Antoine-Nicolas de Caritat,
marquis de, 1743–1794. 3. France--Intellectual life--18th century--Sources.
 4. Statesmen's spouses--France--Correspondence. 5. Revolutionaries--France--Correspondence. 6. Intellectuals--France--Correspondence. 7. Love-letters--France.
 8. France--History--Revolution, 1789–1799. I. Brown, Karen, 1962– II. McClellan, James E. (James Edward), 1946– III. Title.

DC146.C7A4 2008
944.04092--dc22
[B]
                                                              2008041672

Contents

Preface & Acknowledgments   vii

Introduction: The Letters,
Their Author, and Her Times   xi

    THE EDUCATION OF SOPHIE DE GROUCHY   xix
    THE ENLIGHTENMENT BACKGROUND   xxii
    MADAME AND MONSIEUR CONDORCET IN THE
       REVOLUTION   xxv
    THE DIRECTORY, THE IDÉOLOGUES, AND
       NAPOLEON   xxviii
    CONTEMPORARY WIDOWS, WRITERS, AND
       FEMINISTS   xxxiv

Part I   THE PHILOSOPHY OF SOPHIE
        DE GROUCHY   1

    1. ON SYMPATHY   3
       Smith and De Grouchy on the
          Origin of Sympathy   3
       De Grouchy's Empiricism   5
       The Role of Pain in de Grouchy and Smith   9

    The Role of Sympathy in de Grouchy
        and Smith   11
  2. REASON AND SENTIMENTS   19
    The Debate Concerning Reason and
        Sentiments as Basis for Morality   19
    Moral Emotions   22
    Reason and Sentiments   28
  3. SOCIAL AND POLITICAL PHILOSOPHY   35
    Self-Interest, Selfishness, and Helping
        Others   35
    Justice and Beneficence   47
    Inequality, Poverty, and Redistribution   48
  4. MORALITY AND HAPPINESS   59
    Love and Happiness   59
    Ethics and Psychology   62
  5. SOPHIE DE GROUCHY AND
    FEMINIST ETHICS   67
    Caring and the Origin of Morality   68
    Criticism of Liberalism in Moral and
        Political Theory   70
    Integrating Reason and Emotions   76
    Experience and Impartiality   79
    Effect on Political Theory: The Private-
        Public Dichotomy and Social Reform   88
    Sympathy and Feminism   94

Part II   LETTERS ON SYMPATHY (1798)   99

Translator's Preface   101
  LETTER I   107
  LETTER II   115
  LETTER III   123
  LETTER IV   133
  LETTER V   147
  LETTER VI   157
  LETTER VII   167
  LETTER VIII   175

Bibliography   185

Index   193

Preface & Acknowledgments

In 1798 in Paris Marie-Louise-Sophie de Grouchy (1764-1822), the former Marquise de Condorcet, published her translation into French of Adam Smith's *The Theory of Moral Sentiments*.[1] Her translation appeared in two volumes, and she appended eight *Letters on Sympathy* (*Lettres sur la sympathie*) to the second volume. Smith's *Theory of Moral Sentiments* first appeared in 1759; Sophie de Grouchy translated the sixth and last edition of 1790. The translation and the *Letters* were published by F. Buisson, a printer-bookseller. The *Letters* present her views as a moral theorist on the philosophical issues raised by Smith.

The volume at hand presents a critical edition and the first English translation of Sophie de Grouchy's *Letters on Sympathy*. The Introduction that follows, written collaboratively by the

---

1. Sophie de Grouchy is referred to in various ways: Sophie de Grouchy, Sophie de Condorcet, Mme de Condorcet, the Marquise de Condorcet, or "veuve" (the widow) Condorcet. She published the Letters as "S. Grouchy Ve. Condorcet." Because she used her maiden name in the publication, because in France the custom is for married women to keep their maiden names for legal purposes, and above all because we prefer to avoid the patriarchal subordination to her husband, she will be referred to in this book as Sophie de Grouchy.

two of us, more fully describes Sophie de Grouchy's *Letters*, its author, and the context of the times. We aim to show why these *Letters* are of interest and why they and their author merit a wider audience in English.

The *Letters*, however, do not stand on their own. They were not intended for separate publication, and de Grouchy assumes that the reader is familiar with Smith's work preceding the *Letters*. Thus, in order to be fully understood, the *Letters* need to be considered vis-à-vis Smith and what he writes in the *Theory of Moral Sentiments*. Therefore Part I, entirely the work of Professor Brown, first lays out the philosophical issues in Sophie de Grouchy's conversation with Smith and the underlying philosophical thematics of the *Letters*. We concur on seeing Sophie de Grouchy as a philosopher and an original thinker, and Part I seeks to capture her originality, not only in comparing her to Smith, but also as someone who foreshadowed contemporary feminist ethics in powerful and surprising ways. The *Letters* themselves appear in English in Part II of this work, translated by Professor McClellan.

We are grateful to the American Philosophical Society for publishing this work, and we wholeheartedly thank Ms. Mary C. McDonald, Editor, for recognizing that Sophie de Grouchy's *Letters* deserve a critical edition in English and for supporting us in this enterprise. We are indebted to several referees, first at the University of Chicago Press and then through the APS Library committee, for their critical insights that have resulted in significant improvements in this presentation. In particular we would like to express our gratitude to Professor Rita Manning, Dr. Sue Weinberg, and Professor Deidre Dawson for their very helpful comments and suggestions for improving this work.

Karin Brown warmly acknowledges Professor Virginia Held for all her help and support throughout the years, from the beginning of this project as a dissertation to its current state. Professor Held remained involved through the various changes and additions. Brown would also like to thank Eileen O'Neil, who first informed her of de Grouchy's *Letters*, and Maxime LaFantasie at the Fales Library and Special Collections at New York University, who provided access to this rare book. Brown expresses her gratitude to Eliane Golay, her French teacher, who helped with the initial reading and interpretation of the *Letters*. Brown thanks Barbara Edwards for her editorial assistance and Michael Chang for his help and comments. She is also pleased to acknowledge the significant contributions of Dr. Julie Zilberberg, who was very active in formulating the initial proposal for this project and who began the translation. Brown would also like to thank Bernard Roy who contributed to this project by translating the third letter, and Olivier Serafinowicz and Alice Craven who initially provided a translation of the eight letters. Brown is also grateful to Carol Gould for her encouragement and support of this project.

We both have to thank Professor Jean-Paul de Lagrave of the Université de Québec, whose scholarly work and personal interventions at a late stage contributed immeasurably to the solidity of the present study. Similarly, we are delighted to acknowledge Madeleine Arnold-Tétard, not only for her appealing 2003 biography of Sophie de Grouchy but also for her hospitality in hosting us at Sophie de Grouchy's residence at Meulan outside of Paris. We also thank Professor Norman Scofield for the invitation to present some of this material recently to the Center in Political Economy of Washington University in Saint Louis and for the critical response of his group.

Introduction:
The Letters, Their Author, and Her Times

Sophie de Grouchy's *Letters on Sympathy (Lettres sur la sympathie)* appeared in 1798 as an appendix to her translation of Adam Smith's *Theory of Moral Sentiments* (henceforth *TMS*). Smith, the economist and author of *The Wealth of Nations* (1776), published the first edition of *The Theory of Moral Sentiments* almost four decades earlier in 1759. The *TMS* appeared in six English editions, the last one translated by Sophie de Grouchy in 1790.[1] De Grouchy's was the third translation of the *Theory of Moral Sentiments* into French. A first French translation appeared in 1764 by one M.-A. Eidous, and the second in 1774–5 by the abbé Blavet. These earlier translations were considered mediocre, while Sophie de Grouchy's was well received. It remained the standard translation in French for two centuries, from when it appeared in 1798 through three further editions and reprints in 1830, 1860 and 1982. A new French translation from the English original of Smith appeared in 1999.[2]

---

1. The title page announces the work as "Traduit de l'Anglais, sur la septième et dernière Édition." There seems not to have been a formal seventh edition, but apparently notes for a seventh edition of the *TMS* did find their way into de Grouchy's translation; see Forget (2001), (2003) at n.2.

THÉORIE
DES
SENTIMENS MORAUX,
OU
ESSAI ANALYTIQUE

Sur les Principes des Jugemens que portent naturellement les Hommes, d'abord sur les Actions des autres, et ensuite sur leurs propres Actions:

Suivi d'une Dissertation sur l'Origine des Langues;

PAR ADAM SMITH;

Traduit de l'Anglais, sur la septième et dernière Édition,

PAR S. GROUCHY V^e. CONDORCET.

Elle y a joint huit Lettres sur la Sympathie.

A PARIS,

Chez F. BUISSON, Imprim.-Lib., rue Hautefeuille, n°. 20.

AN 6 DE LA RÉPUBLIQUE, (1798.)

FIG. 1-1. Théorie des Sentiments Moraux, Title page of the de Grouchy translation (1798).

Sophie de Grouchy merits our attention not merely as the translator or publicist of Adam Smith, but for her scholarly and philosophical contributions expressed in the appended *Letters on Sympathy*. The *Letters* served as a means to engage Smith and her own contemporaries in reexamining the philosophical and ethical issues Smith treated in his *Theory of Moral Sentiments*. As we will see, she was critical of Smith and developed her own substantive views concerning sympathy. This she effected with an original turn, by appending the *Letters* to her translation. The *Letters* are thought to be written nominally to her brother-in-law, the Idéologue physician P.-J.-G.-Cabanis.[3] The *Letters on Sympathy* contain ideas both in moral and political theory. The first six of these *Letters* concern the disposition of sympathy, and they represent the considered responses of Sophie de Grouchy to Smith's views on the origin and nature of moral behavior. The last two of the appended *Letters* present her social and political views. Given that she and Smith culminated the substantial Enlightenment debate over how to ground ethics and morality make these *Letters* still worthy of consideration today. In addition, the *Letters* are of interest for what they reveal of Sophie de Grouchy as a contemporary feminist and for the light they can shed on the Idéologue movement, and on the work of the Marquis de Condorcet and his famous *Sketch of the Progress of the Human Mind* (1794).

Sophie de Grouchy was well known in her day as the young wife of the Marquis de Condorcet and as an independent thinker in her own right. The Marquis de Condorcet was one of the giants of the Enlightenment, and the pre-Revolutionary salon she maintained with him at the French Mint along the banks

---

2. The new translation is by Michaël Biziou, Claude Gautier, and Jean-François Pradeau, editors and translators. *Théorie des sentiments moraux d'Adam Smith*. Paris: Presses Universitaires de France, 1999. They produced a second edition [Adam Smith. *Théorie des sentiments moraux*, texte traduit, introduit et annoté par Michaël Biziou, Claude Gautier, Jean-François Pradeau, Édition révisée. Paris: Quadrige/PUF] in 2003.
3. The *Letters* are addressed to mon cher "C***," who was taken to be Cabanis until Lagrave (1994, p. 67n) argued that C*** might also have been Condorcet himself. Arnold-Tétard believes the Letters were written to Condorcet as well. Lynn McDonald argues that in correspondence de Grouchy used the designation "GC" for herself and "C" for Condorcet (1998, p. 125). Not everyone agrees—Dawson (1991, p. 158) and Forget (2001, p.2) claim that the *Letters* were written to Cabanis. Forget argues that Cabanis was an expert on the physiology of sympathy and the *Letters* were written after Condorcet's death.

of the Seine welcomed some of Europe's leading thinkers and intellectuals, including Smith.[4] Therefore, it is no surprise that Sophie de Grouchy and her *Letters on Sympathy* have never been lost from sight in French-language literature. The *Letters* were republished in the 1830 and 1860 editions of her translation of Smith's *Theory of Moral Sentiments*.[5] In 1994 Professor Jean-Paul de Lagrave issued a new and accessible modern edition of the *Letters*. French biographical studies of Sophie de Grouchy of varying quality have succeeded one another since the later nineteenth century. Thierry Boissel in his 1988 biography, *Sophie de Condorcet: Femme des Lumières*, lists works in French dealing with her directly that date from 1887, 1889, 1897, 1933, 1950, 1984, and 1987. Jean-Paul de Lagrave in his edition of the *Lettres sur la sympathie* of 1994 adds others from 1897, 1904, 1913, 1922, 1928, 1940, 1943, and 1983.[6] Notable among these are the Antoine Guillois 1897 biography, *La marquise de Condorcet; sa Famille, son Salon, ses Amis (1764–1822)*, as well as the attention de Grouchy and her salon received at the hands of the great historian of the French Revolution, Jules Michelet.[7] Professor Lagrave's modern edition of the *Letters* is itself a milestone in this literature, and Lagrave has contributed greatly in directing scholarly and popularly attention to Sophie de Grouchy before primarily a francophone audience.[8] The appearance in 2003 of yet another biography in French by Madeleine Arnold-Tétard testifies to Sophie de Grouchy's enduring place and reputation in the francophone world and to her comparative invisibility in the literature in English.[9]

Thierry Boissel's study aptly places Sophie de Grouchy among the luminaries of the Enlightenment. It is surprising that Sophie de Grouchy has, until just recently, remained virtually unknown in the world of Anglo-American philosophy and history, even

---

4. On Smith's attendance at the salon of the Marquis and Marquise de Condorcet, see Badinter and Badinter, p. 217; Boissel, p. 103; Dawson (1991), p. 158.
5. The *Letters* were omitted in the subsequent 1982 reprint of the 1860 edition of the translation; see bibliography.
6. See Boissel, p. 294 ("Bibliographie: I. Sur Sophie de Condorcet"); Lagrave (1994), pp. 275–78 ("Biographies et notices biographiques").
7. See references in Boissel, p. 294; Lagrave (1994), p. 278.
8. See Lagrave (1994) and works listed in his bibliography, p. 277. See testimony by Alain Pons to Lagrave's contributions to keeping Sophie de Grouchy in the eye of scholarship and the public, in Lagrave (1994), pp. 7–8.
9. Madeleine Arnold-Tétard. *Sophie de Grouchy, marquise de Condorcet: Dame du coeur*. Paris: Éditions Christian, 2003.

as the wife of the great Marquis. The fact that she took part in Enlightenment thought at the end of the eighteenth century and that she herself was a contributor to contemporary philosophical discussions concerning ethics and morality still largely draws blanks even from historical experts and philosophical specialists who might be likely to know of Sophie de Grouchy.

Sophie de Grouchy has been ignored in different ways by different communities of scholars who do not seem to know of her work or how to incorporate it into their scholarship. The first of these areas is scholarship concerning Smith. Obviously, Sophie de Grouchy should be included as standard reference, not least because she was the translator of a standard French edition of the *TMS* through which French readers have encountered Smith for two hundred years. Unfortunately, this is not the case, and there is essentially no mention of the *Letters* in any secondary literature concerning the TMS! In the otherwise extensive and authoritative 1995 biography of Smith by Ian Simpson Ross, *The Life of Adam Smith*, there is only a brief reference to Sophie de Grouchy that acknowledges her translation of Smith ("said to be the best available in her language"), but not the *Letters*.[10] Sophie de Grouchy's *Letters* provide a substantial and thoughtful contemporary French reaction to *TMS*, and they are a resource for understanding Smith that should be a commonplace. Yet, to take another example, the collection of documents complied by John Reeder, *On Moral Sentiments: Contemporary Responses to Adam Smith* (1997), Sophie de Grouchy and her *Letters* are not included, despite the fact that Reeder's "contemporary" responses run through 1881.[11]

The second of these scholarly areas where Sophie de Grouchy is missing is the history of women philosophers. In recent years historians and philosophers have been making concentrated and extensive efforts to republish works by women that have been ignored in the standard history of philosophy. Much research has been devoted to this cause in order to bring back the voice of women to philosophy and to correct the injustice of a sexist canon. The outcome of this enterprise is that philosophers and historians have found numerous works by women to be incorporated into philosophy and the history of ideas. Yet, Sophie de Grouchy and her contributions are essentially

---
10. Ross, p. 363.
11. See Reeder.

invisible in this literature, too. To share with the reader one's surprise at the absence of Sophie de Grouchy's work from this movement, consider her omission from the seminal four-volume work edited by Mary Ellen Waithe, *A History of Women Philosophers* (1991). To take another example, Noel Hutchings and William D. Rumsey, editors of *The Collaborative Bibliography of Women in Philosophy* (1997), apply a broad definition of philosophy ("Citing fine works by women in all areas of philosophy from ancient times to the present") in its more than 11,000 entries, but there is no mention of Sophie de Grouchy in this otherwise remarkable compilation.[12] The list of works in this category of women in philosophy could easily be expanded without changing the conclusion concerning the invisibility of Sophie de Grouchy and her moral philosophy.[13]

The third area in which Sophie de Grouchy is overlooked is Enlightenment scholarship. The *Letters* are certainly a notable, if overlooked Enlightenment text. But more specifically, there is significant recent interest in sympathy and sensibility in the literature of the eighteenth century, and Sophie de Grouchy is the one contemporary woman philosopher who thought and wrote critically about sympathy. An example of recent interest in Enlightenment and sensibility is the book published in 2002 by Jessica Riskin, *Science in the Age of Sensibility: The Sentimental Empiricism of the French Enlightenment*. This otherwise informed and eye-opening scholarly reinterpretation of the role of sentiment in late-eighteenth century thought is unaware of Sophie de Grouchy or her contributions.

Given Sophie de Grouchy's invisibility in these scholarly areas, it would be unrealistic to expect that yet another literature, the burgeoning philosophical literature concerning the ethics of care, should have noted Sophie de Grouchy and what she has to say to this community and its interests. Yet, as we will see in the concluding chapter of Part I, her voice needs to be heard here, too.

---

12. Hutchings and Rumsey (1997).
13. Along these lines, see also, for example, Else M. Barth, *Women Philosophers, A Bibliography of Books through 1990*; Ethel M. Kersey, *Women Philosophers: A Bio-Critical Source Book*; McAlister, Linda Lopez, ed., *Hypathia's Daughters: Fifteen Hundred Years of Woman Philosophers;* Mary Warnock, ed, *Women Philosophers*; Catherine Villanueva Gardner, *Women Philosophers: Genre and the Boundaries of Philosophy*; Therese Boos Dykeman, ed., *The Neglected Canon: Nine Women Philosophers, First to the Twentieth Century.*

Even though Sophie de Grouchy has not received the attention or credit she deserves, it is no longer true that she is entirely unknown to scholars writing in English. In fact, there has been a recent upsurge of attention recently to Sophie de Grouchy and her *Letters* by scholars from various disciplines. This interest in de Grouchy seems to have sprung up spontaneously in several quarters. Diedre Dawson, a professor of French at Michigan State University, published a pioneering article in 1991, "Is Sympathy so Surprising? Adam Smith and French Fiction of Sympathy," and in 2004 she contributed an article "From Moral Philosophy to Public Policy: Sophie de Grouchy's Translation and Critique of Smith's *Theory of Moral Sentiments*."[14] In the former Dawson provides an excellent summary of Sophie de Grouchy's views of sympathy and their place in moral development; in the latter she explores de Grouchy and the *Letters* more closely, anticipating several of the points developed below. Karin Brown's 1997 thesis and her 2000 "Madame de Condorcet's Letters on Sympathy" were early contributions in English, these from a philosopher. Lynn McDonald, a professor of sociology at the University of Guelph, published a book titled *Women Theorists on Society and Politics* (1998), where she includes a brief presentation of the *Letters* along with several quotations.[15] Evelyn L. Forget, an economist at the University of Manitoba, is another scholar who has contributed to scholarship on Sophie de Grouchy and the *Letters*. In her 2001/2003 "Cultivating Sympathy: Sophie Condorcet's Letters on Sympathy," Professor Forget provides a cogent analysis of the *Letters* and their author's thought.[16] From yet another quarter, in 2003 Laura Schattschneider from New York University Law School and a Mellon Fellow at UCLA's Clark Center for 17th- & 18th-Century Studies published a short, but clear exposition of Smith and de Grouchy.[17] In 2004 Dawson and colleagues Marc-André Bernier and Thierry Belleguic, professors of French at the Université de Québec and Laval University respectively, organized an English-language colloquium dedicated to Sophie de Grouchy at a meeting of the Canadian Society for Eighteenth-Century Studies, and a volume of studies based on their work together is forthcoming.[18] Edith Kuiper, a researcher in the Department of Economics and

---

14. Dawson (1991), (2004).
15. McDonald, 1998.
16. Forget (2001) and (2003a); see also her (2003b).
17. Schattschneider (2003).

Econometrics at the University of Amsterdam, contributed the article "Adam Smith and his Feminist Contemporaries," where she refers the reader to Forget's work on de Grouchy.[19]

Deidre Dawson writes: "An English translation of *Lettres sur la sympathie* is long overdue, for Sophie de Grouchy's work is important not only for its impact on the reception of Smith's book in France, but also because it contributes a major contribution to moral philosophy in its own right."[20] We hope that the present edition of the *Letters* in English will add to this developing and overdue attention to Sophie de Grouchy and her *Letters on Sympathy*. Even with the increased attention, the precise lines of de Grouchy's thinking, particularly vis-à-vis Smith, have yet to be enumerated in full, and for that reason Part I ("The Philosophy of Sophie de Grouchy") explores the course of her thought in detail as the basis for understanding the *Letters*. The *Letters* themselves follow in Part II. We publish them here for the first time in English first and foremost because they are simply not available in English. On looking into them, readers will discover an author and a thinker on par with Smith as someone seeking to analyze serious social and moral issues of the day. In the end it is their content and what they have to tell us substantively that make Sophie de Grouchy's *Letters on Sympathy* worthy of wider consideration and this translation into English. Part of the beauty of the *Letters* is the variety of ways in which they can be read. In coming to grips with the *Letters* we hope readers will discover on their own the various and subtle points espoused by this remarkable late eighteenth-century thinker.

The present introduction continues with a short biography of Sophie de Grouchy and a brief description of the broader intellectual context out of which she emerged and in which her work needs to be set. Subsequent chapters by Professor Brown in Part I explore the particulars of Adam Smith's view given in his *Theory of Moral Sentiments* and Sophie de Grouchy's broader considerations. The chapters are arranged following the structure of the arguments in the *Letters*. Thus chapter one begins where de Grouchy begins, with the question of the origin and nature of sympathy. In looking at both Smith's and de Grouchy's work one can see the ways in which their significantly differ-

---

18. See details at the CSECS/SCEDHS website: http://www.c18.org/scedhs/London2004.html. Dawson, personal communication.
19. Montes and Schliesser, 2006.
20. Dawson, 2004.

ent views result from very different accounts of the origin of sympathy. Chapter Two of Part I is concerned with reason and sentiments, Chapter Three with social and political philosophy, and Chapter Four with morality and happiness. These chapters show not only the differences between Smith and de Grouchy, but also the way in which their different accounts of the origin of sympathy shaped these differences. The final chapter in Part I presents de Grouchy as a feminist philosopher through a comparison of the *Letters* and contemporary theories of ethics of care. Before all that and the *Letters* themselves, however, readers should first be introduced to the remarkable author of the *Letters on Sympathy* and be reminded of circumstances in Old-Regime France out of which she and the *Letters* emerged.

The Education of Sophie de Grouchy

Sophie de Grouchy was born a noblewoman in 1764 into an established, but largely unexceptional family of the French parlementary nobility (the nobility of the robe) just as France began to recover from its losses in the Seven Years War.[21] She had two younger siblings, a sister (Charlotte) and a brother (Henri-François). This noble background imprinted itself strongly on Sophie de Grouchy and on her career. Most immediately, while still broadly conservative, her social origins in the parlementary nobility were tempered with strong doses of literacy, education and liberalism. This orientation sharply distinguished her from other young women out of the upper aristocracy and families of the nobility of the sword. As much as this background of culture and education conditioned the young Sophie de Grouchy and her world, her sensibilities would later turn radical and egalitarian.

Sophie de Grouchy's mother, Marie-Gilberte-Henriette Fréteau, took a keen direct interest in the education of her children, and Sophie received a well-rounded basic education. Sophie was a bright and talented child, reading and writing by the age of six. At the age of eleven in 1775 she nearly died from smallpox, but she recovered without severe scarring to become a notably beautiful woman. In addition to her academic studies, Sophie de Grouchy received painting lessons from Marie-Anne-Élisabeth Vigée-Lebrun (a talented and famous painter herself)

---

21. This account is drawn from Guillois, Boissel, and Arnold-Tétard.

who apparently thought young Sophie was gifted. At another point in her life her skills as an artist would save her life.

Common for a family such as the de Grouchys and given her mother's staunch Catholicism, in 1784 Sophie was sent off to a convent, Neuville-les-Dames-en-Bresse. She went, not to become a nun, but as a pensionner to polish her religious sensibilities and noble manners, as well as to keep her off the marriage market for a while. Sending a young noble or rich bourgeois woman to a religious order was customary at that time, but the priory at Neuville-en-Bresse was a very elite one. It was exclusively for nobles, and one had to prove nobility in order to be admitted. It was very costly, a solid 1700 livres (pounds) a year. (A skilled worker at the time earned around 500 livres a year.) Sophie's father complained that he spent 9000 livres on her in twenty months.

Sophie did not do well at the nunnery. She suffered from eye problms from reading too much under poor conditions. She also became seriously depressed and lonely. Antoine Guillois (her first and best biographer) uses terms such as "seriously sad," "incomprehensible sadness," "melancholy and tears," and "horrible emptiness" to describe her condition with the nuns at Neuville-en-Bresse. Sophie asked to come home. Her parents refused at first. Eventually she fell ill and was allowed to return home and rejoin society. The convent experience proved decisive and had the opposite effect than hoped for by her Catholic mother. Sophie de Grouchy had been vaguely affected by Enlightenment thought in her childhood, but now she was deeply read and of independent mind and spirit. Much to her mother's chagrin, Sophie de Grouchy returned from the convent a heartfelt convert to the *philosophe* movement and a confirmed atheist who unremittingly expressed her discontent with religion.

In 1786 Sophie de Grouchy married Marie Jean-Antoine-Nicolas Caritat, Marquis de Condorcet (1743–1794). The Marquis de Condorcet was then forty-three; she twenty-two. He was already an accomplished mathematician, a well-known political and social theorist, and a philosopher. He was a senior mathematician (*pensionnaire*) in the Académie royale des sciences in Paris, and in 1786 he succeeded to the prestigious post of Permanent Secretary of the institution. He served the state as director of the Royal Mint. He was also the "last of the *Encyclopédistes*" along with Diderot and D'Alembert, to the point where history ultimately conferred on him the epithet, "the youngest *philosophe*."²² The Marquis de Condorcet fell in love with the young Sophie de Grouchy, and he accepted the marriage without a dowry. Sophie's father bestowed 30,000 livres on her as an advance on her inheritance.

They were twenty one years apart in age, but not so strange a couple. They did fall in love and shared a bond of deep affection, and they ultimately had a daughter together. Sophie de Grouchy was a beautiful, intelligent and vivacious woman. The Marquis de Condorcet admired her and stayed very much in love with her. They shared a passion for ideas and ideals, and radical ones at that. Sophie's leanings have already been mentioned. The Marquis de Condorcet himself was a radical feminist, certainly by the standards of his time, for he argued for complete equality between the sexes. Elisabeth and Robert Badinter in their biography of Condorect say that he was "the greatest feminist of his century."²³ He upheld a woman's right to vote and to hold public positions.²⁴ In addition he condemned slavery ahead of his time in 1781, and prior to 1789 and the outbreak of the French Revolution the Marquis de Condorcet was also a radical who secretly favored a republic for France. Clearly, Sophie de Grouchy and the Marquis de Condorcet were nicely matched intellectually as well as socially.

As difficult as it is to evaluate a person's influence, there is no doubt that Sophie was a source of inspiration for the Marquis de Condorcet. She contributed to his ideas and writings throughout their marriage. In his biography, Thierry Boissel suggests that Sophie was more enthusiastic about reform and more extreme in her political views than her husband, and thus she pushed him further in expressing his views and in pursuing political activities that eventually led to the order for his arrest.²⁵

They were an intellectually and politically active couple, and after their marriage they held forth in their salon (in reality her salon), at the Mint (the Hôtel des Monnaies) in Paris. Keith Michael Baker, the Marquis de Condorcet's biographer, labeled the gatherings there the most influential salon in the pre-revolutionary period.²⁶ It was an international intellectual

---

22. The labels of "the youngest *philosophe*" and "the last of the *Encyclopédistes*" are from Baker, p. 27 and Badinter and Badinter, p. 56.
23. Badinter and Badinter, p. 228.
24. Brookes has studied the feminism of the two.
25. Boissel, pp. 105–107; see also Lagrave (1989).

center, a salon in which English was spoken half of the time. Among the foreigners who visited the salon were Thomas Jefferson, Benjamin Franklin, Thomas Paine, and so it seems, Adam Smith. As the French Revolution began to unfold both Sophie and the Marquis de Condorcet took part in creating and supporting the Paris Lycée, the famous establishment devoted to adult education (the equivalent to continuing education today), where the Marquis de Condorcet and other premier scientists and scholars instructed the public in the sciences, mathematics, and history. Sophie de Grouchy became the standard bearer for the Lycée and the Lycée movement in Paris with the sobriquet of Venus Lycée.

The Enlightenment Background

Sophie de Grouchy was a product of her times and the European Enlightenment. She and her *Letters* first and foremost need to be situated in the context of that great intellectual movement of the eighteenth century, the *Siècle des Lumières*.

As a rich world of scholarship has shown, the Enlightenment movement grounded itself in the Scientific Revolution of the previous century. Enlightenment *philosophes* took inspiration particularly from Francis Bacon, René Descartes, and Isaac Newton, whom they revered and completely endorsed. The remarkable success of seventeenth-century scientific intellectuals in overturning traditional authority and applying reason to developing superior understandings of the natural world provided a powerful model for rational inquiry in general.

What Newton and his fellow men of science had achieved the century before in establishing heliocentrism and an explanatory physics set the stage for a broader range of investigations for eighteenth-century thinkers. Indeed, led by John Locke,

---

26. The literature on salon culture in eighteenth-century France especially is rich; see Sutton for a starting point. Commentators recognize the French salons of the seventeenth and eighteenth centuries as social space occupied and run by women. Mary Terrall (1995b) in particular differentiates the female world of contemporary salons from the male-dominated world of the academies, a point relevant to Condorcet's life as an academician and Sophie de Grouchy's as keeper of their salon. In this connection Sophie de Grouchy may be compared not just to the enlightened salonnières of her own time, but with the other strong and educated women who preceeded her, notably that other 'scientific' marquise, the marquise du Châtelet; on the latter point see Terrel (1995a) and Badinter and Muzerelle.

David Hume, Voltaire, Montesquieu and others from across Europe and America, but particularly in France and England, the Enlightenment constituted a program of secular inquiry and action. It consisted of critically evaluating received notions by the light of human reason, articulating more rational alternatives, and pushing for them in law and in the new court of public opinion. This program the *philosophes* developed across a broad front of what we would call the social sciences, the political sciences, and the sciences of man. To the battle cry of "Écrasez l'infâme" ("crush the infamous thing," meaning superstition and the Catholic Church), Voltaire and his followers mounted a frontal attack on received Christian religion. Other *philosophes* variously promoted skeptical inquiry into the organization and foundation of human society, the nature of the laws, the basis of political association, human psychology, and a range of other topics, including ethics and the nature of moral behavior. Not everyone agreed, as the iconoclastic Rousseau made plain, but Enlightenment *philosophes* were nonetheless united in their commitment to reason, to combating authority and superstition, and to ameliorating the human condition. In 1784 Immanuel Kant gave the most general, yet profound answer to the question, "What is enlightenment?" For Kant and his contemporaries, the Enlightenment signaled humankind's coming of age, its maturity. His claim, "dare to know" captures the excitement and climate of contemporary intellectual life that surrounded Sophie de Grouchy as she grew up and that she adopted as her own in the years before 1789.

Beyond such a broad-brush landscape, one particular stream in the various currents of the Enlightenment—contemporary sensationalist psychology—needs to be highlighted as key to understanding Sophie de Grouchy's *Letters on Sympathy*. As is well known, this stream springs from John Locke and his *Essay on Human Understanding* (1690). Locke in his *Essay* argued that all knowledge originates in experience, specifically in sensation and reflection. He held against the existence of innate ideas and in favor of the notion that the mind at birth is a "tabula rasa." For Locke the entire content of the mind is begotten from experience. Even though Locke's main interest in writing the *Essay* was epistemological, he realized that his theory bears on morality as well. If there are no ideas in the mind prior to experience, then there are no innate moral ideas as well, and morality is learned. This, we will see, turned into a pivotal point in Sophie de Grouchy's *Letters* that lies at the basis of her moral and political theory. Sophie de Grouchy is certainly a successor to and part of this Lockean school of thought.

It is not necessary here to recapitulate the entire scope of sensationalist psychology across the eighteenth century. Suffice it to say that Locke's empirical psychology became the psychology of the Enlightenment and was taken up critically and enthusiastically by the French (but not only the French). Étienne Bonnot de Condillac (1715–1780) and Claude Adrien Helvétius (1715–1771) are especially to be noted as French thinkers who developed the tradition in the generation immediately prior to Sophie de Grouchy. Condillac published his Lockean *Essai sur l'origine des conniassances humaines* in 1746 and his *Traité des sensations* in 1754; Helvétius, his contemporary, took the same epistemological positions and concerns for human equality and education, and pushed them to the limits of mechanism and godlessness. Sophie de Grouchy was aware of all of this literature and, as is plain in the *Letters*, added her voice to the conversation. As the *Letters* reveal, Sophie de Grouchy adopted a nuanced view of sensationalism to include internally generated feelings that mixed with outside stimuli perceived through the senses, combined with Lockean reflection.

Likewise central to Sophie de Grouchy and her *Letters* are the moral implications of Locke's views. French *philosophes* believed in progress and reform for which sensationalism provided a basis. Locke's view that people are born "blank slates" renders two very important consequences. One, with such a clean start, people can be seen as a product of the environment. Two, Locke's *Essay* lies at the heart of liberal thought, for if people are born blank slates, then they are also born equal. The connection between natural and political equality is apparent in the Marquis de Condorcet's *Sketch*, where he argues that natural equality serves as a basis for human and civil rights. He argues against domination and exploitation of African and Asian nations and for equality between the sexes. Inequalities, being unnatural, stem from inequalities of wealth, social status, and education. For Condorcet and Sophie de Grouchy there is no sound basis for prejudice and discrimination; these stem from ignorance, tyranny, and corruption. The passion for reform seen in the *Sketch* and in the seventh and eighth *Letters* show to what extent Locke's views became prevalent in France. His philosophy became the platform for theories of progress.

Optimism concerning social reform was prevalent during the Enlightenment to an extent of an explicit belief in the perfectibility of man. The *Letters* in their entirety are well placed within the sensationalistic school of thought.

Madame and Monsieur Condorcet in the Revolution

The French Revolution swept many people into its tumult, but few people more so than Monsieur and Madame Condorcet. Their world, as for so many others, became convulsed and then utterly transformed as the Revolution unfolded from its outbreak with the storming of the Bastille in 1789, through the failure of the constitutional monarchy and the creation of a republic in 1792, and then on through 1794 and the Terror, the overthrow of the Jacobins, and a new order beginning under the Directory, the five-person executive ruling France from 1795 through 1799.

Curiously, the Marquis de Condorcet took himself out of a direct role in the first phases of the Revolution. He did not stand for elections to the Estates General, and so did not end up in the Constituent Assembly that tried to govern France from 1789 through September of 1791. He was elected to the succeeding National Assembly and so entered actively into political life under the constitutional monarchy while Louis XVI was still king of the French. But the Marquis de Condorcet and Sophie staked out the radical left of the moment. They particularly befriended the radical American, Thomas Paine, and Sophie de Grouchy translated into French all of Paine's correspondence and his speeches to the National Assembly. Sophie's and the Marquis' early call for a republic has been mentioned, but it is worth recording as well that Sophie de Grouchy and her daughter were present at the Champ de Mars demonstration (today's Place de la Concorde) at the time of the massacre there in July, 1791. They were protesting the king's flight from the capital and were calling for a republic. Sophie and her daughter were lucky. The national guard killed 400 people that day.

The Marquis de Condorcet was an active member of the republican Convention that followed the fall of the monarchy and that sought to organize the new Republic. Condorcet was generally allied with the comparatively moderate Girondin party, especially in 1792–1793. He was involved in the trial of Louis XVI but did not vote to execute the king. Citizen Condorcet chaired a committee to draft a new constitution; the

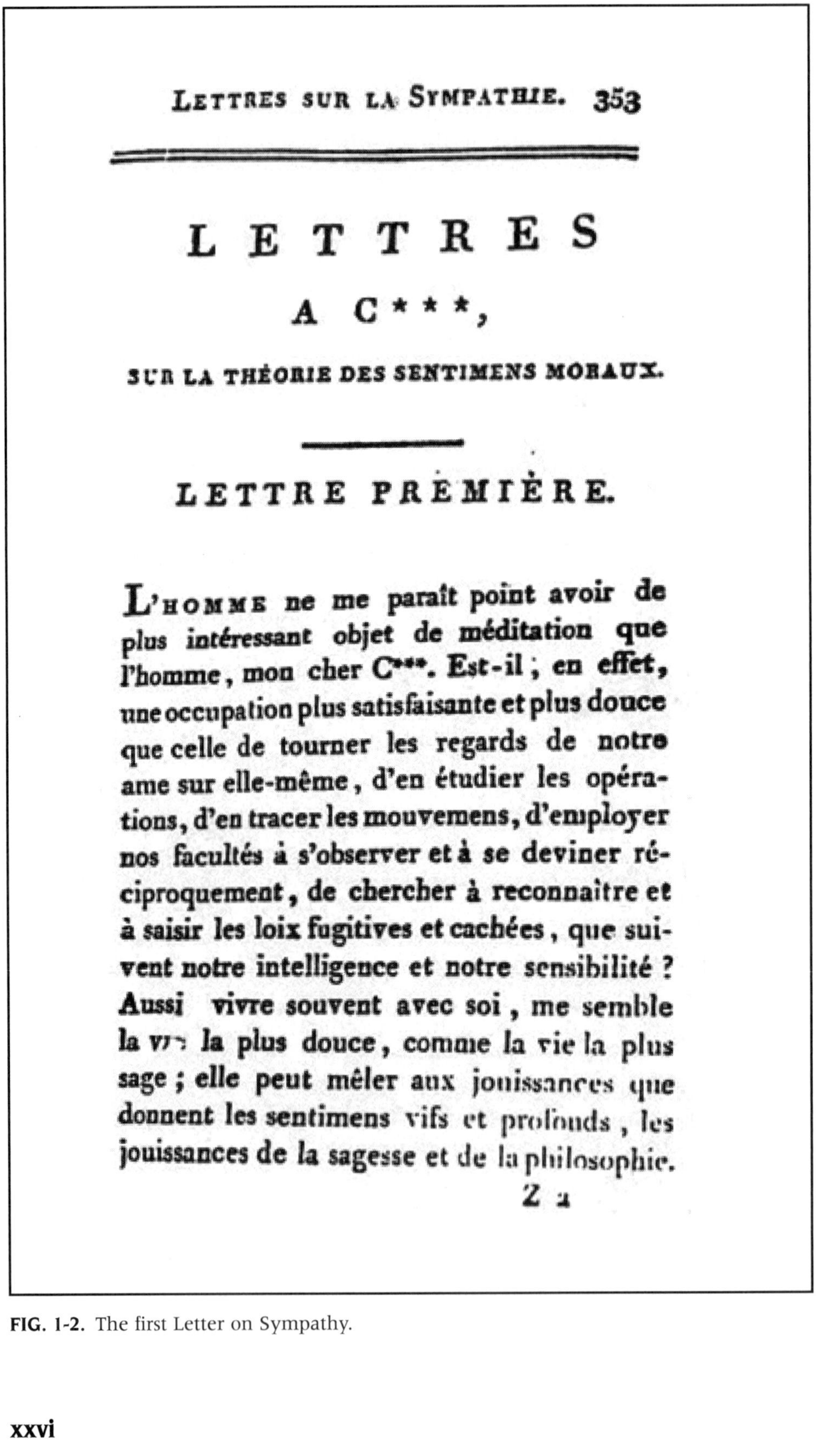

LETTRES SUR LA SYMPATHIE. 353

LETTRES
A C***,
SUR LA THÉORIE DES SENTIMENS MORAUX.

LETTRE PREMIÈRE.

L'HOMME ne me paraît point avoir de plus intéressant objet de méditation que l'homme, mon cher C***. Est-il, en effet, une occupation plus satisfaisante et plus douce que celle de tourner les regards de notre ame sur elle-même, d'en étudier les opérations, d'en tracer les mouvemens, d'employer nos facultés à s'observer et à se deviner réciproquement, de chercher à reconnaître et à saisir les loix fugitives et cachées, que suivent notre intelligence et notre sensibilité ? Aussi vivre souvent avec soi, me semble la vie la plus douce, comme la vie la plus sage ; elle peut mêler aux jouissances que donnent les sentimens vifs et profonds, les jouissances de la sagesse et de la philosophie.

FIG. 1-2. The first Letter on Sympathy.

result was chiefly the work of Condorcet, assisted by Thomas Paine.[27] The former Marquis de Condorcet showed himself more radical than the Girondins when they were purged, but given his credentials out of the nobility, he was not going to be accepted by the radical Jacobin party in the Convention or the sans-culottes (the people of Paris) who were in the throes of saving their revolution from war, civil war, counter-revolution, and economic and overall collapse. When the Jacobins took over the National Convention, they drafted another constitution which Condorcet openly attacked. A warrant for his arrest was issued by Chabot, a Jacobin deputy. Condorcet managed to hide in Paris for nine months, during which he wrote his famous *Sketch of the Historical Progress of the Human Mind*. However, fearing capture, he lit out on a mad dash for freedom. He was arrested in the Paris suburbs after friends refused to take him in. While the local authorities sought to determine his identity, Condorcet was found dead in his cell. It seems that he took poison and committed suicide in prison in order to avoid a certain fate at the guillotine, although it is possible that he died a natural death from a heart attack or exhaustion.

Sophie de Grouchy regularly visited Condorcet clandestinely while he was in hiding, and it was she who persuaded him to write the *Sketch*.[28] They apparently discussed the book together. But in order to survive the Revolution and save some of the family property for herself and her daughter, Sophie on her own initiative took advantage of one of the new liberties the Revolution afforded women, and she divorced her husband, presumed to have emigrated. Theirry Boissel recounts that Condorcet was shocked and heartbroken by Sophie's intention, but went along with her wishes because of the pending danger.

While the Revolution still raged and after the death of Condorcet, Sophie de Grouchy secured modest quarters on the rue Saint-Honoré near where Robespierre lived until his downfall. On her own she survived the Terror by painting portraits and making cameos. Once, when her home was about to be searched by the authorities, she offered to paint the portraits of the members of the town committee and so escaped the danger-

---

27. Schapiro, p. 99.
28. In the margins of a manuscript of the Marquis' political testament she noted that he "[l'a] quitté a ma priere pour écrire L'esquisse des progrès de l'esprit humain." See ms., Institut de France, Bibliothèque de l'Institut, Condorcet papers, Ms. 852, #5; see also, Baker, p. 342.

ous ordeal. She also saved herself by painting portraits of soldiers who had made unreasonable demands on her. She earned some money by going to prisons and drawing portraits of those about to be executed so that the families would have something by which to remember the deceased. She accumulated a modest capital, with which she opened a small lingerie shop. Surely, she was a very skillful and resourceful woman to survive such horrifying personal and socio-political ordeals.

With the end of the frightful period of the Terror and the extreme phase of the French Revolution in 1794 and with a return to relative normalcy, Sophie de Grouchy saw her and Condorcet's property in Paris and in Auteuil restored to her, and she gradually resumed some semblance of her former intellectual and social life. She returned to paying her own servants and to those of d'Alembert, whom Condorcet had been supporting. She established a small salon at her houses in Paris and at Auteuil that grew in importance under the Directory. It was at this point that she turned or perhaps returned to the project of translating Smith's *Theory of Moral Sentiments* and writing her own *Letters on Sympathy*.

The Directory, the Idéologues, and Napoleon

We can situate the immediate context in which Sophie de Grouchy wrote and published fairly precisely, as that from the end of the period of the Terror, through the Directory, and to Napoleon's rise to power between 1794 and 1799. The *Letters on Sympathy* represent an Enlightenment document and a contribution to philosophical discussions going back to Locke and to her own pre-Revolutionary salon, but they also very much bear the imprint of the French Revolution, the Directory period, and Napoleon's rise to power. On 9 Thermidor of Year II of the Republic (27–28 July 1794) a coup ended the reign of terror of Robespierre. The Directory that followed in 1795 tried to steer a liberal, constitutional republic through still troublesome political waters. The executive Directory notably instituted progressive feminist legislation, allowing divorce, a woman to own property and to vote.

The period of the Directory saw the full emergence of the progressive group known as the Idéologues, and the *Letters* have to be seen as very much part of the Idéologue movement. The Idéologues' roots go back to Enlightenment sensationalist psychology, and the term ideology involves references to the science of ideas. A. Destutt de Tracy, Cabanis, P.-S. Laplace, A.-L. Lavoisier and Condorcet (while the latter two were alive), and others formed a distinct scientific and philosophical school whose thought started with an analysis of sensations, then went on to develop the principles of language and logic, and finally to demonstrate the application of these principles to moral and political sciences. Moreover, in 1795 their movement secured a formidable institutional outpost in the second class devoted to the Moral and Political Sciences of the newly established Institut National (what is today the Institut de France). Six sections composed this class, and they encapsulate the logic of Idéologue thought: sensations and ideas, morals, civil society and laws, government, history, and geography. The Idéologues fought for a constitutional government, civil and legal rights, and basic universal education. (At this time Napoleon Bonaparte began winning victories in Italy and moved on to campaigning in Egypt.)

The salon that gathered around Sophie de Grouchy in the period of the Directory became not only a main center of *Idéologie* and liberal political thought but a center of republican, anti-Napoleon opposition. Sophie stuck to her guns politically and was outspoken, even after Napoleon's rise to power. Elisabeth and Robert Badinter record the following exchange between Napoleon and Sophie de Grouchy:

> *Napoleon:* "I don't like it that women meddle in politics."
>
> *de Grouchy:* "You are right in general, but in a country that cops off their heads, it's natural that they would like to know why."[29]

The role of Pierre-Jean-Georges Cabanis (1757–1808) needs to be highlighted both as a leading Idéologue figure, but also for his close personal ties with Sophie de Grouchy. These were family ties in part, as Cabanis married Sophie de Grouchy's sister Charlotte and was her brother-in-law. Cabanis also made regular visits to Sophie de Grouchy's salon between 1794 and 1809. And it is worth recalling that the *Letters* seem nominally addressed to him. This connection with Cabanis is important in understanding the *Letters*.

---

29. Badinter and Badinter, pp. 228–29.

With Cabanis the concept of the science of man took a turn that again is particularly influential in the *Letters*. Peter Gay points out that during the eighteenth century the science of man became a medical study. The *philosophes* demonstrated considerable confidence in medicine as having explanatory value for human life. Gay remarks that the ancient view that health is connected with happiness, combined with modern science, gave rise to the idea that humans can not only be explained within the scope of science, but the specific avenue is the study of medicine.[30] Indeed, if people can be explained within the scope of science, as Enlightenment thinkers held, would not medicine be the most suitable science? Such is the ambition of Cabanis's work, *On the Relations Between the Physical and Moral Aspects of Men* (1802). Cabanis studied medicine, but did not practice. He belonged to the Idéologues group aimed at establishing a science of man that would unite analysis of ideas, physiology, and ethics. Although Cabanis' work was published in 1802, the first six of its twelve memoirs were composed during 1796–1797, at roughly the same time Sophie de Grouchy composed and published her *Letters*. Both works—Cabanis' on the *Physical and Moral Aspects of Man* and de Grouchy's *Letters on Sympathy*—emerged out of their intellectual conversation and interaction. Cabanis clearly influenced de Grouchy; acknowledging her influence on Cabanis is to her credit and of no lesser value.

In this context, Cabanis' thought is worth exploring. To the question of why the science of nature progressed, but not the science of man, Cabanis replies that it is the omission of medicine from inquiry into human nature. More specifically, the human sciences lagged behind the natural sciences because the study of morality was separated from medicine. Any ethical theory assumes a theory of human nature as its basis. Human nature ought to be studied physiologically. The proper science of man is the study of the relations among physiology, sentiments, passions, and intellect, or as Cabanis put it, "...physiology, the analysis of ideas, and ethics are the three branches of a single science, which may justly be called the SCIENCE OF MAN."[31]

Cabanis then undertakes a detailed study of the relationship between physiology and ethics. He argues that ethics, studied

---

30. Gay, pp. 12–17.
31. Cabanis, p. 33.

apart from physiology, is an obscure metaphysical study. Instead of a metaphysical study we need an empirical one. He credits Locke with the turning point in the history of moral theory because Locke was the first one to claim that all ideas, including moral ideas, are a product of sensations. Cabanis mentions that Locke was a doctor who based his studies on the physical man. Locke was concerned with sensations from an external source that impinge on the human organism. Cabanis was concerned with the physiological capacities of the organism to receive and process sensation. In this way, what was sensationalism with Locke turns into sensibility with Cabanis. It is in the concept of sensibility, or physical receptivity to sensation, that one finds the correlation between physiology and ethics in Sophie de Grouchy and Cabanis. The concept of physical sensibility stands at the heart of Cabanis' work and Sophie de Grouchy's moral theory.

What Cabanis and de Grouchy add to Locke's theory is the view that we can receive ideas from internal sensations as well. The material body has the ability to generate sensations, through which the nervous system can influence other organs, including the brain. Thus the production of ideas, emotions, and wishes that give rise to moral activity is engendered by the physical body. More simply put, morality is embedded in instincts. For Cabanis external sensation is not sufficient to account for actions like a newborn reaching for his mother's breast, or for a mother's maternal instincts toward her offspring. Even in the fetal stage, the human body is already comprised of impulses and needs. Ethics is based on these needs. Moral ideas originate in internal sensations, in instincts.

As a materialist, Cabanis studies both external and internal conditions that affect morality and intelligence. He undertakes a detailed study of physical conditions including climate, gender, age, and mental and physical sickness, and he shows how they affect our sensibility, which in turn influences the formation of ideas (including moral ideas). He studies internal physiological conditions that affect ethical behavior such as hereditary traits, the states of internal organs, dreams, illusions, depressions, and unconscious impulses. The moral is derived from physical.

> The study of physical man is interesting both for the doctor and for the moralist and is almost equally

> necessary for both. In striving to discover the secrets of the organization, in observing the phenomena of life, the doctor tries to recognize in what consists the state of perfect health, what circumstances may disturb this equilibrium, what means may maintain or restore it. The moralist endeavors to go back to the more obscure operations that constitute the functions of the intelligence and the conditions of the will. Here he looks for rules that are to direct life and for roads that lead to happiness.[32]

Cabanis believed that the study of the physical body holds the key to moral and intellectual perfectibility. The proper study of humankind and human faculties would yield a better understanding of human needs and reveal the optimal conditions for extracting the full human moral potential. Ethical rules, he writes, can be proved mathematically!

A related question arises, appearing both in Cabanis and in Condorcet: Why has there been progress in the sciences and technology but not in ethics and politics? Their thesis was that man and his moral faculties have not been studied in a scientific manner. For comparable progress to occur in ethics, human nature ought to be studied within the scope of science. Thus, as Peter Gay remarks, the "age of the Enlightenment made the study of man into a science."[33]

Sophie de Grouchy begins with an empirical analysis of morality in order to find out in what way we attain our moral disposition, how we sustain it, and how we can develop morality further. She sees human nature as law-like, thus understandable and predictable. Future progress and happiness depend on a proper analysis of human beings. She opens the *Letters* on this note:

> Man does not appear to me to have any more interesting object of meditation than man himself, my dear C***. Is there, in effect, an activity any more satisfying and agreeable than to turn the soul's gaze upon itself, to study its operations, to trace its movements...and to seek to identify and grasp the hidden furtive laws that guide our intelligence and our sensibility?

---

32. Cabanis, p. 7.
33. Gay, p. 167.

FIG. 1-3. "La Maisonnette," Sophie de Grouchy's house in Meulan. Photo courtesy of Christian Arnold-Tétard.

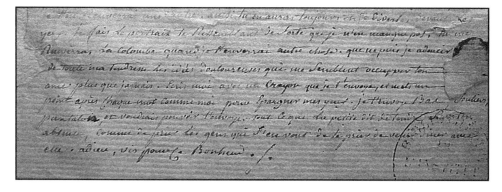

FIG. 1-4. A letter, probably of early 1794 from Sophie de Grouchy to the Marquis de Condorcet, in hiding, with its touching closing, "Farewell, live for happiness." Bibliothèque de l'Institut Ms, 852.

Both Sophie de Grouchy and Condorcet argue that freedom and liberty are basic needs and that the role of the law is to preserve freedom and equality. In order to ground morality in fact, to establish a firm foundation and to ensure reform, Sophie de Grouchy and other Enlightenment *philosophes* saw the study of morality and politics as a form of science. Martin Staum, the biographer of Cabanis, writes that "scientific principles about human nature did in fact justify a political commitment to natural rights, to liberty and equality before the law."[34] The *Letters* should be read in this light.

It was against this background that Sophie de Grouchy produced for publication her translation of Smith's *Theory of Moral Sentiments* and her own *Letters on Sympathy*. Her work appeared in 1798, as we know. The *Letters* formed part of and were self-evidently intended to address the Idéologue movement, especially as it represented an extension of Enlightenment moral and psychological inquiries. Of course, Napoleon seized power in the coup d'état of the 18 of Brumaire (November 9–10, 1799), becoming Consul, First Consul and then Emperor by 1804. In 1803 Napoleon crushed the Idéologues and overturned the progressive legislation of the previous fourteen years. He eliminated the Idéologues' institutional base in suppressing the Class of the Moral and Political Sciences in the Institute. He restored slavery and reestablished relations with the Catholic Church. In 1804 he instituted the Code Napoleon where he reduced the status of woman to that of possessions of their fathers and husbands, and thus, it may be said, ended the Enlightenment era in France. The *Letters* that Sophie wrote on sympathy would not have seen light in the period of the Napoleonic empire. They are one of, if not the last Enlightenment documents, very much the product of their time. The *Letters* of Sophie de Grouchy could not have been written at a later date.

Contemporary Widows, Writers and Feminists

After the Terror Sophie de Grouchy had her own life to lead. In 1798 she was single, attractive, and in her middle thirties. She wanted another man in her life, and for several years she was the lover of the second-rate lawyer and archivist Maillia

---

34. Staum, p. 9.

Garat (1763–1837).³⁵ She was eventually rebuffed by the ingrate Garat, however, and she remained a widow for the rest of her life. She devoted the remainder of her days to her family and to preserving her husband's opus. She edited and published Condorcet's collected works and published them posthumously with an introduction of her own, the *Oeuvres complètes de Condorcet* in twenty-one volumes (1804). She also reedited and published separately the *Esquisse d'un Tableau Historique des Progrès de L'Esprit Humain*, the historic book Condorcet wrote while he was in hiding. Sophie de Grouchy also wrote a treatise on education (to her daughter) that remained in manuscript and is lost today.³⁶ She was devoted to her daughter and family. Towards the end of her life she was not in good health, and she died in September, 1822.

Sophie de Grouchy was plainly an independent and intelligent woman with ideas of her own who made herself felt in French intellectual life in the 1780s and 1790s. This was no small accomplishment, one that makes her relative obscurity today that much more difficult to understand. We can gain an enriched sense of her talents, her accomplishment, and her place in the history of philosophy by triangulating Sophie de Grouchy's place in a constellation of other contemporary women luminaries.

One obvious point of comparison would be with that other famous scientific widow of the day, Mme Lavoisier. The parallels are striking. Marie-Anne Paulze (1758–1836) did not emerge out of the parlementary nobility, but from a cultured bourgeois family of Farmers General, and she, too, was inclined to liberal thought.³⁷ She married an up-and-coming young Farmer General and man of science, Antoine-Laurent Lavoisier, and like Sophie de Grouchy, she married young…at the age of fourteen to a man twice her age.

The Lavoisiers were socially prominent, if somewhat less so than the Condorcets, and Marie-Anne organized the Lavoisiers' salon at the Arsenal that mirrored Sophie's at the Mint. Mme Lavoisier likewise assisted her husband in his work, acting as his secretary and laboratory assistant, and

---

35. See Lagrave (1994), pp. 187–245.
36. Some few of Sophie de Grouchy materials are in the Bibliothèque de l'Institut in Paris, but others that have not been studied are in private hands; see Lagrave (1992).
37. This portrait of Mme Lavoisier is abstracted from Poirier, pp. 281–325.

she became quite proficient in chemistry at the time of the Chemical Revolution. Although not as talented as Sophie de Grouchy, Mme Lavoisier studied painting with Jacques-Louis David, and is known for a portrait of Benjamin Franklin. Like de Grouchy, Mme Lavoisier also became a translator, rendering from English into French Richard Kirwan's *Essay on Phlogiston* (1788). And as the world knows, Lavoisier, like Condorcet, also perished in the Revolution, guillotined on May 8, 1794 as a General Farmer. Mme Lavoisier suffered even more during the Revolution than did Sophie de Grouchy, being herself arrested and imprisoned, and only the 9th of Thermidor saved her from execution.

After the Revolution, like Sophie de Grouchy, Mme Lavoisier struggled to recover her property, and she worked on a posthumous edition of her husband's works that appeared in 1803. Mme Lavoisier succeeded in marrying again, a disastrous union with the American royalist and man of science, Benjamin Thompson, who also was Count Rumford, and who died shortly thereafter. The two women settled into in their own social circles, the difference being that Mme Lavoisier's was not at odds with Napoleon. But Mme Lavoisier did not have any ambitions or anything to say on her own, and she published nothing and is known for nothing original. Childless, she became isolated and something of a laughing stock in her declining years, a relic of a bygone age, a shell without substance. By way of contrast, Sophie de Grouchy's translation of Adam Smith and her own *Letters on Sympathy* earned her a reputation as an independent intellectual and marked her out strongly in comparison with her sisterly widow of science and the French Revolution.

Sophie de Grouchy rather merits comparison with two more accomplished contemporary women writers and intellectuals. One person with whom she deserves to be linked is Germaine de Staël (1766–1817).[38] Mme de Staël was the daughter of the famous Swiss financier and on-and-off Minister of Finance for France, Jacques Necker. She received the very best education available to anyone, man or woman, at the time. At the age of twenty she married a German count and diplomat who

---

38. Badinter and Badinter, p. 218, note similarities between Sophie de Grouchy and Mme de Staël; see also. Boissel, p. 102. Lefebvre,, p. 62, underscores political, Idéologue sympathies linking the de Grouchy and de Staël salons.

was thirty-seven years old. Mme de Staël was politically active and oversaw her own illustrious salon in pre-Revolutionary Paris. She lived in Paris through the first phases of the French Revolution, but she fled France in 1792 after the September massacres. She returned to oppose Napoleon, who had her exiled, and they remained bitter enemies. Germaine de Staël knew Sophie de Grouchy, and at one point the two lived and had separate salons close by each other. Relations between the two were cool because of Condorcet's views of her father, but Mme de Staël was taken by the *Letters on Sympathy*. She sent a letter to Sophie de Grouchy from Switzerland. Written sometime between 1798 and 1806, it deserves to be quoted at length:

> Madame, I just read the 8 letters that you added to the translation of Smith, and they gave me such great pleasure that I need to talk with you about them. You are someone insensitive to praise, but you will not be to have attained the goal you set for yourself to convince and to touch. You know me to be too emotional to count as a success what I felt, but my father is less flighty, and in listening to your work that I just read to him he did not cease remarking on both your considered thoughts and the well evinced feelings. You will be more obliged than ever to accept my respects when I see you. In these letters there is an authority of reason, a sensibility that is true, but controlled that make you an exceptional woman. I think of myself as talented and intelligent, but I govern nothing of what I possess. I am part and parcel of my faculties, but I cannot guide their use. In the end I admired you both for your views and for a returning to myself, and as I have the good nature not to be at all jealous, I only felt pleasure in thinking that I knew and loved someone so rare. I also think that these Letters are really useful. If I had in me the possibility of happiness, they would have developed it, calmness without being cold, reason without being dry. In the ideal nature of the good and the beautiful this unites many opposites. Oh, how far we are from all these social institutions to shape mankind as you would like. I have an extreme need to converse with you; tell me in your letters when I will see you again. Your character inspired your Letters, and they confirm your

character... Finally, whatever happens to me, through you I have rediscovered a long-lost emotion and the admiration that the heart and virtue are led to feel.[39]

Mme de Staël became a prolific and celebrated author, writing novels, critical essays, travelogues, and important historical/cultural studies on Germany and on the French Revolution. The fame of Mme de Staël is deservedly greater than that of Sophie de Grouchy, but their intellectual and life trajectories were more similar than different. Mme de Staël and Sophie de Grouchy were absolute contemporaries, riding the tempests of their times, and like Mme de Staël Sophie de Grouchy was a serious, engaged citizen and intellectual.

Finally, Sophie de Grouchy may also be profitably situated alongside her famous English contemporary, Mary Wollstonecraft (1759–1797). Mary Wollstonecraft was, of course, a pioneering

---

39. Note that in a postscriptum Mme de Staël asks to be reminded to Cabanis. This manuscript letter is dated only "Canton Leman, Coppet ce 20 May 1 prairial," and hence could not be after the termination of the Revolutionary calendar in 1806. Two copies of this letter are preserved, Institut de France, Bibliothèque de l'Institut, Ms. 2475, #44 and 45; see also Guillois, pp. 181–83; parts are quoted in Lagrave, p. 41. The original French is as follows: "Je viens de lire Madame les 8 lettres que vous avez ajoutées à la traduction de Smith et elles m'ont fait un si grand plaisir que j'ai besoin de vous en parler. Vous êtes une personne insensible à la louange, mais nous ne le serez pas à atteindre le but que vous vous êtes proposé convaincre & toucher—vous me savez trop facile à l'emotion pour compter comme un succès celle que j'ai eprouvée [sic], mais mon père est moins mobile et dans la lecture que je viens de lui faire de votre ouvrage il n'a cessé de remarquer et les pensées réflechis & les sentimens heureusement exprimés—vous serez plus obligée que jamais de me passer mon impression de respect en vous voyant. Il y a dans ces lettres une autorité de raison, une sensibilité vraie mais dominée qui fait de vous une femme à part. Je me crois du talent et de l'esprit, mais je ne gouverne rein de ce que je possède, j'appartiens à mes facultés mais je n'en puis guider l'usage—enfin je vous ai admiré et dans vous et par un retour sur moi, et comme j'ai la bonne nature de n'etre point jalouse, je n'ai eu que du plaisir en pensant que je connaissais et que j'aimais une personne si rare—je crois aussi que ces Lettres sont d'une utilité véritable—Si j'avais en moi la possibilité du bonheur elles l'auraient développée, c'est du calme sans froideur, de la raison sans sécheresse—C'est ce qui compose dans toute la Nature l'idéal du bien & du beau la réunion de quelques contraires. Oh, que nous sommes loin de toutes ces institutions sociales qui doivent former l'homme tel que vous le voulez. J'ai un besoin extrême de causer avec vous, parlez moi [dans] vos lettres quand je vous reverrai, votre caractère vous les a inspiré & elles doivent confirmer votre caractère....—enfin quoiqu'il m'arrive vous m'avez fait retrouver un plaisir depuis longtems perdu l'emotion & l'admiration que le coeur & la vertu font éprouver."

feminist and author of the landmark work of 1792, *A Vindication of the Rights of Women*. Although more notable as a philosopher and moral theorist, Sophie de Grouchy herself (along with the Marquis de Condorcet) stood on the contemporary vanguard of radical feminism. A later chapter in Part I explores Sophie de Grouchy's feminist thought, but it is not too much to remark here that her foci on education, egalitarian marriages, universal human rights, the objectification of women, and the role of women as citizens parallel the analytical perspectives that have immortalized Mary Wollstonecraft. According to Jean-Paul de Lagrave, through the agency of Thomas Paine, Mary Wollstonecraft became familiar with the Condorcets and their radical views on women in 1790. Wollstonecraft was in Paris in the later part of 1792 where, given her Girondin sentiments, she doubtless met and interacted with Sophie de Grouchy and her husband.[40]

The world knows and remembers well Mme Lavoisier, Mme de Staël, and Mary Wollstonecraft. Outside of the francophone world, however, until relatively recently Sophie de Grouchy might well have never existed. The premise of the present study and the accompanying translation of her *Letters on Sympathy* is that she must rank high in our consideration along with her more famous sisters.

---

40. Lagrave (1994), p. 69. Sophie de Grouchy was probably also connected with the important French feminist of the Revolutionary period, Marie-Olympe de Gouges (1748–1793), the author of the *Declaration of the Rights of Women (1791)*. This connection remains speculative; however, given de Gouges' Girondin affiliations, she and Sophie de Grouchy doubtless did know and influence one another.

Part I

The Philosophy of Sophie de Grouchy

Chapter 1

On Sympathy

As outlined in the introduction, Sophie de Grouchy's eight *Letters on Sympathy* of 1798 emerged out of a long and complex tradition of sensationalist psychology and epistemology that stretched back to the seventeenth century and John Locke. At the same time, her *Letters* are framed by and represent her specific responses to the positions staked out by Adam Smith in his *Theory of Moral Sentiments*. This rich background shaped de Grouchy's views very differently from Smith's, and the differences begin with their account of the origin of sympathy.

Smith and De Grouchy on the Origin of Sympathy

Both Adam Smith and Sophie de Grouchy provide a moral theory based on sympathy. Their views on sympathy, however, vary significantly. The differences between them begin with their initial assumptions concerning the foundation of sympathy. To de Grouchy, Smith did not sufficiently tend to the topic of the foundation of morality, and she opens the *Letters* by criticizing Smith for failing to provide an account of the origin of sympathy. Due to this omission, she claims Smith was not able to show that sympathy necessarily exists and is always present. Her argument at the outset is not merely a criticism of this omission but a claim concerning the consequences of Smith's theory that follow. She writes:

> You know that the subject of the opening chapters of Smith's book is sympathy. Smith limited himself to noting its existence and to showing its principal effects. I regretted that he did not dare go further, to penetrate its first cause, and ultimately to show how sympathy must belong to every sensible being capable of reflection. You will see how I had the temerity to fill in these omissions (*Letters*, 357/108).

The idea that sympathy is deeply embedded in our nature is developed throughout the *Letters* and renders de Grouchy's ethical, social, and political views different from Smith's. A full comparison between Smith and de Grouchy shows that the differences between their moral and political views are rooted in their conceptions of the origin of sympathy. The quote above should be read in contrast to Smith's opening statement in *TMS*. There, Smith simply assumes the existence of sympathy:

> How selfish soever man may be supposed, there are *evidently* some principles in his nature, which interest him in the fortune of others, and render their happiness necessary to him, though he derives nothing from it except the pleasure of seeing it…That we often derive sorrow from the sorrow of others, is a matter of fact too obvious to require any instance to prove it.[1]

For Smith, then, sympathy exists self-evidently. On the other hand, de Grouchy devotes the first two *Letters* to explaining the causes and origin of sympathy. She provides an empirical explanation for the origin of sympathy, showing how sympathy originates in experience, first in sensations of pleasure and pain. Grounding morality in experience was an important task in the context of the Enlightenment in order to grant the environment a significant role in shaping individual morality. This task begins with Locke. In his *Essay Concerning Human Understanding*, Locke attempts to explain the origin of moral ideas in experience, an issue which he does not complete. In Book Two of the *Essay* Locke writes:

---

1. Page references to the *Letters* are first to original French edition of 1798 amd then to translation on Part II. Smith, *TMS*, p. 9. KB italics.

1. On Sympathy

> Amongst the simple I*deas*, which we receive both from S*ensation* and R*eflection*, *Pain* and P*leasure* are two very considerable ones…Things then are Good or Evil, only in reference to Pleasure or Pain. That we call G*ood*, which *is apt to cause or increase Pleasure*, or *diminish Pain in us.*[2]

Locke then establishes a correlation between sensations of pleasure and pain and moral ideas. But, how is this connection made in experience? In what way does it translate into a moral theory? The quotation above represents the extent of Locke's attempt to include ethics in his work, and the *Essay* remains mainly an epistemological work. Condorcet goes further than Locke and opens the *Sketch* with the following statement:

> Man is born with the ability to receive sensations; to perceive them and to distinguish between the various simple sensations of which they are composed…Sensations are attended by pleasure or pain; and man for his part has the capacity to transform such momentary impressions into permanent feelings of an agreeable or disagreeable character, and then to experience these feelings when he either observes or recollects the pleasures and pains of other sentient beings.[3]

Condorcet goes on to explain that morality develops based on this capacity to feel for others. He does not develop this argument further, and it is possible that at this point he was already influenced by de Grouchy. Hume and Smith are empiricists as well, yet they do not incorporate an empirical analysis of the origin of morality. Hume offers more than Smith, but he does not provide a complete explanation. With a detailed account of the empirical origin of moral ideas de Grouchy provides an original contribution to this discussion.

De Grouchy's Empiricism

Like Locke, de Grouchy claims that morality originates in sensations of pleasure and pain. Further than Locke, she fully develops the link between sensations and human morality. What becomes a unique feature of her theory is her analysis of pain and suffering and the ways in which they motivate

---
2. Locke, *An Essay Concerning Human Understanding*, Book II, pp. xx, 220.
3. Condorcet, *Sketch*, p. 3.

sympathy. It is by virtue of being able to feel pain and then detect it in others that we come to care about them. Pleasure plays a lesser role. She begins with an analysis of physical pain as follows:

> Every physical pain produces a compound sensation in the person who experiences it. It first produces a local pain in that part upon which the cause of pain acts initially. Beyond that, it produces a painful general impression in all our organs, an impression very distinct from the local pain and that always accompanies the latter, but that can continue to exist without it. (*Letters*, 357/108)

De Grouchy explains that "a general impression of pain" can be renewed upon recalling a pain we have suffered; hence results the experience of a painful memory. Further, de Grouchy argues that seeing another person suffer will provoke a painful sensation as well. This observation, in effect, is the heart of de Grouchy's concept of sympathy: sympathy consists in feeling pain upon seeing another person suffer:

> In the same way as the memory of an injury we have felt reproduces the painful impression that affected all our organs and that formed part of the local pain this injury caused us, so, too, we feel this painful impression again when, being in a position to notice the signs pain, we see an impressionable being suffer or whom we know suffers. (*Letters*, 359/109)

In other words, for de Grouchy morality begins with sensitivity to suffering and consists in identifying or being able to feel with another. In fact she defines sympathy as "the disposition we have to feel as others do."

Her terminology in the first *Letter* and her discussion of pain and bodily organs can be better understood in the context of her exchanges with Cabanis. Her nineteenth-century biographer, Antoine Guillois, suggests that the *Letters* reflect conversations de Grouchy had with Cabanis over the subject of physical pain.[4] Cabanis in *On The Relation Between The Physical and Moral Aspects of Man* (1802) sets out to map the relation between physiology and the formation of character and ideas or "...the systematic development of his organs with the analogous development of

---

4. Guillois, *La Marquise de Condorcet*, pp. 121–22.

1. On Sympathy

his sentiments and passions."[5] He explains morality as a biological phenomenon, and he also provides a physiological explanation for the origin of sympathy.

At the heart of Cabanis' theory (and also of de Grouchy's) stands the concept of sensibility. Sensibility according to Cabanis is our ability to feel sensations. Sensibility is what enables us to receive impressions from both internal and external sources and these constitute the content of the soul or mind. Without sensibility we would neither survive nor have a single idea.

> Without the sensibility we would not become aware of the presence of external objects; we would not even have a means of perceiving our own existence, or rather we would not exist. But from the moment at which we feel, we are.[6]

In an attempt to explain feelings, Cabanis claims that the main organ of sensations is the brain, but it is the nervous system that transmits sensations throughout the body. The nerves feel and the brain perceives sensations. Sensations, then, make us feel. Cabanis points out that sensitive organs, via the nervous system, can produce feelings in other organs, a phenomenon which he labels as "sympathetic communication of the affections from one organ to another."[7]

> It must appear natural that the excess of action in an important organ brings on a proportional excess of influence, on its part, over the other organs that are sympathetically linked to it.[8]

In his view, through sympathetic communication between and among organs, the entire body participates in feeling pain. It is in this sense—an appeal to physiological phenomena followed by an emotional reaction—that we are to understand de Grouchy's claim that a general impression of pain in all our organs follows a local pain.

Cabanis' explanation of sympathy is very similar to de Groucy's. He also appeals to sensations of pleasure and pain in his account of sympathy. As pleasure and pain are impor-

---

5. Cabanis, *On the Relations*, p. 33.
6. Ibid., p. 51.
7. Ibid., p. 135.
8. Ibid., p. 664.

tant for the preservation of the animal, we cannot conceive of our nature without them. Pleasure and pain are also essential for sensibility. When we detect these feelings in others, we sympathize.

> The signs thus recall the sensations; they make us FEEL again...Other [sensations] manifest themselves externally; to help him communicate with others. Among the latter....those of pleasure and pain, which are remarked in the features, the attitude, the cries of different animate beings, make us feel with them, SYMPATHIZE with their joys and sufferings.[9]

The similarity between de Grouchy and Cabanis sheds light on her use of sensationalism but does not continue much further. Cabanis remains a materialist and explains that just as parts of matter tend toward one another, so do living beings. Sympathy then "falls within the domain of the instinct."[10] Cabanis also places sympathy at the core and base of morality. He writes that sympathy is one of the greatest assets of sociability, but otherwise Cabanis does not develop this issue. We can see de Grouchy's influence on the analysis of sympathy in Cabanis' work. When Cabanis writes about moral sympathy, for example, he refers the reader to the work of Scottish philosophers, and especially to that of de Grouchy:

> These [sympathetic] tendencies are in fact, then, what is understood by the expression MORAL SYMPATHY—a principle celebrated in the writings of the Scots philosophers—whose great power in eliciting the sentiments was recognized by Hutcheson; of which Smith carried out an analysis that was full of wisdom, though incomplete for this lack of success in relating it to physical laws; and which Madame Condorcet by simple yet rational considerations has been able in great part to draw out of the vagueness in which the THEORIE DES SENTIMENTS MORAUX (THEORY OF THE MORAL SENTIMENTS) had left it.[11]

---

9. Ibid., p. 68.
10. Ibid., p. 585.
11. Ibid., p. 598.

The Role of Pain in De Grouchy and Smith

De Grouchy claims that pain is a phenomenon that has "moral presence." As noted, by virtue of the fact that we are able to perceive and react to pain in others, "Pain and adversity are such effective schools for making men more compassionate and more human" (*Letters*, 362/110). De Grouchy places our sensitivity to pain at the heart of her moral theory. Ultimately our willingness to help others and our aversion from harming others will depend on our feelings for those who suffer.

De Grouchy notes that repeated experiences of feeling pain produce "an abstract idea of pain." She uses an empirical analysis to suggest that we construct general ideas from particular instances through the process of abstraction. Again we observe that de Grouchy is using Lockean terminology and frames of reference, for as Locke puts it:

> ...the Mind makes the particular *Ideas*, received from particular Objects, to become general; which is done by considering them as they are in the Mind such Appearances, separate from all other Existences, and the circumstances of real Existence, as Time, Place, or any other concomitant *Ideas*. This is Called ABSTRACTION, whereby *Ideas* taken from particular Beings, become general Representatives of all of the same kind....[12]

Thus, from particular instances of pain we form an abstract idea of pain. For de Grouchy the point is that an abstract idea of pain, such as pain we have not experienced ourselves, the pain of people we do not know, or the suffering of a whole group of people will evoke our sympathy as well. Upon learning of any of the above, we also feel pain. De Grouchy keeps reminding us that what is triggered by the idea of suffering is a "general impression of pain on all our organs." Thus, she is in a good position to explain what is meant when one claims that the sight or idea of atrocities is "sickening." It is the abstract idea of pain that has a moral presence:

> In effect, as soon as the development of our faculties and the repeated experience of pain permit us to have an abstract idea of it, that idea alone renews in us the general impression made by pain on all our organs.

---
12. Locke, *Essay*, p. 159.

> Here, then, is an effect of pain that follows equally from both its physical presence and its moral presence. One understands here by its moral presence either the idea that our memories give us of pain or that which we can have of it by the sight or knowledge of another's pain (*Letters*, 359–60/109).

Smith, in contrast, makes no use of the concept of physical pain. He writes:

> Nothing is so soon forgot as pain. The moment it is gone the whole agony of it is over, and the thought of it can no longer give us any sort of disturbance. We ourselves cannot then enter into the anxiety and anguish which we had before conceived.[13]

We see then that for Smith physical pain serves no function. Smith devotes a section in *TMS* entitled "Of the Passions which takes their origin from the body" to explain that bodily sufferings excite very little or no sympathy in others, compared to what is felt by the sufferer. For Smith, a physical sensation does not arise in the spectator as a response. We do not become hungry, he notes, by reading about famine. Suffering in general for Smith stems from the imagination. A disappointed love calls for much more sympathy than the greatest bodily evil.

Smith emphasizes that we sympathize through our imagination, not through our bodies:

> The frame of my body can be but little affected by the alterations which are brought about upon that of my companion:...The person who has lost his whole fortune, if he is in health, feels nothing in his body...our imagination can more readily mould themselves upon his imagination, than our bodies can mould themselves upon his body."[14]

For Smith then, physical pain and emotional pain are two separate, unrelated phenomena. In his theory Smith manifests the traditional mind–body dualism, whereas de Grouchy does not. Both Smith and de Grouchy write a moral theory based on sentiments, but in the *Letters* the idea that morality is always felt and not merely thought is developed much further.

---

13. Smith, *TMS*, p. 29.
14. Ibid., p. 29.

The Role of Sympathy in De Grouchy and Smith

From her sensationalism and the preceding account of physical pain emerges the aspect of human relations in the *Letters*. This is an additional dimension in de Grouchy's philosophy, not present in any of her contemporaries, including Cabanis, and does not appear elsewhere until twentieth-century feminist ethics. As we have seen, the sensationalists argued that morality originates in sensations of pleasure and pain. De Grouchy pays novel attention to the context in which sensations of pleasure and pain arise, pointing out that sympathy emerges when these sensations are first felt at the hands of caretakers. That is to say, our moral disposition develops out of a relation to another human being. In addition, for de Grouchy dependency on others is a significant aspect of human relations that has moral repercussions. Each person depends on many others from the fulfillment of basic needs to welfare in general. Dependency, she notes, "begins in the crib" and broadens throughout one's life as the circle of people we are dependent upon expands, De Grouchy argues that we cannot be indifferent to those who contribute to our happiness and welfare. We develop a capacity to care for them, and we are led in turn to care for their well-being and happiness. The claim that morality is embedded in dependency on others is a fundamental point in her philosophy, because eventually we depend on many other individuals. From this perspective, people's willingness to help those in need stems from an understanding of the extent of their dependency on others, or in fact, on the rest of humanity. De Grouchy here integrates ideas from two traditions, French sensationalism and British sentimentalism, to argue that morality originates in both physical sensations and sympathy, but claims that the most significant aspects of our moral disposition are dependency on others and our relations to them.

For Smith the perception of pain is not the basis for our capacity to sympathize, and neither are human relations. For Smith imagination is the basis for sympathy, because he claims that we do not directly perceive what another person feels. Imagination, he explains, functions to overcome what we do not naturally feel:

> As we have no immediate experience of what other men feel, we can form no idea of the manner in which they are affected, but by conceiving what we ourselves should

feel in the like situation. Though our brother is upon the rack, as long as we ourselves are at our ease, our senses will never inform us of what he suffers. They never did, and never can, carry us beyond our own person, and it is by the imagination only that we can form any conception of what are his sensations....By the imagination we place ourselves in his situation, we conceive ourselves enduring all the same torments, we enter as it were into his body, and become in some measure the same person with him, and thence form some idea of his sensations, and even feel something which, though weaker in degree, is not altogether unlike them. His agonies, when they are brought home to ourselves, when we have thus adopted and made them our own, begin at last to affect us, and we then tremble and shudder at the thought of what he feels.[15]

In order to be able to imagine what another person feels we need to change places with the sufferer and only then we can begin to sympathize. Thus, seeing a person on "the rack" is not disturbing to Smith until he can imagine what it would be like to be tortured. For de Grouchy our reaction is direct and immediate: "The first manifestations of particular sympathy arise at the very instant objects capable of stimulating it present themselves to us" (*Letters*, 386/123). The difference between our two authors lies in their perception of the difficulty involved in coming to sympathize with another, along with the function of sympathy altogether.

In *TMS* Smith provides a theory of moral judgment based on sympathy.[16] The first step for Smith is judgment of whether sympathy is appropriate at all. After providing a strong expression of what a sympathetic reaction can be, Smith continues to qualify his view and claims that without knowing what caused the person's

---

15. Ibid., p. 9.
16. Leonidas Montes in a recent article, "Das Adam Smith Problem: Its Origins, The stages of the Current Debates, and One Implication for Our Understanding of Sympathy," argues that viewing of Smith's concept of sympathy as moral judgment is a too narrow interpretation and that sympathy for Smith also serves as motive for action. We will see in Chapter Three that for Smith feeling sympathy can in some cases motivate us to help. Nevertheless, for the most part in *TMS* Smith applies sympathy as basis for judgment. Smith's claim that first we judge whether sympathy is appropriate at all still holds.

1. On Sympathy

grief, sympathy is "extremely imperfect." Sympathy is imperfect because you do not really know what happened. Naturally you would ask, "What has befallen you?"[17] What we ought to imagine is how we would feel under the same circumstances. In effect the question is: is this person justified in feeling grief? Smith gives an example of witnessing a person in anger, perhaps a violent expression of anger. We first need to determine whether we would be angry under the same circumstances. Should we determine that we would not feel the same in that case, then we would not sympathize. That is, sympathy depends on our own speculated reaction to the same causes. Indeed, Smith claims:

> Nature, it seems, teaches us to be more averse to enter into this passion, and, till informed of its cause, to be disposed rather to take part against it…Sympathy, therefore, does not arise so much from the view of the passion, as from that of the situation which excites it.[18]

Smith carries the full implications of his views in *TMS*. He concludes that we might sympathize with someone even if they do not think they are suffering. For instance, a person might be poor but happy. Nevertheless, when imagining ourselves in their situation, we feel compassion. We might judge that a person is not angry enough given his circumstances.

> We sometimes feel for another, a passion of which he himself seems to be altogether incapable; because, when we put ourselves in his case, that passion arises in our breast from the imagination, though it does not in his from the reality.[19]

Smith goes as far as insisting that a perception of feeling is not necessary to elicit sympathy, and thus he claims that we can even sympathize with the dead! We can sympathize with one who feels nothing, solely based on imagination of what it would be like to be in their situation:

> We sympathize even with the dead…It is miserable, we think, to be deprived of the light of sun; to be shut from life and conversation; to be laied in cold grave, a prey to corruption and the reptiles of the earth; to be no more

---

17. Smith, *TMS*, p. 11.
18. Ibid., pp. 11–12.
19. Ibid., p. 12.

> thought of in this world, but to be obliterated, in a little time, from the affections, and almost from memory, of their dearest friends and relations.[20]

Sympathy for Smith clearly correlates to a person's situation rather than to his or her emotions. It is also a conditional sentiment. In Smith's conception of sympathy we actually bypass the expression of pain to examine the causes and determine whether the person's reaction is appropriate and whether sympathy is warranted.

Smith's insistence on learning of someone's circumstances before sympathizing makes sense in the context of his system. T.D. Campbell argues that because Smith's *TMS* is a theory of moral judgment based on sympathy, sympathy has to be conditional.[21] Sympathetic feelings are the standards by which we judge one another; thus our feelings and theirs cannot coincide. Smith writes that in order to sympathize with another we need to check that their passions "are suitable to their objects." He then continues to offer a detailed and complex theory of moral judgment where we judge the propriety or impropriety of an action according to the sympathy (or lack of it) we feel with a person's intentions, and we judge merit or demerit of an action by the sympathy or lack or it we feel about the consequences of the action.

By contrast, for de Grouchy the role of sympathy is one of moral motivation. The sympathy we feel motivates us not only to help another person, but also to refrain from inflicting pain on another.

> But when we have freed them from some harm or evil, our pleasure, like theirs, arises from the cessation of pain, and it is even more natural [because of] the satisfaction of having made pain stop...Because the sight or idea of another's misfortune makes us experience a painful reaction, the feeling is more intense when we are the voluntary or even involuntary cause of this misfortune (*Letters*, 435–6/148–9).

We can see here the implications of the concept of sensitivity to pain in the *Letters*. If indeed through sympathy we too feel pain with another human being who suffers, then sympathy entails

---

20. Ibid., p. 12.
21. T.D Campbell, *Adam Smith's Science of Morals*, pp. 95–96.

1. On Sympathy

that we would not be able to bear the sight of suffering. The goal is: "Render them [children] easily remorseful and sensitive to the voice of honor and integrity so that they are unable to see suffering without being compelled to relieve it" (*Letters,* 366/112). Moreover, not only would we be driven to help, we would also have a more compelling reason to refrain from inflicting pain. A painful sensation or the fear of it are the "motive behind prudence" (Ibid., 437/149). In other words, de Grouchy views sympathy as a powerful force that can both motivate to help and serve as a deterrent from harm. The merit of this view is the idea that sympathy is a strong enough force that it can curtail cruelty. For de Grouchy, being able to experience sympathy rules out indifference to pain.

Smith would not necessarily object to the idea that sympathy compels us to help. The problem with his view is twofold: one, even though sympathy is a natural disposition, it is not so easy to achieve; and two, in the end sympathy is not a strong enough sentiment itself to motivate us to action. Smith presents the following limitation for sympathy. He claims that for sympathy to work, a "correspondence" of sentiments needs to take place. For example, he reminds us how good it feels when people are in agreement, share the same views, and laugh at the same jokes. If someone laughs too hard, Smith thinks, it would be hard to relate to that person. Since for Smith we access sympathy only through imagination, and given the difficulty in relating to another, what we feel is much weaker.

> After all this, however, the emotions of the spectator will still be very apt to fall short of the violence of what is felt by the sufferer. Mankind, though naturally sympathetic, never conceive, for what has befallen another, that degree of passion which naturally animates the person principally concerned. That imaginary change of situation, upon which their sympathy is founded, is but momentary... The person principally concerned is sensible of this, and at the same time passionately desires a more complete sympathy...But he can only hope to obtain this by lowering his passion to that pitch, in which the spectators are capable of going along with him. He must flatten, if I may be allowed to say so, the sharpness of its natural tone, in order to reduce it to harmony and concord with the emotions of those who are about him.[22]

---

22. Smith, *TMS*, pp. 21–22.

Both parties must tone down their reactions so they can relate to each other. Smith is uncomfortable with a strong expression of emotions. He conveys a lack of capability to sympathize with strong expressions of pain. In effect, in his opinion it is indecent to grieve or lament violently. The same goes with sympathy for happiness. Smith writes that "It gives us the spleen...to see another too happy or too much elevated."[23] This is a significant point in Smith's theory since out of this effort to produce a harmony of sentiments the impartial spectator is born. We come to consider the way a spectator would feel in our situation. We realize then that "If the passion is too high, or if it is too low, he [the spectator] cannot enter into it."[24] Propriety, Smith argues, consists in moderating the emotions. If we need to control the expression of our emotions so another person can sympathize with us, then the result is that what they feel only correlates to the display of emotions and not to what we really feel. Hence, for Smith sympathy is much weaker than the real experience of the other.

De Grouchy does not encounter the same difficulty in relating to another. Sympathy is a direct reaction: "Lastly, since we sympathize with the passions of others, the signs of those passions move us and suffice to make us feel them" (*Letters*, 426/142). Sympathy is also unconditional because it is a direct response to suffering, as opposed to Smith's conception of sympathy as indirect (via the imagination) and conditional. In de Grouchy's philosophy one again sees the background of sensationalism and her ideas of the origin of sympathy. Our first ties to others are ties of sympathy. Also, when feeling for another a physical reaction is present. De Grouchy starts with the assumption that before everything else we are similar and connected. What we feel is just as strong as the original sensation in the other. Smith, instead, assumes we are alone first, and therefore he requires imagination to bridge the gap. In the end, for Smith, we feel little and our emotions are "languid" compared to what the sufferer feels. If one agrees that the stronger the feeling, the more one would be compelled to help, then in de Grouchy's conception of sympathy we would reach much further with moral goals, and this point is completed in her *Letters* on progress, as we will demonstrate in Chapter Three.

---

23. Ibid., p. 16.
24. Ibid., p. 27.

1. On Sympathy

De Grouchy recognizes limits to sympathy, too. She could not live through a bloody revolution, witness a horrifying massacre, and be personally threatened and think that sympathy is prevalent and achieved with ease. For de Grouchy sympathy needs to be cultivated. She recognizes that people can become hardened. One of the recurring themes in the *Letters* is that sympathy needs to be exercised in order to develop, or even exist at all. She provides an analogy between physical exercise and exercising our sensibility to indicate that the vivacity of our moral disposition depends on tending to it.[25] From the point of view of the *Letters*, whether people end up with a disposition of the kind Smith describes or the kind de Grouchy espouses depends on one's goals of moral development and the effort and engagement in the process. Her conception of sympathy is of a disposition that can develop, that becomes habitual, and that eventually can constitute an integral part of one's interactions with other human beings. Quoting Smith, D.D. Raphael notes that Smith views beneficence in terms of what is "recommended by nature" and that Smith's sense of moral obligation follows.[26] Smith treats sympathy as a steady disposition. It entails choice, but not improvement. We judge according to what we feel or do not feel as a result of imagination and thought. In de Grouchy's view of sympathy, beyond what we feel instinctively, there is room to ask what we ought to feel. For her, education and cultivating sensitivity in others is one of the goals of morality.

Finally in this connection, de Grouchy claims that sympathy is augmented by enthusiasm, which she also labels a moral phenomenon. Enthusiasm, defined as "a sentiment of the soul," is a capacity to imagine all the pleasures and all the pains that may arise from a certain situation. Through enthusiasm one can imagine an event in an exaggerated manner, thus multiplying the effects of what one sees or conceives. One can immediately imagine what it would be like to experience events that in reality can take a lifetime to occur. Her explanation and terminology are not entirely clear in the *Letters* alone. It is easier to understand what enthusiasm signifies by looking at Voltaire's definition of enthusiasm in his *Philosophical Dictionary*. Voltaire

---

25. For a good summary of cultivating sympathy through education see Evelyn Forget, "Cultivating Sympathy."
26. D.D. *Raphael, The impartial Spectator*, p. 76

sees enthusiasm as an emotional state, an ability to react emotionally to an event.

> It is the rarest of things to unite reason with enthusiasm. Reason consists of always seeing things as they are. The drunkard is deprived of this reason when he sees things double. Enthusiasm is precisely like wine: it can excite so much tumult in the blood vessels, and such violent vibrations in the nerves, that the reason is entirely destroyed...This is what happens in great outbursts of eloquence, and above all in sublime poetry.[27]

Although differences are noted, enthusiasm explains the non-rational workings of the passions. De Grouchy applies enthusiasm to explain the workings of sympathy. She explains that enthusiasm predisposes us towards unreflective sympathy, and thus it increases the effects of sympathy. What we multiply here would be the images or thoughts of people's suffering. In all these aspects of the *Letters*, then, sympathy and the extent and depth of a sympathetic disposition are matters of choice and training.

The differences between Smith and de Grouchy's conceptions of sympathy affected their social and political views, as we will see. But first, we need to examine de Grouchy's criticism of Smith's views on reason.

---

27. Voltaire, *Philosophical Dictionary*, p. 188.

Chapter 2

Reason and Sentiments

Recent scholars such as Emma Rothschild and Jessica Riskin show that the Enlightenment can be better understood by incorporating the role sentiments and sensibility played in contemporary discussions. In this regard, the *Letters* become an interesting case study. But more particularly, de Grouchy's views concerning reason and sentiments need to be placed in the context of British philosophy, where an actual debate concerning the predominance of these dispositions took place.

The Debate Concerning Reason or Sentiments as Basis for Morality

Adam Smith wrote *The Theory of Moral Sentiments* in the context of a long debate during the seventeenth and eighteenth centuries over whether morality was grounded in reason or sentiments. This debate began after the Reformation and the Scientific Revolution, and was a reaction to these developments. Modern philosophers set out to establish a secular foundation for morality, with science rather than theology as a model to emulate. Leslie Stephen provides a lengthy discussion of this shift in his *History of English Thought in the Eighteenth Century*. Stephen notes that during the Middle Ages, when moral theories were theologically based, questions such as "Why ought we be good?" and "What does goodness mean?" received complete and satisfactory answers in theology.

For Stephen, the idea that revelation and divine command were no longer sought as an explanation of human morality became a difficult challenge to moral theory, since no other dictates are as compelling. Thus Stephen claims that developments in moral philosophy at that time can be seen as an attempt to provide a non-religious foundation for morality. He writes:

> The prohibition of murder is no longer uttered by a visible Deity from Mount Sinai. Why, then, should we not commit murder? and how do we know that it is wrong? Hell no longer yawns before us; what punishment has the murderer to dread?...How could order be preserved when old sanctions are decaying? Can a society of atheists be maintained?...How, to put the question less bluntly, should morality survive theology?[1]

Indeed, one can look at the history of moral philosophy from Hobbes onward as an attempt to provide a secular foundation for morality, independent of divine origin, and as stemming purely and variously from human rationality, sentiments, or social contract theory. The issue of the relation between religion and morality lingered through the eighteenth century, as one finds that references to God or a deity are prevalent in the literature. It has also been a source of controversy in interpreting philosophers such as Hobbes, Hume, and Smith. Smith, for instance, refers to God as the author of our nature and our judge, and he speaks of the afterlife as a place where justice will be done to everyone. Yet, Smith does not base his moral theory on religion. Instead Smith, among others, saw the foundation for morality in human nature.

The interest in establishing a rational basis for morality as natural is also a reaction to Hobbes's claim that we are amoral, apolitical beings.[2] But the question is, what is it in human

---

1. Stephen, *History of English Thought In the Eighteenth Century*, 2:1–2. KB emphasis.
2. For more on Hobbes' impact on the British Moralists see Bernard H. Baumrin, *Introduction*, Selby-Bigge 1964.

2. Reason and Sentiments

nature that gives rise to morality? Various answers were given and precipitated the aforementioned debate of whether morality was grounded in reason or sentiments. Hence, two schools of thought emerged, the rationalists and the sentimentalists. Both schools formed part of what is termed in the literature as British Moralists, Smith being one of them. D. D. Raphael, following and amending Selby-Bigge, divides moral philosophy during this time along these lines:

> When I judge that I ought to do a certain action, do I make this judgement of the basis of knowing, or of feeling, or of sensing something? This question played an important part in the discussions of the eighteenth-century moralists and gave rise to what is known as the controversy between sense and reason in morals. The main participants in the controversy were Shaftsbury, Hutcheson, Hume and Adam Smith on the side of sense and feeling, and Samuel Clarck, Wollaston, Balguy, Richard Price and Reid on the side of reason or knowledge.[3]

Virtually all moral philosophers at the time acknowledged taking part in this debate. Hume, for example, opens his *Inquiry Concerning the Principles of Morals* with the following statement:

> There has been a controversy started of late, much better worth examination, concerning the general foundation of Morals; whether they be derived from Reason, or from Sentiments; Whether we attain the knowledge of them by a chain of argument and induction, or by an immediate feeling and finer internal sense; whether, like all sound judgment of truth and falsehood, they should be the same to every rational intelligent being; or whether, like the perception of beauty and deformity, they be founded entirely on the particular fabric and constitution of the human species.[4]

Hume tells us that he is interested in the above question since "moral speculation" ought to affect our behavior; for Hume,

---

3. Raphael, *The Moral Sense*, pp. 1–2. The division into rationalists and sentimentalists is general. There are finer nuances in these schools of thought, such as intuitionists among the rationalists and moral sense theorists among the sentimentalists.
4. Hume, *Inquiry Concerning the Principles of Morals*, p. 2.

morality is "a practical study." With the aim of attaining virtue and avoiding vice, Hume asks whether we are influenced by reason or by our feelings. The question in effect is two-fold: it concerns moral motivation and moral epistemology. That is, whence stems the desire to be moral and how do we figure out what is the moral course of action? One finds Smith's account of this debate in section VII of Smith's *Theory of Moral Sentiments*.

Since *TMS* was written within the context of this debate, in translating and commenting on Smith's work de Grouchy integrates herself into this controversy as well. Reading the *Letters* as a part of this debate is particularly important since, while acknowledging the controversy, de Grouchy objects to this dichotomy and does not align herself with the choices her contemporaries established. She argues that neither reason nor sentiments on their own are sufficient to create a moral constitution, but both are required. Thus she bridges the gap between the rationalists and the sentimentalists.[5] Smith stays loyal to the sentimentalist tradition, explaining the entire scope of morality through sentiments, and this becomes a source of criticism by de Grouchy. A comparison between Smith and de Grouchy's views on the moral emotions and the role of reason and sentiments in one's moral disposition will again reveal de Grouchy's originality and critical engagement with Smith.[6]

Moral Emotions

The most prominent point of comparison between Smith and de Grouchy on moral emotion is found in their discussion of remorse. Morality in general for Smith is learned in a social context rather than in solitude. Smith compares society to a mirror to indicate that without a mirror we would not have any idea

---

5. This debate resurfaced in the latter half of the twentieth century with philosophical work concerning justice and care. Recently philosophers have been suggesting that both justice and care are pertinent to ethics. With this point and others, De Grouchy was prescient and an innovative thinker. This theme will be discussed in a last chapter on feminist ethics.
6. The term moral emotions is a twentieth-century term. Recently philosophers such as Robert Solomon, Amélie Rorty, Michael Stocker, Bernard Williams, and others argue that emotions possess a cognitive content (when one is angry or scared he or she is angry or scared about something) and as such can serve as the basis for judgment. For de Grouchy emotions such as regret and remorse are moral emotions since an indication of right and wrong is necessarily embedded in them.

of the beauty or deformity of our own face. Likewise, without society we would not have any idea of the goodness of our character, conduct or sentiments. In solitude there is no one to reflect on or respond to our conduct and no criterion is provided to judge our actions. But as soon as we are placed in society, Smith argues, we consider our passions and conduct in light of what other people think of us. Smith makes the assumption that we are endowed with a natural disposition to care about the way in which we appear in other people's eyes. We crave being loved and dread being hated. He makes a further distinction; we not only desire love, but wish to become a person who deserves love. This desire for praise and the aversion to blame ensures our future actions will become ones that merit people's approval. This is Smith's view of remorse: we come to regret actions that result in social scorn.

Smith illustrates his view of remorse with his example of murder. Murder, he writes, is the most atrocious crime because death is the greatest evil a human being can inflict upon another. Smith claims that after killing someone, the murderer, when reflecting on his actions, would sympathize with what other people think of him, which is hatred and abhorrence. Smith thinks that through sympathy people internalize the way others feel about them. As a result, the murderer feels hatred and abhorrence toward himself. The pertinent distinction here is that even though Smith claims that the murderer would sympathize and feel pity for the victim, the most dominant aspect of remorse is the effect of internalizing people's judgment.

> The thought of this [having murdered] perpetually haunts him, and fills him with terror and amazement. He dares no longer look society in the face, but imagines himself as it were rejected, and thrown out from the affections of all mankind. He cannot hope for the consolation of sympathy in this his greatest and most dreadful distress. The remembrance of his crimes has shut out all fellow-feeling with him from the hearts of his fellow-creatures...His own thought can present him with nothing but what is black, unfortunate, and disastrous, the melancholy foreboding of incomprehensible misery and ruin.[7]

---

7. Smith, *TMS*, p. 84.

The murderer would like to run away and hide, but solitude seems more horrifying. He remains in society full of feelings of shame and remorse. Smith writes:

> The horror of solitude drives him back into society, and he comes again into the presence of mankind, astonished to appear before them, loaded with shame and distracted with fear, in order to supplicate some little protection from the countenance of those very judges, who he knows have already unanimously condemned him.[8]

Remorse for Smith is a powerful emotion that haunts and torments. Similarly, a good deed is followed by anticipation of sympathy, gratitude, and approval. Viewing one's deeds from the point of view of others creates feelings of confidence, harmony, and satisfaction.

So far, Smith provides a powerful description of the effect of remorse, but then he compromises the role of emotions with his theory of the impartial spectator. Underlying Smith's theory of the impartial spectator is his belief that many ethical problems stem from a selfish and thus distorted point of view. Moreover, Smith notes that "self-deceit, this fatal weakness of mankind, is the source of half the disorders of human life."[9] One cannot become moral with a vision clouded with selfish tendencies, and thus the individual is in dire need of self correction.

Since for Smith we cannot judge our own motives unless we remove ourselves from our own situation, the impartial spectator constitutes an essential role in his philosophy. Indeed, Smith is so convinced that better morality would result from incorporating an objective point of view that he claims, "If we saw ourselves in the light in which others see us, or in which they would see us if they knew all, a reformation would generally be unavoidable."[10] As a result, Smith assigns only a contingent role to emotions because they need to be judged in light of the impartial spectator. The effect of Smith's quest for objectivity is that the perspective of the impartial spectator takes precedent over emotions.

> It is he [the impartial spectator] who shows us the propriety of generosity and the deformity of injustice;

---

8. Smith, *TMS*, p. 85.
9. Smith, *TMS*, p. 158.
10. Smith, *TMS*, pp. 158–59.

> the propriety of resigning the greatest interests of our own, for the yet greater interests of others, and the deformity of doing the smallest injury to another, in order to obtain the greatest benefit to ourselves. It is not the love of our neighbor, it is not the love of mankind, which upon many occasions prompts us to the practice of those divine virtues. It is a stronger love, a more powerful affection, which generally takes place upon such occasions; the love of what is honourable and noble, of the grandeur, and dignity, and superiority of our own characters.[11]

Smith then claims that we do not help others because we love them. We help them because we love the general, objective point of view of the impartial spectator.

The same applies to deterrence. For Smith the way in which the impartial spectator becomes effective in shaping human morality is through fear of the most dreadful consequence, which is social condemnation. Smith writes: "We dread the thought of doing any thing which can render us the just and proper objects of the hatred and contempt of our fellow-creatures."[12] In the end, we are motivated to help because we admire social praise, and we avoid harming because we fear blame. Smith's moral philosophy is still based on sentiments. Loving praise and dreading blame constitute emotional motivation. But in the end it is not our own sentiments that affect us, but the ones we adopt following the impartial spectator.

There are two points of comparison to de Grouchy. First, how is remorse triggered? De Grouchy again provides an empirical explanation for moral emotions. Because sympathy consists in feeling pleasure or pain with another, it follows that we feel an even more intense pleasure in contributing to the happiness of others and a more intense pain in harming them. For de Grouchy, remorse stems from sympathizing with the victim's pain and the idea that we caused it. This is in contrast to Smith, for whom remorse stems from social scorn.

The second point of comparison concerns the effect of remorse. De Grouchy argues that in addition to the pleasure of doing good we also feel pleasure of having done good, which remains in us as a *general and abstract sentiment*.

---

11. Smith, *TMS*, p. 137.
12. Smith, *TMS*, pp. 117–18.

> We thus feel a natural pleasure in doing good. But there yet another sentiment arises from its pleasure: the satisfaction of having done good. Just as is the case of physical pain, beyond the immediate, local impression, an unpleasant general sensation arises throughout our body…Thus, the long-lasting satisfaction of having done good joins the pleasure of doing good. This feeling becomes, in some way, general and abstract since we feel it anew at the mere recollection of good actions without recalling their particular circumstances (*Letters*, 434–5/148–9).

In her explanation of abstract sentiments, de Grouchy first refers the reader back to her discussion of the abstract idea of pain to indicate that she is speaking of the same process. From a particular instance of doing good follows a general feeling and sense of what it is like to do a good deed. Similarly, having done wrong produces a painful sentiment, a feeling of regret and remorse. Remorse, then, can also become a general and abstract feeling that is not related to the specific action that gave rise to it.

> Just as the satisfaction of having done a good integrates itself into our existence and makes us feel good, so, too, the recognition of having done something wrong attaches itself to us and upsets our existence. It produces sentiments of regret and of remorse that bother us, afflict us, disturb us, and make us suffer, even when we do not retain a distinct memory of the initial impression of pain that our wrongs make us feel (*Letters*, 437–8/150).

The point is that general and abstract sentiments are triggered upon thinking about good or bad deeds, in the same way as the memory or sight of pain triggers a general impression of pain. In this way, abstract sentiments for de Grouchy serve as moral motivation or deterrence.

> The remorse of wrongdoing and the satisfaction of the good we have done can also exist without reimagining the details of these actions. We no longer have even the general memory of having done something good or evil, but are motivated by the more abstract and even more general feeling of having done well or not done well (*Letters*, 444/153).

2. Reason and Sentiments

What de Grouchy wishes to establish with her notion of an abstract sentiment is that we can have a feeling that something is right or wrong prior to and independent of thinking about it. We develop an instinctive feeling for the moral appropriateness of a particular action. For instance, consider the issue of torture of political prisoners or terrorists. What de Grouchy would hope is that before we come to think rationally about human rights, for instance, we would reject torture because it would feel very wrong. Thus, the effect of remorse (and positive feelings as well) are the abstract sentiments that constitute a tendency to do good and avoid harm. Feelings of regret, remorse, or joy always accompany our actions and serve as indication of right and wrong. Out of the pleasure and pain we feel for helping or hurting someone, a moral conscience is born.

> The fear of remorse suffices to distance all men from evil...The satisfaction associated with good actions and the terror created by the memory of bad ones are two effective motivators for shaping all our actions. These two sentiments are universal. They constitute the principles and the foundation of morality for the human species (*Letters*, 438/150).

De Grouchy's theory of abstract sentiments can be considered against Smith's impartial spectator. For Smith, we are deterred from harming by the wrath of the impartial spectator. For de Grouchy we are deterred by an abstract sentiment and by the bad feeling we get from the thought of doing harm. In contrast, for Smith we do feel bad, but initially as a result of an external, objective point of view.

For de Grouchy abstract sentiments develop out of our own experience and out of the recollection of a good action. For this recollection to occur, sentiments "must be linked to our existence" (*Letters*, 434/148). The effect of this linkage is two-fold. One, de Grouchy claims that in this way we take a personal interest in others. And two, moral sentiments become ingrained in us and an integral part of our being, and consequently they become habitual. De Grouchy here further develops her initial claim that morality is deeply rooted in our nature.

> The idea that this action is *good* implies a secret satisfaction; the idea that it is *bad* suggests remorse in precisely ways that the mere idea of physical pleasure

or pain produces in the present and for the future, a painful or pleasant sensation. In some respects, what happens here is what happens in the sciences that use certain methods and certain principles that are relied on for their exactness and truth, without recalling the proof we once worked through. Similarly, one follows general sentiments without thinking of the manner by which they were formed at and all that justifies them . (*Letters*, 443–4/152–3)

The use of emotions in the *Letters* is a powerful resource, and de Grouchy certainly appeals to the heart in terms of morality. Yet she does not leave all to the emotions, as we will see next.

Reason and Sentiments

Smith stays loyal and consistent with regard to sentimentalism throughout his theory. Smith's failure to adequately acknowledge the role and significance of reason is a source of a notable criticism by de Grouchy. The following is Smith's critique of reason and morality. In addressing the rationalist's challenge that emotions might not be consistent or reliable, Smith concedes the point and claims that we need general rules of morality to direct our conduct. He recognizes that we might not always possess the appropriate feelings and states that rules are able to compensate in the absence of sentiments. Smith provides several examples to illustrate his point. When a friend visits and you are not in the mood to socialize, you will still receive your friend kindly out of deference to a rule. Or, Smith speaks of a case of a man who receives a great benefit but does not feel gratitude in his heart. If properly educated he would still manifest gratitude and the social grace called for. For instance, he might make regular visits to his benefactor.

Smith carries this thought to personal relationships, claiming that a wife who does not feel a tender regard for her husband will, if virtuously educated, act as if she felt it. By virtue of following rules people will not fail in their duties. However, Smith insists that rules are derived from sentiments as well. They are not rational constructs. Again, with regard to murder Smith explains that one detests a murder first, and then a general rule is formed:

> To the man who first saw an inhuman murder, committed from avarice, envy, or unjust resentment...who beheld the last agonies of the dying person...His detestation of this crime, it is evident, would arise instantaneously and antecedent to his having formed to himself any such general rule. The general rule, on the contrary, which he might afterwards form, would be founded upon the detestation which he felt necessarily arise in his own breast, at the thought of this, and every other particular action of the same kind.[13]

Smith stays close to Hume in his criticism of rationalism. For Smith reason is instrumental only; moral truths are indicated solely by sentiments.

> But reason cannot render any particular object either agreeable or disagreeable to the mind for its own sake. Reason may show that this object is the means of obtaining some other which is naturally either pleasing or displeasing, and in this manner may render it either agreeable or disagreeable for the sake of something else. But nothing can be agreeable or disagreeable for its own sake, which is not rendered such by immediate sense and feeling.[14]

For Smith then, reason is morally neutral. Smith also needs to address the charge that sentiments do not yield objectivity and universal moral precepts. According to Smith, we overcome subjectivity and moral relativism through rules and the impartial spectator. The impartial spectator is also based on sentiments as judgment is formed based on the way the impartial spectator would feel, not think.

De Grouchy provides a lengthy explanation of the manner in which distinctions between good and evil have already been made by sentiments. But she asks, are sentiments sufficient? She labels this question "the most important question in moral theory" because she sets out to show that "reason alone united with sentiment can still lead us to the good by more sure, pleasant, easy, and less complicated means that are liable to fewer errors and dangers." (*Letters*, 468/164)

---

13. Smith, *TMS*, pp. 159–60. Also see Hume, *Treatise*, III.i.1, where Hume compares judgment of murder to an aesthetic judgment.
14. Smith, *TMS*, p. 320.

De Grouchy's argument rests on the assumption that we necessarily reflect on sentiments that arise, and thus ideas of good and evil emerge:

> Thus, my dear C***, sentiment alone already creates a distinction among our actions since some are accompanied by pleasure and followed by an internal satisfaction, while others are accompanied by anguish and followed by an always disagreeable and often painful feeling. But this more lasting feeling of satisfaction or of pain connected to the recollection of the good or harm we have done to others is necessarily modified by reflection. And the modifications which reflection entails lead us to the idea of the moral good or evil. (*Letters*, 439–440/150–1)

Ideas of good and evil, then, emerge when reflecting on feelings of right and wrong. De Grouchy argues that when we submit sentiments to the scrutiny of reason we thus obtain ideas of good, evil, justice, and rights. De Grouchy claims that concepts such as justice and rights are rational constructs first because they require a more complex thought process. Justice and injustice are more specific application of ideas of good and evil.

> In evaluating moral good or evil, we submit the natural sentiment of sympathy to reason, and reason then directs it toward the most pressing claim. In evaluating the just and the unjust, we submit this sentiment to reason, itself guided by general rules, notably a preference founded on general and logical grounds that aim for the greatest good, that is to say, directed by the rule of *right*. (*Letters*, 457/159)

In addition, concepts such as justice and rights are the domain of reason since de Grouchy sees reason as universal and its dictates as necessary truths. Thus she argues, ideas such as human rights and equality could never be contingent. They are true for all beings at all times.

> The morality of our actions, the idea of justice, and the desire to be just are the necessary outcomes of sensibility and of reason. In this regard every reasonable and impressionable being will have the same ideas. The limits of these ideas will be the same, and these ideas can thus become the object of an exact science because

2. Reason and Sentiments

> they have an invariable basis. Indeed, one can express by the word *just* whatever idea one wants, but everyone who reasons well will have a common notion of justice. Given that moral ideas are not arbitrary, their definitions can vary only in the more or less clear or more or less general way of presenting them. (*Letters*, 463/162)

De Grouchy criticizes Smith for not deriving the concept of justice from the general rules of morality. (Smith argues that our sense of justice stems from sentiments and specifically that injustice stems from resentment of injury.)[15] She accuses Smith of being too vague with regard to the foundation of justice because she expects the concept of justice to be unequivocal and, for this reason, necessary.[16]

Against the pure sentimentalists de Grouchy claims: "As if reason could approve leaving to a sovereign (who, sometimes, can be a tyrant) no other restraint than his remorse, the progress of Enlightenment, or the despair of his victims." (*Letters*, 457/159) Sentiments are necessary but not sufficient for social action. Against the pure rationalists de Grouchy claims that moral thinking is unlike any other rational thinking because we are not indifferent to it.[17] Assent to moral truths is different from assent to mathematical proofs because affect is always involved. Perhaps the question of whether light consists of particles or waves might leave us indifferent, whereas to questions regarding abortion or capital punishment we have emotional reactions. Indeed, de Grouchy argues that moral truths are always preceded and followed by an emotional reaction.

> This first building block needed to be put in place. The origin of our moral sentiments had to be shown to lie in our natural and unreflective sympathy for the physical pains of others, and the origin of our moral ideas to lie in reflection. Assent to a moral truth especially had to be shown to differ from assent to a mathematical or physical truth in that an inner desire to harmonize our

---

15. Smith, *TMS*, p.79.
16. De Grouchy's criticism is not charitable enough to Smith. Smith does claim that justice is a universal value (*TMS*, p. 79) In addition, de Grouchy's criticism is based on *TMS*, Smith has a more developed and complex theory of justice in his *Lectures on Jurisprudence*.
17. For the rationalists the analogy between ethical truths and mathematical truths lies in their necessity. The fact that love is good and hate is bad is not a contingent matter. See D.D. Raphael, *Moral Philosophy*.

conduct accompanies it, along with the desire to see others so align theirs, as well as a fear of not doing so and a regret of having failed to do so. Yet, one cannot say that morality is founded on sentiment alone, since it is reason that shows us what is just or unjust. But, even less can one maintain that morality is founded uniquely on reason because reason's judgment is nearly always preceded and followed by a sentiment that indicates and confirms it and because reason initially acquires moral ideas from sentiments, ideas it then elevates into principles. (*Letters*, 463/162)

Moral sentiments, then, originate in sympathy, and moral ideas originate in reflection. There are two aspects to de Grouchy's objection to the dichotomy between reason and sentiments, one empirical, the other theoretical. Empirically, she provides an extensive description of the way in which moral ideas are formed and proves that they are not derived solely from reason but are based on sentiments as well. To claim that morality stems solely from human reason is overlooking human nature and moral development. In encountering moral truths there is both an emotional desire to fulfill a goal and a fear of avoiding it. Thus moral truths are always accompanied by feelings that prompt us to act accordingly. Theoretically, for de Grouchy without emotions one would lack humanity, and without reason one would not be able to formulate theories concerning universal rights and equality. By not taking feelings into consideration we loose a powerful moral force, and without proper reasoning a violation of people's rights might occur. For de Grouchy one cannot be a moral agent without human sentiments and without a rational understanding of the necessity of general laws.

In addition, de Grouchy claims that the process of abstraction occurs and is necessary in both rational and non-rational spheres. Experiencing an abstract and general sentiment versus forming abstract and general ideas is what distinguishes hearts from minds. Without general and abstract sentiments hearts might remain egotistic. On the other hand, hearts capable of general sentiments always follow conscience. Without the capability of generalizing, minds cannot arrive at general rules. Minds that are capable of calculating, comparing, and conjuring results are able to form well-supported general truths. However, de Grouchy cautions, both faculties, reason and sentiments, are fallible. Passions can stifle intelligence, and prejudice can blind reason.

> In some sense one must first seek in their passions the forces that can extend and renew their intelligence weakened by inaction or and degraded by error. One can then have them adopt the truth...One of the primary goals of education should thus be to provide the ability to acquire the general idea and to experience these abstract and general sentiments that I have discussed. (*Letters*, 449–50/155)

Although she does not develop a complete theory of education in the *Letters*, de Grouchy lays heavy emphasis on moral education. The goal of education for her is acquiring this power of abstraction both intellectually and emotionally. She blames educators for teaching children logic and grammar while neglecting to develop their sensitivity and consideration for others.

We can see in her discussion of reason and sentiments the full development of her empiricism and sensationalism. In the opening of the fifth *Letter* she claims that moral theorists (except Rousseau) did not examine the origin of moral ideas, and this research is the only one capable of explaining the connection between sentiments and moral ideas. Pleasure and pain accompany our actions, and through sympathy and abstract sentiments they serve as an indication of right and wrong. Moral ideas arise when reflecting on sentiments. Here she completes what Locke began by showing in what way ideas of good and evil arise from sensations of pleasure and pain.

The basis of de Grouchy's polemic against this long-standing debate, which lasted about one hundred and fifty years and in which Smith clearly took sides, is that reason and sentiments are inseparable. De Grouchy realizes that our moral constitution is complex and prevails through various aspects, including reason, sentiments, and conscience. The strength and depth of her moral theory lie not only in her seeing that both reason and sentiments are necessary to form a moral action, but also in her showing how in and of themselves neither reason nor sentiment are sufficient to generate moral action. She does not reduce morality either to reason or to sentiment. Instead of the aforementioned dichotomy between the two faculties, she shows how both reason and sentiments are complementary and how they enhance each other to provide a better moral constitution. In adding to the rationalists the importance of emotional experience and in adding to the sentimentalists the role of reason, she bridges the gap between the two schools of thought.

The full significance of de Grouchy's theory of reason and sentiments can be better appreciated in the context of the last two *Letters*, where we can see the implications for social and political theory. We turn to an examination these *Letters* next.

Chapter 3

Social and Political Philosophy

Scholars today read Smith primarily as a philosopher and more specifically as a moral philosopher, claiming that one cannot understand Smith's economics apart from his ethics. Several scholars have shown that Smith has been misinterpreted through studying his economics in isolation. This approach has resulted in reading certain issues such as the role of self-interest and the invisible hand out of context, resulting in distorted views of Smith.[1] Consequently, there are new interpretations of key issues in Smith which vary. Sophie de Grouchy, as Smith's contemporary and as someone who probably knew him personally, adds a unique insight to Smith's work. Reading the *Letters* adds to today's debates in Smith scholarship.

Self-interest, Selfishness and Helping Others

Selfishness and self-interest are of major concern in *TMS*, and these themes are addressed throughout the work. Smith views selfishness as a natural disposition, but in writing a moral theory

---

1. On this point, see Emma Rothschild, Charles Griswold, Samuel Fleischacker, Leonidas Montes, Jerry Evensky and John Jill.

he sets out the goal of overcoming it: "...to feel much for others and little for ourselves, that to restrain our selfish, and to indulge our benevolent affections, constitutes the perfection of human nature."[2] There are two important points to consider here: One, even though Smith sees selfishness as natural, he does not view it as the only disposition, but one among others. He offers three categories: social, unsocial, and selfish passions. Selfish passions, Smith claims, are to be ranged between social and unsocial ones.[3] Secondly, since selfishness is not a moral disposition, nor is it conducive to moral behavior, Smith devotes good portions of TMS to explaining when and how we over come selfish tendencies. The issue here in comparison with de Grouchy is that Smith provides an analysis of human nature and morality that begins with a conflict between a selfish tendency and the goal of altruism.

De Grouchy avoids this problem. We saw in Chapter One that de Grouchy constructs sympathy as *relational* disposition, that is, sympathy presupposes a human interaction, as opposed to Smith's concept of sympathy which is *individualistic*. Smith does speak of the primacy of family relationships, claiming that we are habituated to sympathize with family members first and that sympathy with family members approaches what a person feels for themselves.[4] Still, family comes after the self, and in the end people are most concerned about themselves. According to Smith,

> Every man, as the Stoics used to say, is first and principally recommended to his own care; and every man is certainly, in every respect, fitter and abler to take care of himself than of any other person. Every man feels his own pleasures and his own pains more sensibly than those of other people. The former are the original sensations; the latter the reflected or sympathetic images of those sensations. The former may be said to be the substance; the latter the shadow.[5]

If sympathy arises within the individual, as Smith argues, and not out of a relation to another person, then one's primary concern would be towards oneself. The idea that one's moral

---

2. Smith, TMS, p. 25.
3. Smith, TMS, p. 40.
4. Smith, TMS, p. 219.
5. Smith, TMS, p. 219.

3. Social and Political Philosophy

disposition leads one to care for oneself first follows. If sympathy arises out of a relation to another, as de Grouchy claims, then relations and connections to other human beings serve as the foundation for morality. If we are connected before we are alone, then one's primary concern would be both towards oneself and others. Smith's concept of selfishness and later self-interest logically follows from his individualism. Recent commentators indicate that Smith should not be viewed as a radical or atomistic individualist in the sense Hobbes conceived of it. Smith indeed thinks that we are social beings. Nevertheless, he views sympathy as a disposition that arises within the individual prior to social interaction. In de Grouchy's philosophy there is no point at which we can consider ourselves in isolation, since this circumstance is never the case empirically. We previously saw in Chapter One that this is a main source of criticism by de Grouchy. Further differences between Smith and de Grouchy on social issues follow from this initial conception of sympathy.

The most prominent difference between Smith and de Grouchy pertains to feeling sympathy with distant people or people whom we do not know. Consequently, they hold different views concerning our motivation to help strangers. Caring for one's family or sympathizing with those we love, with friends, or with other close connections is not as difficult as sympathizing with people we do not know. For both Smith and de Grouchy this disposition comes naturally and hence is not such a great challenge to moral theory. The more difficult question derives from issues such as famine, political oppression, or crimes against humanity in a distant place. Why should we care? How are we to react to suffering taking place in a distant country? Are we obligated to help those with whom we have no relations? Both de Grouchy and Smith address this issue in their theories in different ways.

Smith addresses the question of sympathy for distant persons explicitly in Part III of *TMS*, which deals with the impartial spectator and our sense of duty. In this section, Smith first establishes that the impartial spectator has a dual purpose, i.e., self-judgment and judgment of others. Smith then raises the question: how do we make a proper comparison between our own interests and those of others? To this question he replies that we are obviously biased in our own favor, and only the impartial spectator offers an objective perspective and is in a position to compare our interests to others. And more specifically, given our starting point of partiality towards ourselves, the question arises: what is our duty toward others? We see then that the initial conception of a conflict between selfishness and altruism translates into seeing our interests as separate from or in conflict with others, and hence Smith faced the task of setting moral parameters to self-interest.

In an earlier discussion in *TMS* on human nature, Smith observes that sympathy depends on a connection with people. Hence, in cases were there is no connection, Smith fails to detect sympathy:

> Men, though naturally sympathetic, feel so little for another, with whom they have no particular connexion, in comparison of what they feel for themselves; the misery of one, who is merely their fellow-creature, is of so little importance to them in comparison even of a small conveniency of their own.[6]

Since Smith eliminates sympathy in the absence of an apparent connection, and given his view of human nature, when considering distant people we are left with considerations of self-interest and the ethical question: how much self-interest is acceptable?

In his discussion of duty, Smith claims that a small loss of our own appears to us much worse than a disaster for someone with whom we have no connection. To illustrate, he provides the following scenario. Suppose that the empire of China with all its inhabitants was suddenly swallowed by an earthquake. Upon hearing the news, the European humanitarian would feel sorrow. At first, all kinds of thoughts and humanitarian sentiments might appear, but they would not last for too long.

> And when all this fine philosophy was over, when all these humane sentiments had been once fairly expressed, he would pursue his business or his pleasure, take repose or his diversion, with the same ease and tranquility, as if no accident has happened. The most frivolous disaster which could befall himself would occasion a more real disturbance. If he was to lose his little finger to-morrow, he would not sleep to-night; but, provided he never saw them, he will snore with the most profound secu-

---

6. Smith, *TMS*, p. 86.

> rity over the ruin of a hundred million of his brethren, and the destruction of that immense multitude seems plainly an object less interesting to him, than this paltry misfortune of his own. To prevent, therefore, this paltry misfortune to himself, would a man of humanity be willing to sacrifice the lives of a hundred millions of his brethren, provided that he had never seen them?[7]

Smith replies that, of course, no such person exists. People do sacrifice their own interests for the benefit of others all the time. And it is through the impartial spectator we overcome selfish tendencies:

> When we are always so much more deeply affected by whatever concerns ourselves, than by whatever concerns other men; what is it which prompts the generous, upon all occasions, and the mean upon many, to sacrifice their own interests to the greater interests of others? It is not the soft power of humanity, it is not that feeble spark of benevolence which Nature has lighted up in the human heart, that is thus capable of counteracting the strongest impulses of self-love. It is a stronger power, a more forcible motive, which exerts itself upon occasions. It is reason, principle, conscience, the inhabitant of the breast, the man within, the great judge and arbiter of our conduct.[8]

Smith appeals to the impartial spectator because he thinks that benevolence is not a strong enough force to counteract selfishness and partiality. For Smith, without the impartial spectator we would take little interest in our neighbor. Appealing to the impartial spectator is consistent with the theory of *TMS* since, as seen in Chapter One, sympathy is constructed as mostly moral judgment and not necessarily as a motivational force. So lack of feelings should not strip us of potential foreign aid.

But Smith does not conclude that the impartial spectator would indicate an obligation to help distant trouble. Instead, he makes the following distinction between cases in which the other's calamities depend on us and cases where they do not. In the former case we should not prefer our own interests to theirs, but in the latter, we should. Smith poses the question

---

7. Smith, *TMS*, pp. 136–37.
8. Smith, *TMS*, p. 137.

clearly: How should we feel about remote suffering that we did not cause?

> When the happiness or misery of others, indeed, in no respect depends upon our conduct, when our interests are altogether separated and detached from theirs, so that there is neither connexion nor competition between them, we do not always think it so necessary to restrain, either our natural and, perhaps, improper anxiety about our own affairs, or our natural and, perhaps, equally improper indifference about those of other men.[9]

As mentioned, this section of *TMS* focuses on our sense of duty as well, and Smith claims that our sense of duty can motivate us to act in case of absence of sentiments. But here too, Smith does not apply his ideas concerning duty to the remote. After Smith acknowledges that we do not necessarily feel anxiety on behalf of misfortunes we did not cause, he affirms that we also do not have a duty to feel any anxiety:

> Whatever interest we take in the fortune of those with whom we have no acquaintance or connexion, and who are placed altogether out of the sphere of our activity, can produce only anxiety to ourselves, without any manner of advantage to them. To what purpose should we trouble ourselves about the world in the moon? All men, even those at the greatest distance, are no doubt entitled to our good wishes, and our good wishes we naturally give them. But, if, notwithstanding, they should be unfortunate, to give ourselves any anxiety upon that account, seems to be no part of our duty.[10]

In *TMS*, Smith clearly struggles with this issue of caring for the distant, and he struggles with it because of his initial conception of a conflict in our very nature between selfish and benevolent passions. *TMS* also contains a theory of virtue, and Smith addresses this issue again in the section on virtue. In a section entitled "Of Universal Benevolence" Smith notes and views negatively the fact that people are generally more concerned for the welfare of their own society, and are seldom concerned with trouble outside their own country.

---

9. Smith, *TMS*, pp. 138–39.
10. Smith, *TMS*, p. 140.

3. Social and Political Philosophy

Benevolence is one of the virtues Smith lists. Our good will, Smith thinks, should extend universally, and we should be willing to sacrifice our own interests for the interests of all sentient and intelligent beings. "He should, therefore, be equally willing that all those inferior interests should be sacrificed to the greater interest of the universe, to the interest of the great society of all sensible and intelligent beings."[11] But Smith is not able to accommodate such a view in this theory, and he resolves the tension between the sentiments expressed above and his individualism by an appeal to God: This is a world "of which God himself is the immediate administrator and director."[12] In the end he claims:

> The administration of the great system of the universe, however, the care of the universal happiness of all rational and sensible beings, is the business of God and not of man. To man is allotted a much humbler department, but one much more suitable to the weakness of his powers, and to the narrowness of his comprehension; the care of his own happiness, of that of his family, his friends, his country.[13]

When it comes to people outside one's country, self-interest takes precedent. Recent commentators caution about misinterpreting Smith's conception of self-interest. First, self-interest and selfishness are different concepts for Smith and should not be conflated. In addition, self-interest is a complex notion in Smith. Patricia Werhane points out that Smith's concept of self-interest ought to be understood as a desire for self preservation or bettering one's condition, which in and of itself not a negative disposition. Werhane shows that self-interest in the context of Smith's moral theory does not have free reign. We are restrained by a desire for approval, and we are motivated by virtues such a prudence and parsimony. Above all, self-interest in Smith functions in an environment of cooperation, since we are also social animals.[14]

Similarly, Athol Fitzgibbons notes that the concept of self-interest in Smith is self-love mitigated through virtues such as prudence, justice, and beneficence. Indeed, Smith argues that

---

11. Smith, *TMS*, p. 235.
12. Smith, *TMS*, p. 235.
13. Smith, *TMS*, p. 237.
14. Wehane, pp. 88–89.

we possess "love of virtue" as well.¹⁵ In addition, for Smith self-interest is a matter of long-term planning and ought to proceed following general rules, rather than passion.¹⁶ Leonidas Montes in "Das Adam Smith Problem: Its Origins, the Stages of the Current Debate, and One Implication for Our Understanding of Sympathy" argues that rules for Smith mitigate self-love, and because sympathy is the basis for the formation of the general rules of morality, "Self-interest, and virtues in general, cannot be detached from the social implications underlying the concept of sympathy."¹⁷ In any reading of Smith one realizes that even though self-interest is an acceptable motive, it is only a part of a more complex system. In Smith's favor, it would be implausible to argue that we should not care for ourselves, and most of us would agree with Smith that "self neglect is improper." But we saw that neither the impartial spectator nor duty indicate a moral obligation in the absence of a connection. Regarding virtue, Smith writes that universal benevolence is weak, and in addition the general rules concerning virtue are loose and inaccurate.¹⁸ While it is possible to enlighten us regarding the misconception that Smith's philosophy is based on self-interest, it is not possible to deny that in his philosophy, the further one gets from one's immediate circle the weaker the moral obligation. Smith did not provide us with tools to deal with global issues. The subject of caring for the remote is a shortcoming in Smith's theory, one that stems from his individualism, because the initial consideration is of the self in isolation.

De Grouchy's views vary significantly. First, with the relational approach to human morality de Grouchy does not view selfishness as a natural disposition. The argument is completed in the final two *Letters* where she argues that people become selfish through growing up in a climate of grave injustices (or, one might add, through a philosophy that endorses it). The root of the problem with regard to selfishness is social institutions and not human nature. According to her philosophy, in addition to the idea of a reciprocal relation between individuals and social institutions, an economic system that is built on the workings of self-interest will compound this disposition in people.

---

15. Smith, *TMS*, p. 306. Also see Fitzgibbons, *Adam Smith's System of Liberty.*
16. Smith, *TMS*, p. 173.
17. Montes, "Das Adam Smith Problem," p. 86.
18. Smith, *TMS*, p. 174.

3. Social and Political Philosophy

Selfishness is socially constructed via legislation and social institutions, as we will see shortly. In the *Letters*, self-interest or personal interest is viewed and referred to negatively. She treats it as a disposition to overcome.

Nevertheless, whatever the origin, de Grouchy recognizes hat selfishness exists and instead of general rules or the concept of the impartial spectator, she offers sympathy as the very faculty that amends selfish tendencies:

> What do we not owe to sympathy, even in its faintest glimmerings, since for that moment sympathy is the first cause of the feeling of humanity, the effects which are so precious. It compensates for a portion of the evils issuing from personal interests in large societies....(*Letters*, 369/113).

Overcoming selfish tendencies through the impartial spectator and general rules, or through sympathy as de Grouchy argues, renders a different approach to those whom we do not know. The former leaves us with little or no recourse or reasons to care. The latter creates feelings that lead us to care. De Grouchy does think we can and should sympathize with the remote, and hence she argues an obligation would follow. Here is what de Grouchy has to say about people who are remote:

> As the general impression of pain upon our organs repeats itself at the sight or just the recollection of pain, our abstract idea of pain can also reproduce it, and consequently so can the after-effects and situations where pain is inevitable. In this case, although this impression usually reproduces itself in a more vague and indeterminate manner (because the abstract idea of pain brings it home to us only in a weak way), nonetheless, if this idea offers us a new and extraordinary combination of pains, its effect can equal an existing pain. Such is the cause of the disquieting sensation we experience when, without thinking precisely of such and such an individual, we turn our thoughts to the class of men doomed to both the harshest labors and to poverty, or at least to dreading poverty (*Letters*, 373/116–7).

With her abstract idea of pain de Grouchy claims that any kind of pain and suffering provokes a sympathetic reaction. Distance and the number of people are not obstacles to sympathy. She could not agree less with Smith concerning strangers:

"The most abstract idea of physical pains, i.e., their possibility for an individual who is a stranger to us, thus more or less strongly renews the general impression of pain on our organs. The idea of moral pain also produces the same effect" (*Letters*, 374/117). However, like Smith, she recognizes that the effects of witnessing a disaster can be lesser and short lived. Smith, as we saw above, thinks that after the initial shock, we go about our lives as usual because we do not really have a duty to feel for others when we did not cause the disaster and when we otherwise have no connection with them. After stating that sympathy alone can be too brief, de Grouchy expresses the following position. We ought to continue to reflect on the situation of which we were made aware, and through reflection we sustain the ideas of suffering. Feelings for people may not be enough. We need to think about their situation as well:

> Reflection comes to the rescue of our natural volatility and activates our compassion by offering anew a scene that had made a merely momentary impression. At the sight of pain reflection reminds us that we, like the downtrodden being we perceive, are subject to the tyranny of death, and so reflection draws us closer to the sufferer by means of an inward emotional and affective turn that leads us to be concerned with his pains...And finally, reflection conditions our sensitivity by prolonging its activity and so installs humanity in our souls as an active and permanent sentiment that, eager to apply itself, spontaneously seeks the happiness of men... (*Letters*, 370–1/115).

In *Science of A Legislator*, Knud Haakonssen points out that Smith's concepts of justice are not based on a regard for the public, since moral judgment occurs through sympathy among individuals; therefore, the individual bears moral primacy.[19] Charles Griswold notes that in Smith's discussion of the impartial spectator, concern for all sentient beings is not a goal for Smith. Further, Griswold points out that for Smith, "Humanity *qua* humanity is last on the list."[20] Samuel Fleischacker makes a similar point in asking "*why* is benevolence economically so unimportant."[21] He replies that economic networks are vast

---

19. See Haakonssen, *The Science of A Legislator*, p. 89.
20. Griswold, *Adam Smith and the Virtues of the Enlightenment*, p. 208.

and extend over large societies. Thus it is not possible to apply "particular benevolence," and "general benevolence" is too weak. De Grouchy opens the third *Letter* with a distinction between particular sympathy and general sympathy. If particular sympathy is properly cultivated, it renders us more attuned to "the ills and needs of all humanity" (*Letters*, 386/123). The fact that we do not naturally or easily care about those who are remote she views as a shortcoming to be addressed. For de Grouchy one of the goals of sympathy, then, is to arrive at the point of caring about those with whom we have no immediate connection. For her no human being ought to be excluded from our consideration.

The differences between the theories of Smith and de Grouchy are significant when it comes to the issues of social reform. We can see again the way in which de Grouchy's views of dependency and the moral obligation that follows serve as criticism of Smith. If we view people as separate first, then the question that frames our inquiry becomes: What do we owe each other? This question does not appear in the *Letters*, nor could it be raised according to de Grouchy's philosophy. She starts with the assumption that we have a concern for others, which can be diminished or augmented according to our education and goals.

We can see that whether we have a connection with people or not is key to both Smith's and de Grouchy's conception of moral obligation. We saw above that Smith claims that since we do not feel any anxiety on behalf of the distant unfortunate, we lack motivation to help. He also explicitly claims that our desire to promote happiness and prevent misery in others is a direct outcome of sympathy, which in turn is an outcome of a relationship:

> Our desire to promote the one [happiness] and to prevent the other [misery]; are either the actual feeling of that habitual sympathy, or the necessary consequences of that feeling. Relations being usually placed in situations which naturally create this habitual sympathy, it is expected that a suitable degree of affection should take place among them.[22]

---

21. Fleischacker, *On Adam Smith's Wealth of Nations*, p. 95.
22. Smith, *TMS*, p. 210. Here is a case in which Smith states that sympathy can serve as moral motivation and not merely moral judgment.

So, without a relationship we would not feel sympathy, and relationships weaken once one moves beyond one's immediate circle and becomes nonexistent outside of one's country.

As mentioned, lack of feeling should not necessarily pose a problem in Smith's theory because he does not rely solely on sympathy. The impartial spectator has a central role in Smith's concept of moral motivation, and so does his concept of duty and his appeal to general rules. The weakness in *TMS* lies in the following set of considerations. In the last section of *TMS* on the systems of moral philosophy, Smith notes that there are two basic questions in morality: What does virtue consist of? And, by which faculty is it recommended or communicated to us (self-love, reason, moral sense, or sympathy)? The second question, he notes, is theoretical only and has no influence on practice.[23] As we saw, in writing a moral theory that is based on sympathy, Smith provides a criticism of rationality that is very similar to Hume's. He concedes that without feelings we would not be able to distinguish between right and wrong. Consistent with Smith's criticism of rationality, we have no rational motive to care and help people "on the moon." First Smith rejects reason, and then claims that sentiments are not effective enough. What is left then? Smith claims that only the first question mentioned above—what is virtue?—pertains to affecting our conduct. But Smith argues that universal benevolence is a weak force and his concept of justice, as we will see below, is minimal.

Other virtues Smith lists, such as prudence, self command, and parsimony also do not indicate global concern. In the end Smith's view of moral obligation does not extend far enough. De Grouchy calls for the cultivation and augmentation of sentiments because she thinks such training is the only way to bring forth social reform. While Smith does see the relation between sentiments and social reform, he never tells us we ought to feel for those who are not connected to us. One of the main messages one gets from the *Letters* and the major point about sympathy is that you must think about others, and Smith does not always require it.

One can trace back these differences between Smith and de Grouchy to two issues in their original conception of sympathy. One is Smith's individualism, and the second is his view of sympathy as conditional. Criticism of individualism and the limits

---

23. Smith, *TMS*, p. 315.

Justice and Beneficence

Smith's views concerning the remote are rooted in his theory of virtue and society. In *TMS* Smith considers the significance of two basic virtues, justice versus beneficence. Beneficence cannot be extorted by force, and its violation is not considered injury. Not so with justice, which can be enforced, and violating justice is punishable. In addition, Smith argues that justice is the most necessary and fundamental virtue of a society. Men are social creatures by virtue of needing each other's assistance. If we assist each other out of love we would have a happy society. However, without love society would not dissolve. If we injure each other, then we could not exist, for a society of robbers and murderers cannot survive. So, Smith concludes that:

> Beneficence, therefore, is less essential to the existence of society than justice. Society may subsist, though not in the most comfortable state, without beneficence; but the prevalence of injustice must utterly destroy it.[24]

Smith sees benevolence as a natural disposition and a virtue, but given his claim that beneficence is "always free," the following becomes its role:

> It is the ornament which embellishes, not the foundation which supports the building, and which it was, therefore, sufficient to recommend, but by no means necessary to impose. Justice, on the contrary, is the main pillar that upholds the whole edifice. If it is removed, the great, the immense fabric of human society...must in a moment crumble into atoms.[25]

Moreover, Smith completes this discussion in a section about general rules in which he claims that general rules of justice are accurate and analogous to the rules of grammar, whereas rules concerning virtues are vague and not accurate.[26] Smith, then,

---

24. Smith, *TMS*, p. 86.
25. Smith, *TMS*, p. 86.
26. Smith, *TMS*, p. 175.

does not choose benevolence or sympathy as the primary disposition that creates social bonds. He chooses justice instead.

On the other hand, de Grouchy places sympathy at the very core of human relations and makes it an integral part of human interaction. She argues that in order to be concerned with the pains of others one has to feel for them first, "and so reflection draws us closer to the sufferer by means of an inward emotional and affective turn that leads us to be concerned with his pains" (*Letters*, 370/115). De Grouchy agrees that benevolence cannot be forced (Ibid., 454/158). But rather than leaving this point as is, she argues that benevolence must be cultivated. De Grouchy thinks that sentiments and our beneficent inclinations are necessary for social order (Ibid., 416/137). Evelyn Forget notes that de Grouchy was interested in the question of what holds societies together. Forget concludes that "Sympathy…is, in her mind, the indispensable cement that holds a society together."[27] Compared to Smith, for de Grouchy sympathy is the disposition that should be "the main pillar that upholds the whole edifice."

Inequality, Poverty and Redistribution

Poverty is certainly a concern in Smith's writings. Fleischacker notes about Smith: "But by far the most important contribution Smith made to the history of the state welfare programs was to *change the attitudes toward the poor* that underwrote the restrictive, disdainful policies by which the poor were kept poor."[28] Fleischacker points out that it was seeing the poor as persons, as one's equal, and restoring dignity to them that made it possible to view poverty as a harm to be addressed.

In *TMS* Smith addresses poverty with his metaphor of the invisible hand. Smith explains that the rich do not share their wealth out of humanity or justice, but they do out of "luxury and caprice":

> The rich only select from the heap what is most precious and agreeable. They consume little more than the poor, and in spite of their natural selfishness and rapacity, though they mean only their own conveniency, though the sole end which they propose from the labours of all the thousands whom they employ, be the gratification

---

27. Forget, "Cultivating Sympathy," p. 322.
28. Fleischacker, *On Adam Smith's Wealth of Nations*, p. 206.

3. Social and Political Philosophy

of their own vain and insatiable desires, they divide with the poor the produce of all their improvements. They are lead by an invisible hand to make nearly the same distribution of the necessities of life, which would have been made, had the earth been divided into equal portions among all its inhabitants, and thus without intending it, without knowing it, advance the interest of the society, and afford means to the multiplication of the species.[29]

Scholarship concerning Smith's invisible hand is vast and controversial. Mark Skousen claims that the invisible hand is a central element in Smith's philosophy.[30] By contrast, Werhane notes that Smith was less optimistic concerning the invisible hand in the *Wealth of Nations* (*WN*). The invisible hand is only a side effect of the free market and not the principle that governs economic behavior. Werhane argues that the market can unintentionally promote economic growth only if it functions within the framework of five conditions: natural liberty, justice, self restraint, competition that ought to take place among more or less equal participants, and the market that can only function through cooperation. Werhane notes that far from being free from morality the competitive free market depends on and is a result of moral conditions.[31] Similarly, Fleischacker agrees that Smith did not retain the same optimism in *WN* and that the invisible hand can only be understood as operating in a system wherein each person labors for all. Fleischacker adds that Smith did not intend to argue that the invisible hand holds in all cases.[32] Emma Rothschild generated an extensive discussion in the literature by claiming that the whole concept of the invisible hand is one which Smith himself did not take seriously. She devoted a chapter in *Economic Sentiments* to building the case that Smith used the concept of the invisible hand as a "mildly ironic joke."[33]

First one must consider the context in which the passages of the invisible hand are written. The passage above appears in

---

29. Smith, *TMS*, pp. 184–85.
30. Skousen, *The Big Three in Economics*, p. 21.
31. See Werhane, *Adam Smith and His Legacy*, p. 102–7.
32. See Fleischacker, *On Adam Smith's Wealth of Nations*, p. 141.
33. Rothschild, *Economic Sentiments*, p. 116. Also see symposium on Emma Rothschild's *Economic Sentiments*, in Vivienne Brown, *The Adam Smith Review*.

Part IV of *TMS* which is on utility. Here, Smith claims that utility pleases and that everyone desires basic conveniences in life, including the poor. Seeking wealth promotes economic growth and the rich end up with excess which they distribute since the "eye is larger than the belly"; hence, the invisible hand. From here Smith continues to discuss his view that society is like a system that works well when agents act out of respect for the system. Public welfare is achieved while acting out of "love of system" rather than sympathy. Smith notes that "It is not commonly from a fellow-feeling with carries and waggoners that the public-spirited man encourages the mending of high roads."[34] Smith continues to explain that when the legislator provides subsidies to encourage the production of linen or wool, his conduct does not proceed from sympathy. The metaphor of the invisible hand makes sense in the context of this section and fits well with Smith's philosophy in general. Walter Eltis notes that in *WN* the invisible hand appears in a crucial chapter and the context indicates that Smith intended the argument to be persuasive.[35]

Deidre Dawson reports that the idea of a free market was prevalent at the time and that Condorcet was a great supporter of Turgot's ideas on liberalization of commerce and free market and a great admirer of *WN*.[36] Similarly Gareth Stedman Jones claims that Condorcet was a disciple of Smith.[37] Condorcet argues in the S*ketch* that restrictions on the market are one of the causes of poverty, and hence he argues for free trade.[38] Note the resonances of this line of thinking in the following passage from de Grouchy's seventh *Letter*:

> But it has been proven in our day and the evidence shows that the lack of wages or their transitory insufficiency is caused almost entirely by restrictive laws that inhibit commerce and industry. These same laws further undermine the general welfare by allowing the slow

---

34. Smith, *TMS*, p. 185.
35. Eltis, "Emma Rothchild on Economic Sentiment," pp. 154–5. For a more in-depth discussion on the invisible hand one might consider the question of whether Smith held a concept of natural order that he thought economic order could emulate. See Werhane; Montes (2004).
36. Dawson, "From Moral Philosophy to Public Policy," p. 265.
37. Jones, "An End to Poverty," p. 196.
38. Condorcet, *Sketch*, p. 180, for a more recent translation of the Tenth Epoch, see Keith Michael Baker (2004).

> accumulation of wealth in the hands of a few men who can freely use their riches as a means of oppression. Through the unrestricted interplay of competing interests these resources would otherwise have remained, if not equal, at least common to all. (*Letters*, 476/169)

De Grouchy echoes here Smith's invisible hand and ideas concerning the free market. Given the context of her time, it makes sense that she would see needed reform in lifting the current restrictions that created an unfair advantage. Regarding legislation she points out that restrictions on commerce and industry result in insufficient wages for the poor. In addition, unequal distribution of taxes and unjust heredity rights leave the poor with few resources and no means of improvement. Laws are geared towards allowing accumulation of wealth in the hands of the few. Thus in the context of that time an unrestricted economy would be more conducive to a good distribution of resources. As is the case with self-interest, one cannot isolate the idea of the invisible hand and interpret it outside the context of Smith's complex system, and in this regard points by recent scholars are well taken. The problem with Smith and the invisible hand is not this metaphor per se, but his vision beyond it. The differences between Smith, de Grouchy, and Condorcet are embedded in the question of whether minimal provisions for the poor are enough or are there further goals? More specifically, Smith and de Grouchy differ on their stance concerning redistribution.

We saw earlier that Smith places justice as the cardinal virtue in society. Smith defines justice as commutative justice. Commutative justice pertains to prevention of injury. In *TMS* Smith argues that justice is a negative virtue, and in his *Letters on Jurisprudence* (LJ) he defines commutative justice against distributive justice.[39] Smith draws a distinction between perfect rights and imperfect rights, the former pertains to commutative justice, the latter to distributive justice. For Smith the beggar may be an object of charity, but he has no right to demand it. Consistent with the argument above that benevolence is always free, justice ought to be limited to what can be defined and enforced.

Not legislating redistribution does not mean that Smith did not advocate it in other ways. Jerry Evensky states that

---

39. Smith, *LJA*, p. 9.

"Smith believes that the liberal plan is the best constitution for the working class because it produces the greatest wealth for the nation and distributes the wealth most justly."[40] Patricia Werhane claims that Smith believed that the laboring poor will be better off in an unregulated economy.[41] John Hill argues that Smith's philosophy is community oriented and that ideas concerning the free market are geared towards everyone's welfare. Hill reminds us that Smith's work is entitled "'not wealth of individuals' but an *Inquiry into the Nature and Causes of the Wealth of Nations.*"[42] In addition, several scholars pointed out that Smith advocated public schooling, higher taxes on luxury goods, and progressive taxation in general.[43] Charles Griswold claims that Smith was committed to the view that everyone ought to enjoy a basic, decent standard of living, but that he did not advocate redistribution for both considerations of justice and efficiency.[44] Instead, Griswold notes Smith leaves distributive justice to private benevolence.[45] Werhane notes as well that Smith reserves distributive justice to morality rather than law.[46] But comparison to de Grouchy indicates that Smith's reasons for not advocating redistribution go beyond his faith in an unregulated economy and his advocacy of benevolence. Rather, they are rooted in his conception of sympathy and its role.

Deidre Dawson argues that de Grouchy manifests strong egalitarian principles and finds two main reasons in the *Letters* in favor of redistribution. First, Dawson points out that according to de Grouchy in order to properly develop sympathy people must be freed from concerns for basic survival, and this goal could be achieved only "through radical redistribution of wealth."[47] Dawson sites de Grouchy's claim that if people are busy taking care of the basic necessities in life they cannot sufficiently develop their sensitivity and reflection. (*Letters*, 372/116) Dawson interprets de Grouchy as arguing strongly against legislation that favors inequalities of fortune. She quotes an important claim from the second letter: "One of the primary goals of the laws

---

40. Evensky, *Adam Smith's Moral Philosophy*, p. 13.
41. Werhane, *Adam Smith and His Legacy*, pp. 85, 161.
42. Hill, *Democracy, Eqaulity and Justice*, p. 91.
43. See Griswold, Rothschild, and Fleischacker.
44. Griswold, *Adam Smith and the Virtues of the Enlightenment*, p. 250,
45. Griswold, *Adam Smith and the Virtues of the Enlightenment*, p. 229.
46. Werhane, *Adam Smith and His Legacy*, p. 57.
47. Dawson, "From Moral Philosophy to Public Policy," p. 275.

should thus be to establish and maintain an equality of wealth amongst citizens." (*Letters*, 372/116) Secondly, Dawson points out that in the *Letters* inequalities of wealth affect the moral disposition of citizens and are conducive to promoting crime.

De Grouchy certainly opposes large gaps in socio-economic status. The discussion in the seventh and eighth *Letters* is framed by the issue of just and unjust behaviors and the question of under which conditions is justice maintained and under which conditions are people inclined to violate justice? This question is further framed by her view that human nature is basically conscientious and morally inclined. Thus, de Grouchy sets out to show that injustice is a product of legislation and social institutions and the ways these lead to various inequalities. More specifically she lists four reasons for being unjust: love (when corrupted), money, ambition, and self-love or vanity. All of these motives are aggravated by social inequalities.

Money leads to crime because inequalities of wealth result in a class of people who lack basic means of subsistence, but here de Grouchy notes that committing an injustice for survival needs is understandable. Inequalities of fortune and an unjust legal system also create a class of people who have nothing to loose by committing a crime. Inequalities also create a class of people who would violate justice just for the sake of becoming richer and accumulating more and not out of need. Here, de Grouchy argues that the culprits are unfair laws that allow corruption with impunity. She notes that crimes committed to gain wealth presuppose the possibility of success. Money becomes a source of corruption because the laws enable it. Ambition becomes a motive for injustice because inequalities of wealth and status also violate fairness in the job market. De Grouchy notes that positions are obtained through unfair hereditary rights or social status rather than qualifications. People do not choose their professions freely, and thus the means that are necessary to succeed are already unfair and corrupt. When social institutions are designed to allow wealth and social status, rather than qualifications, to entitle people to positions, the foundation of a merit-based society with professional virtues is compromised. Vanity and self love also flourish in a system which is based on considerations of self-interest .

Concerning love as a source of injustice, de Grouchy argues that marriage is also adversely affected by inequalities. The institution of marriage corrupts love. Marriages are entered into for convenience and economic considerations. The passion of love, instead of prevailing, is sacrificed. In place of love as a motivation for marriage, greed and ambition substitute. This circumstance leads men to a desire to possess a woman rather than love her. De Grouchy finds that the institution of marriage is not only altered but is also oppressive for women. For de Grouchy this inequality between the sexes is produced by the laws, which she proposes to reform by abolishing the dowry and by allowing divorce and short-term relationships without social stigma. Here, too, inequality creates distance between the sexes and "barriers …that render almost impracticable the mutual understanding of hearts and minds." (*Letters*, 485/173) De Grouchy thinks marriage effects or corrupts both sexes. Of course, women are disadvantaged by marriage, but she points out that men in a loveless marriage are led to vanity, ambition, and wandering.

For de Grouchy, then, individual moral inclinations are stifled and corrupted under social inequalities created by unjust legislation. Unjust social institutions promote vices rather than virtues, and individual justice is shaped and affected by social justice. But her second question remains, if human nature is basically conscientious, why is it that conscience is not sufficient to override the inclination to be unjust even in the face of poor legislation and social inequalities?

The connection between the first six *Letters* on sympathy and the last two which are more concerned with social progress becomes very clear at this point. Inequalities diminish ties of sympathy which for de Grouchy are the basis of morality. She argues that because extreme economic gaps create a distance between classes men are estranged from one other. (*Letters*, 501/180) The powerful aristocrat and the ordinary worker are too distant to judge one another; hence their respective duties become unclear. It is easy for the rich to oppress without remorse and for the poor to deceive while believing they are doing right. Along these lines, she notes that those who own property are more prone to respect another's property. For de Grouchy, we cannot feel sympathy without an awareness of another's situation, and with great gaps in social classes, when the wealthy have but a vague notion of what it is like to be desolate, awareness of the other's situation cannot develop. Thus, if the distance between classes is too great, ties of sympathy and compassion cannot prevail.

3. Social and Political Philosophy

> Simply eliminate the extreme inequality that separates the poor too far from the rich for them to be seen or known or for the voice of humanity to touch the latter's hearts, and unforeseen misfortunes will become rarer and more definitely rectified. (*Letters*, 499/179)

One might raise the following objection: according to what was said above concerning the suffering of others in distant lands in de Grouchy's philosophy, distance between people should not pose an obstacle to sympathy. Yet, social distance seems to be an obstacle to that very sympathy. But now we see that certain conditions are necessary for sympathy to prevail. We see that de Grouchy views human moral tendencies as basically good, but not immune to negative influences of an unjust society. She repeats the point several times that the legal system and the social structure have a profound effect on people's moral sense and behavior. In order to emphasize this point further, de Grouchy asks why it is that people take pleasure in seeing their fellow human beings tortured? A faulty legislative system, she claims, has separated the interests of individuals, creating a situation in which people are opposed to each other rather than being united. From childhood people are accustomed to seeing the misfortunes of some against the good fortune of others. This situation can desensitize people and distort their sense of justice, "…because in society a vicious system of legislation, instead of uniting interests of individuals, has for too long separated them and set them at odds." (*Letters*, 414/137) People who are constantly exposed to injustice tend to become accustomed to it, and conscience and remorse can be dulled. Over time, immoral behavior is ingrained and turns into habit. De Grouchy offers interesting insights regarding what becomes acceptable and how people easily deceive themselves, overlook considerations of justice, and comply with norms under a corrupt system.

> Here, depraved institutions complete what they started. They furnish the means for lasting self-deception over one's own heart. They give us leave to consider as inevitable, necessary, politically neutral, or even useful the evil for which they are responsible and for which they then become the excuse. Besides, habit alone dulls every sentiment…." (*Letters*, 487–8/174)

De Grouchy then targets a good portion of her views concerning social reform to reforming legislation that create inequalities. Her insight is further clarified in making the comparison to Condorcet. Condorcet addresses the issue of inequality as well and raises an astute quandary. Looking at history of societies he notices times during which rights were embedded in the law but hardly in practice; equality was established by political codes but did not exist among individuals. Reflecting on our own times, one might think of discrimination which is illegal, yet, unfortunately, not unheard of. Condorcet offers the following reasons for this discrepancy. He blames inequality of wealth, inequality of status, and foremost inequality of education. According to Condorcet, then, equality among people is important in order to ensure that human rights and civil rights are respected. De Grouchy's theory offers a more in-depth explanation for the discrepancy between law and practice. She is able to explain why inequality of wealth, status and education cause the violation of people's rights. We saw above that de Grouchy argues that great social distance among people diminishes sympathy and humanitarian feelings, and so it becomes easy to exclude people. As important as laws are, they alone cannot compensate for what is lost in the absence of moral sentiments. De Grouchy addresses the root of the problem, and for her discrimination begins with the discrepancy between what is legal and what people care about. Indeed, how else are people to deal with prejudice and discrimination without addressing the way they actually feel towards those whom they view outside their social circles?

For Smith the issue of social equality is a matter of justice and liberty. For these considerations, the gap between rich and poor is not a problem as long as everyone if better off. On this point Fleischacker compares Smith to John Rawls.[48] De Grouchy concedes the significance of justice and liberty. She speaks of justice extensively and argues that "the first need of the human heart is freedom." (*Letters*, 403/131) But for de Grouchy ensuring that everyone has the bare minimum is not enough because too large economic gaps will dull sentiments that she sees as essential for a society to function well. Sympathy is a prerequisite for justice and liberty. Redistribution, then, is for the purpose of allowing the necessary conditions for sympathy to develop. In other words, liberty for all would not be possible without a certain amount of equality.[49]

Smith makes an odd remark in *TMS*. After noting that humanity, justice, generosity, and public spirit are all qualities that are useful to others, he claims that humanity is the virtue of women while generosity is the virtue of men. Humanity consists in sympathy and "the most humane actions require no self-denial, no self-command, no great exertion of the sense of propriety. They consist only in doing what this exquisite sympathy would on its own accord prompt us to do."[50] Meanwhile, self-denial, self-command, and propriety are essential to Smith's moral theory. On the other hand, Smith claims that generosity requires self-command and the impartial spectator. Smith notes that propriety, generosity, and public spirit are founded on the same principles as justice. By contrast, the feminine attributes of sympathy and humanity "consist merely in the exquisite fellow-feeling...."[51] Smith thus distinguished between sympathy and humanity on the one hand and "manly" virtues on the other, and he applies virtues politically, but not sympathy.

In place of Smith's impartial spectator, virtues, and his theory of justice, de Grouchy speaks of the "sentiment of humanity" as a moving force. Dawson notes that Smith emphasized self control rather than considerations of humanity.[52] De Grouchy argues that it is the power of humanity we ought to enlist. The goal of morality and progress in the *Letters* is to become a humanitarian. The goal of becoming a humanitarian, she thinks, is achieved through sympathy. De Grouchy opens the *Letters* by claiming that Smith did not go far enough in developing his concept of sympathy. By the end of the *Letters* she shows to what extent sympathy is essential to social and political relations.

* * *

One cannot claim that Smith provides an economic theory devoid of ethics. Rothschild has shown that Smith's economics is far from a cold rational calculation and is based on sentiments.

---

48. See Fleischacker, *On Adam Smith's Wealth of Nations*, p. 225.
49. Note that it is not entirely clear from the *Letters* how egalitarian de Grouchy thinks society ought to be. She states the principles of redistribution and provides an argument for it but not an economic theory to follow. It is possible to interpret her as being closer to Smith in believing that a free market will go along way in creating equality. She does claim in the seventh *Letter* that without restrictions on the market everyone would have means of subsistence. Yet the difference between Smith and de Grouchy remains in the need and reasons for redistribution.
50. Smith, *TMS*, p. 191.
51. Smith, *TMS*, p. 190.
52. Dawson, "Is Sympathy so Surprising?"

Montes rightly claims that "were he alive today, Smith would certainly lament the divorce of economics and ethics."[53] John Hill agrees with Fitzgibbons that Smith "implied that moral considerations were superior to economic ones."[54] But Smith did separate benevolence and sympathy from economics while keeping justice the operative principle. De Grouchy argues that justice cannot properly operate without sympathy. A return to Smith's theory with its emphasis on justice would certainly be an improvement over today's forms of capitalism and would lead us to significant social reform. But following de Grouchy's pleas for legislation that is more conducive to equality and the spread of sympathy will take us much further.

---

53. Montes, *Adam Smith in Context*, p. 163.
54. Fitzgibbons, quoted in Hill, *Democracy, Eqaulity and Justice*, p. 143.

Chapter 4

Morality and Happiness

The relation between morality and happiness is, of course, not a new theme in philosophy. Smith and de Grouchy address this issue in the context of their theories and again offer different views concerning the questions of what happiness consists of, and why it is that being moral brings forth happiness. The interest in these questions is twofold; one is to ground morality in human nature, particularly in sentiments rather than religion; and two, to provide a compelling reason for acting morally.

Love and Happiness

Smith and de Grouchy begin with what happiness does not consist of. Notably, it does not consist of money or wealth. Smith argues that power and wealth offer conveniences in life, but if one has to sacrifice tranquility and peace of mind and if obtaining wealth involves fatigue and anxiety, then wealth is more trouble than it is worth and is counterproductive.[1] For de Grouchy, too, happiness is not achieved through wealth but by means of the heart: "Let the gentle habit of doing good teach them [children] that it is by means of their hearts that they can be happy, and not by their titles, luxury, high rank or riches" (*Letters*, 366/112). Both Smith and de Grouchy take the issue further, however, and because they view people as social beings, happiness comes from human relations and particularly from the strongest bond possible—love.

The following is Smith's version. We saw in Chapter Two that Smith claims that we dread social scorn and doing things that would render us an object of hatred. This fear will be a deterrent even if we are assured that we will not be caught, even if we could be convinced that there is no God.[2] (Hence a secular foundation for morality is possible.) By the same token we love praise and love being worthy of it. Thus we desire not only to be approved of, but also to be what ought to be approved of. From here Smith continues to argue that to merit moral praise is to deserve love, and here happiness is embedded: "What so great happiness as to be beloved, and to know that we deserve to be beloved? What so great misery as to be hated, and to know that we deserve to be hated?"[3] And more specifically, even if we come across more fortune Smith warns: "If the chief part of human happiness arises from the consciousness of being loved, as I believe it does, those sudden changes of fortune seldom contribute much to happiness."[4] In general Smith thinks that "humanity does not desire to be great, but to be beloved."[5]

De Grouchy begins the issue of love with particular sympathy. She defines particular sympathy as occurring in a relationship as opposed to general sympathy for remote people or humanity as a whole.

> Today, my dear C***, I wish to speak to you about particular sympathy, the one that establishes intimate bonds between men that are necessary for their perfection and happiness. It draws hearts together and entwines them with the most tender affections. (*Letters*, 386/123)

Particular sympathy leads to friendship and friendship to love. For de Grouchy, love (like sympathy) depends on merging of hearts and minds, tastes and opinions: "…finally the rapture of feeling everything together as if feeling everything for each

---

1. Smith, *TMS*, p. 181.
2. Ibid., p. 118.
3. Ibid., p. 113.
4. Ibid., p. 41.
5. Ibid., p. 166.

4. Morality and Happiness

other can by themselves satisfy the demands of love" (*Letters*, 404–5/131). Being able to love is dependant on knowing how to enjoy the happiness of another: "…only the felicitous capacity of sharing the happiness of others can establish in these hearts the solid, true, and durable affections, independent of place, time, and the interests of each, and that are suitable for enchanting life or at least to temper it" (Ibid., 397/128).

De Grouchy develops the link between happiness and morality further. Her first point is that happiness stems from helping others and from being moral:

> [The pleasure of doing good] is the only sensation capable of recompensing humanity for the ills it suffers. It is the only one constantly at our disposal, that never lets us down, that is always responsive, that calms and fills our hearts, and that is, finally, an indissoluble tie between ourselves and our fellow men. Happy is he, my dear C***, who carries this sentiment unwaveringly at the bottom of his heart and who dies feeling it! He alone has lived! (*Letters*, 436/149).

Then, de Grouchy claims that only moral beings are capable of loving. In other words, one's ability to love depends on one's moral disposition: "Only generous souls are capable of loving" because "only generous hearts capable of being touched by the happiness of others really know how to love" (*Letters*, 396–7/128). De Grouchy includes a discussion of the pleasure of loving, which to her consists in making others happy: "It is so true…that the pleasure we take in making other people happy by being affectionate is, in large measure, the cause of pleasure we find in loving" (Ibid., 396/128). Love, for de Grouchy, is more about giving than receiving. Even though both Smith and de Grouchy mention both loving and being loved, there is certainly a striking difference in emphasis in their discussion of love and happiness. Smith emphasizes happiness as stemming from being loved, while de Grouchy emphasizes happiness as stemming from loving. The discussion of love and happiness follows their ethical theory, because for Smith the most important and desired aspect in a relationship is approval, and so being loved follows. For de Grouchy our goal is to feel sympathy, and so feeling love follows.

In addition, their approach to love in general varies because of their different views on sympathy. Smith argues that we do not sympathize with love. This is consistent with his views of sympathy and the difficulty he perceives in achieving a bona fide sympathetic connection, as seen above. For Smith sympathy stems from the imagination, and he argues that we cannot imagine love. We need a "correspondence of sentiments," and we also need to judge that the "passion is suitable to the object." Smith notes that if a friend has been injured we can sympathize with his resentment, or if he received a benefit we can sympathize with his gratitude. But how can we judge love?

> But if he is in love, though we may think his passion just and reasonable as any of the kind, yet we never think ourselves bound to conceive a passion of the same kind…but the man who feels it, entirely disproportioned to the value of the object; and love…is always laughed at, because we cannot enter into it.[6]

De Grouchy criticizes Smith's argument about our lack of sympathy with someone in love. And here, too, the major differences in their approach to sympathy in general are manifest.

First, once again for de Grouchy sympathy stems from experience and not merely imagination. Thus for her, if one experienced love, then one should be able to sympathize with love. She responds to the quote above: "It is surprising that love's passion always seems to have a touch of ridiculousness [to Smith]… One would think that such an opinion is shared only by this frivolous youth that judges love before having loved" (*Letters*, 411/136). We saw in Chapter One that sympathy is a direct and immediate reaction to another, and consequently sympathy consists in feeling with another "we suffer in watching him suffer" and so "love pleases us and awakens visions of pleasure in us" (Ibid., 405/132, 411/136). Unlike Smith, for de Grouchy sympathy is easy to achieve, and there is no need to judge whether a person is justified in being in love. The approach to love accentuates the different views concerning the depth of a connection possible between people, and consequently the potential for moral relations.

Ethics and Psychology

Both Smith and de Grouchy address the connections between moral emotions and happiness and between character and

---

6. Ibid., p. 31.

happiness. Both recognize a relation between morality and psychological or emotional well-being in general. For Smith the virtuous person is happy, and the unvirtuous one is miserable.[7] But there is more depth in de Grouchy's moral psychology. She first complains:

> [Moralists] have not been sufficiently concerned with demonstrating that the principles of virtue and the internal pleasures they provide are a necessary consequence of our moral constitution and that the need to be good is an almost irresistible inclination for men subject to wise laws and raised without prejudices (*Letters*, 433/147).

We already saw that for de Grouchy doing good and the sympathy we have with those who benefited from our actions in turn makes us feel good. De Grouchy makes a further claim, that doing good leads one to a state of peace and security. The moral person:

> ...lives amidst the good he has done or hopes to do so, and always has an inner sense of peace and security. He can remain alone with himself experiencing neither emptiness nor indolence because one of his most active thoughts always centers on virtue. He is certainly liable to pain, but at least pain cannot penetrate the sanctuary of his conscience....Life and all its disappointments and people and all their weakness cannot disturb or embitter him (*Letters*, 470/165).

Conversely, the unethical person suffers a painful and agitated existence. The reason is that the immoral person is lonely and distrusting and has enemies rather than friends. While the moral agent sees in other people potential for a relationship that can be a source of joy, the immoral person cannot trust others. In fact, his distrust of others is inspired by the distrust he actually deserves. Instead of seeking love and friendship, the immoral person conducts his relationships through cunning calculation. The immoral person, rather than being related to others through love or sympathy, ends up isolated and tormented. In the end, the social relations of such a person are so distorted that ultimately this person will lose reason in order to stifle his own conscience:

---

7. Ibid., p. 187.

> Even more guilty and unfortunate is when, tired of loathing and self-hatred and too far removed from virtue to be touched or enlightened by it, he seeks to lose his reason and sensibility by becoming a brute so as to stifle the remorse that inevitably outlives the feelings and ideas that engendered it (*Letters*, 472/166).

For de Grouchy one cannot be happy in isolation, and one cannot be integrated to society and connected to other people without morality. She makes a further point about psychological health. If immorality separates us and makes us feel lonely and sympathy creates ties and is a source of happiness, then it follows that giving and being kind towards others are ways to emerge out of a sense of emptiness and depression. The joy and satisfaction of giving are ways to overcome feelings of loneliness. Being kind and helping others can fulfill a void in one's life:

> ... [The moral person] considers men, not so much relative to what they could be or to what can be expected of them, than with regard to the happiness he can provide them. Thus, in his relations he is neither prickly nor anxious, and... he becomes happy in making others happy....(*Letters*, 470/165).

For de Grouchy mental health is dependent on a good moral disposition, and immorality leads to emotional turmoil. Being selfish and mean leads to an agitated and stressful existence, while being just, kind, and benevolent is conducive to positive mental states such as satisfaction, peace, and love.

De Grouchy further supports her view with her discussion of *ennui*. The Littré French dictionary defines ennui as: 1) torment of the soul caused by the death of loved ones, by their absence, by the loss of hope, by whatever misfortune, and 2) a sort of emptiness which is felt in the soul deprived of action or of interest in things.[8] In his biography, Thierry Boissel describes de Grouchy's father's reaction to her birth:

> The baby snuggled at her half-conscious mother's breast under the stunned look of the Marquis. Here he is a father, finally, the first big event of his life. A renaissance for him in some sense. But did it take time in coming!

---

8. Littré, Paul-Emile, *Dictionnaire de la langue française* (Versailles: Encyclopaedia Britannica France, 1977) Vol. II, 2092–2093.

> Ennui that frequently overcame him these past years vanished like magic.⁹

The best contemporary equivalent for this sense of *ennui* is probably depression, and the term is so translated in the *Letters* in Part II. De Grouchy does not define *ennui* but does state that "Depression [*ennui*] is thus one of the most cruel ailments of the human heart (*Letters*, 382/120). In an attempt to account for the causes of *ennui* she writes that when we are contented with physical needs, moral needs torment us, and thus we become liable to feeling *ennui*. She explains this position by claiming that people manifest a need for being moved. It is this need that causes people to be interested in tragedy, poetry, and novels. Earlier we saw that she argues that people possess a need to do good. Moral needs, then, have to be satisfied, and if neglected lead to a state of ennui. "The human heart in some fashion is drawn to what agitates it and stirs it up. It senses that these exotic emotions distract it from habitual impressions it often finds disagreeable or insipid. These emotions, it feels, will save it from 'ennui'" (Ibid., 383–4/121). De Grouchy treats morality as an activity that can add meaning to one's life, that can fill a void, and that can even help with depression. She establishes a relation between morality and happiness via the positive psychological state we reach through moral actions or the misery we suffer through immoral actions.

De Grouchy brings sensationalism to its full development. We saw that originally, morality emerges out of sensations of pleasure and pain, and these sensations accompany our actions and choices and ultimately continue to construct our happiness or misery. In being able to experience the pleasure and pain of others, sympathy is created. De Grouchy takes us from sensations to sympathy and from sympathy to happiness:

> Let us stop here for a moment, my dear C***, to see how this single faculty of experiencing pleasure and pain at the idea of another's pleasures and pains, in perfecting itself through reason and magnifying itself by reflection and enthusiasm, becomes not only a rich source of delightful or angry feelings for us, but guarantees an always pleasant and peaceful existence (*Letters*, 469/164–5).

---

9. Boissel, *Sophie de Condorcet*, p. 18.

De Grouchy ends where she begins. Human well-being leads to sympathy, and sympathy leads to well-being. She opened the *Letters on Sympathy* with an explanation regarding the origin of morality, and she closes these *Letters* with a discussion of the end to which morality can lead. Anyone who is interested in the subject matter of ethics would agree that without morality life would not be possible. De Grouchy links morality to our existence in a fundamental way. One might claim that Cabanis also grounds morality in human nature with his view that morality is biological. But de Grouchy reminds us that before anything occurs in our lives, someone must care for us. This view as a basis for morality did not reappear until the twentieth century, in feminist ethics and psychology. We turn to this topic next.

Chapter 5

Sophie de Grouchy and Feminist Ethics

Half a century ago the historian Louis Gottschalk distinguished between posthumous reputation and historical or philosophical influence.[1] No one can claim that Sophie de Grouchy influenced modern feminist ethics in any way since no historical connection is apparent, and indeed, as pointed out in the introduction, until recently de Grouchy has been invisible for all intents and purposes. However, I wish to establish de Grouchy's posthumous reputation as a feminist ethicist. In this chapter I point out several common denominators linking de Grouchy with feminist ethics today. In using the term feminist ethics, I am referring to two major themes: one is the concern with the status of women in society and the other is applying women's experiences to moral theory, which results in the ethics of care. Both themes are found in the *Letters*.[2]

---

1. Gottschalk, *Understanding History*, p. 234.
2. I chose the ethics of care for the purpose of comparison to de Grouchy, but would like to note that the ethics of care does not represent the entire scope of feminist moral theorists. As Virginia Held points out, some feminists defend versions of Kantian, Utilitarian, Contractarian or liberal moral theories. See Held (2006).

In a recent article Virginia Held provides a historical account of the emergence of feminist ethics out of the feminist movement in the late 1960s in the United States, which she notes was a revolutionary social movement. More specifically, Held locates the beginning of inquiry into the ethics of care in Sara Ruddick's article, "Maternal Thinking," published in 1980.[3] Shortly after, Carol Gilligan's book, *In a Different Voice* (1982), generated a significant and in-depth discussion concerning the ethics of care. Contemporary feminist ethics, then, emerged not so long ago out of both a revolutionary movement and empirical research in psychology pointing to a distinctive feminine voice. De Grouchy lived and wrote over two hundred years earlier, yet shares similar feminist ideas and revolutionary circumstances.

Comparing de Grouchy and trends in feminist ethics today further illuminates the originality of her thought and the relevance of the *Letters* to the twenty-first century, particularly as her ideas apply to current social issues and philosophical debates. Since the literature in feminist ethics is vast and growing it is not possible to treat all feminist philosophers who share a common point with de Grouchy. However, it is possible and it turns out to be fruitful to examine the most outstanding common denominators.

Caring and the Origin of Morality

We saw that de Grouchy addresses the causes of morality as a criticism of Smith for omitting an important part of human morality. In contemporary ethics of care, attention to the origin of morality is part of the criticism of rationalism and contractarianism in ethics for similar reasons. In order to explain the primary human moral tendency, de Grouchy and contemporary feminists look at the way and the context in which morality arises. Contemporary feminists identify care as the context and capacity in which morality first develops, and in de Grouchy's version it is sympathy. Both argue that human infants show love and affection and are capable of sympathy and could not survive without it. Infants cannot yet think, and rationality is a much later development; rationality thus is added to and complements the emotions.

Recall that de Grouchy traces moral development to early experiences with our caretakers, and she claims that sympathy

---

3. Held, "The Ethics of Care,", *Oxford Handbook for Ethical theory*, p. 558.

5. Sophie de Grouchy and Feminist Ethics

arises from memory of these experiences when triggered by seeing another person suffer or prosper. Being cared for and remembering having been cared for lies at the foundation of Nel Noddings' moral theory as well. Noddings opens her 1984 work, *Caring: A Feminine Approach to Ethics & Moral Education*, with the following claim: "Human caring and the memory of caring and being cared for, which I shall argue form the foundation of ethical response, have not received attention except as outcomes of ethical behavior."[4]

For Noddings, omitting the element of caring leaves us with a principled approach to morality that is too remote and abstract and that compromises our moral potential. Noddings argues that morality does not begin with principles, but with caring. Her argument rests on the distinction between natural caring and ethical caring, and the claim that ethical caring emerges out of natural caring and would not come into existence otherwise. Caring for another out of a natural sentiment, Noddings notes, such as a mother caring for a child, is not particularly moral or human, for we share this behavior with animals as well. Ethical caring emerges out of the memory of being cared for.

> This memory of our own best moments of caring and being cared for sweeps over us as a feeling—as an "I must"—in response to the plight of the other…I recognize the feeling and remember what has followed it in my own best moments. I have a picture of those moments in which I was cared for and in which I cared, and I may reach toward this memory and guide my conduct by it if I wish to do so.[5]

For both de Grouchy and Noddings morality would not exist without its affective causes. The idea that a moral reaction follows memories of being cared for, what Noddings describes as the feeling of "I must," is found in the *Letters* as well. De Grouchy, in speaking of those who cared for us, notes that we "cannot be indifferent to their presence or to the very idea of them. These people unfailingly make him feel pain or pleasure" (*Letters*, 376/117). This core feeling extends to other people throughout life and renders us sensitive to others.

In the previous chapter we noted the way in which moraliy for de Grouchy is linked to happiness, love, and well-being in

---

4. Noddings, *Caring*, p. 1.
5. Ibid., p. 79.

general. For de Grouchy the most essential part of our existence is human relations that cannot be healthy or sustained without morality. Nel Noddings takes the same approach:

> The relation of natural caring will be identified as the human condition that we, consciously or unconsciously, perceive as "good." It is that condition toward which we long and strive, and it is our longing for caring—to be in that special relation—that provides the motivation for us to be moral.[6]

For de Grouchy and Noddings morality and well-being are intricately linked through the desire for and centrality of human connections in our lives. Both realize that without morality we could not sustain relationships, and without relationships we would suffer a lonely and meaningless existence.

In addition, tracing human morality to a natural reaction of caring entails that human potential involves caring or having a sympathetic nature, depending on education and social institutions. De Grouchy specifically argues that the capacity to sympathize can diminish or expand according to education and social structure. Rita Manning espouses the same view in her book, *Speaking From the Heart: A Feminist Perspective on Ethics*:

> What is implied in both Hume and Noddings is that when sentiment and natural caring do motivate us, we freely follow their dictates. Both of them admit that this capacity can stagnate and die or it can flourish, and, accordingly, we have an obligation to support this capacity in ourselves.[7]

How much is expected of people bears on the question of what people are capable of. For de Grouchy and feminist ethics, people are capable of much more caring and sympathy than currently found in individuals and in our social structure.

Criticism of Liberalism in Moral and Political Theory

One of the main themes in recent literature in feminist ethics is criticism of liberalism for giving rise to the concept and

---

6. Ibid., p. 5.
7. Manning, *Speaking From the Heart*, p. 68.

consequently the ideology of individualism. In the liberal tradition, beginning with social contract theory, morality originates with rational, independent, self-sufficient and, of course, equal adults. Social and political institutions follow as a cooperative venture of these independent and free moral agents. The attention to the initial status of people as free and equal individuals is the basis for the arguments that people deserve equal rights. It is also the basis for the conception of political organization as voluntarily entered into through a contract for the purpose of best preserving freedom and rights. The problem, as Alison Jaggar claims, is that "the assumption in this case is that human individuals are ontologically prior to society; in other words, human individuals are the basic constituents out of which social groups are composed."[8] For Jaggar it follows that in this atomistic conception of persons one can conceive of people as existing independently and outside of a social context. It is also conceivable that in principle people can satisfy their needs independently of other people: "What I mean by political solipsism is the liberal assumption that human individuals are essentially solitary, with needs and interests that are separate from if not in opposition to those of other individuals."[9] There are two points of criticism regarding the liberal conception of human nature and the origin of morality to be addressed here. One, from a feminist perspective, is that liberals provide an inaccurate depiction of when and how cooperation begins with human beings. The second point concerns the political values and ideological consequences inherent in the liberal view of persons. Regarding the first point, human beings should be first viewed as relational and dependent, or to quote Jaggar again:

> As soon as one takes into account the facts of human biology, especially reproductive biology, it becomes obvious that the assumption of individual self-sufficiency is impossible. Human infants resemble the young of many species in being born helpless, but they differ from all other species in requiring a uniquely long period of dependence on adult care.[10]

---

8. Jaggar, *Feminist Politics and Human Nature*, p. 28.
9. Ibid., p. 40.
10. Ibid., pp. 40–41.

Virginia Held likewise notes that the ethics of care views persons as relational first, rather than self sufficient individuals:

> The ethics of care, in contrast, characteristically sees persons as relational and interdependent, morally and epistemologically. Every person starts out as a child dependent on those providing care to this child, and we remain interdependent with others in thoroughly fundamental ways throughout our lives.[11]

The argument regarding the centrality of dependency is found in the *Letters* as well:

> ...each individual finds himself depending upon many others for the necessities of life, for his well-being, and for life's conveniences. This dependency, in truth more extensive and more marked in childhood, continues to a certain degree into later years and remains more or less strong insofar as moral development sets it aside or lets it subsist (*Letters*, 375/117).

Rosemarie Tong in her article, "Feminist Ethics," goes further and places the relational and dependent view of the self at the core of feminist thought:

> Apparently, most of the thinkers who have forwarded a woman-centered approach to ethics have rejected the ontological assumptions that the more separate the self is from others, the more fully developed that self is...In place of these assumptions, they have instead embraced the ontological assumption that the more connected the self is to others, the better that self is....[12]

In contrast to liberalism, this different concept of the self entails a different conception of human nature. Rita Manning writes: "We can see that an ethic of care requires a new conception of human nature, and such an account would involve a picture of humans as essentially involved in relationships with other humans."[13] Thus instead of individualism leading to self-interest as the foundation of morality, Manning argues that "an ethics of care involves a morality grounded in relationship and

---

11. Held, "The Ethics of Care," p. 9.
12. Rosemarie Tong, "Feminist Ethics," *Stanford Encyclopedia of Philosophy*, On-Line, Nov 16, 2005, p. 4.
13. Manning, *Speaking from the Heart*, p. 67.

response."[14] The result is a different approach toward the problem of selfishness. Manning goes so far as to say that if viewing ourselves as involved in relations with others is prior, then an ethics of care is incompatible with a philosophy that is based on maximizing self-interest. Care, which comes first, would take precedence over self-interest. Manning writes:

> If our primary desires are to care and be cared for in relationships with other humans, then we cannot fulfill our desires independently of other humans. We should not be seen as seeking to maximize self-interest either, because caring involves the suspension of self-interest in many cases.[15]

Manning's view reinforces the idea that the differences observed between Smith's and de Grouchy's philosophy concerning self-interest are a direct consequence of the concept of the self as individualistic or relational.

The second critical point follows from this initial view of people as independent individuals first, i.e., the political values and ideological consequences inherent in the liberal view of persons. Jaggar reminds us that "the liberal conception of human nature sets the terms of liberal political theory. It constitutes the ground of the basic moral and political values of liberalism."[16] Jaggar's argument is that liberalism leads to an egoistic conception of human nature. For Jaggar the assumption that people seek to maximize their individual self-interest is tantamount to assuming universal egoism. If one starts with the individualistic conception of persons, then social cooperation becomes in need of explanation:

> Instead of community and cooperation being taken as phenomena whose existence and even possibility is puzzling, and sometimes even regarded as impossible, the existence of egoism, competitiveness and conflict, phenomena which liberalism takes as endemic to the human condition, would themselves become puzzling and problematic.[17]

---

14. Ibid., p. xiv.
15. Ibid., p. 67.
16. Jaggar, *Feminist Politics and Human Nature*, p. 33.
17. Ibid., p. 41.

Virginia Held notes that once this individualistic ideology is embedded and defines our social institutions, it affects people's conceptions of social relations: "That we can think and act as if we were independent depends on a network of social relations making it possible for us to do so."[18] De Grouchy devotes the seventh and eight *Letters* to a discussion of the way in which social institutions affect people's mind sets and behaviors. She, too, thinks that once an ideology is embedded in social institutions it determines what becomes acceptable and common practice. In the closing paragraphs of the eighth *Letter* (which is also the closing of the entire work) de Grouchy offers a nicely developed discussion of this issue. She argues that social institutions are based on contingencies of birth and fortune and are corrupted by self-love. In turn, social institutions "exalt self-love to the point of turning it into a dominant passion" (*Letters*, 503/181). Institutions and the customs they embody establish people's ideas of happiness and well-being. With a series of rhetorical questions, de Grouchy provides her insight that, once practices of privilege and self-interest become possible, they are very hard to resist: "Yet, who in society, in an honest self-examination, will not find that he bears within himself their principal traits?" (Ibid., 504/182).

The subject of liberalism becomes more complex and interesting in the *Letters* because, after her criticism of the liberal conception of human nature and the origin of morality based on individualism, de Grouchy continues to endorse the liberal ideals of equality, rights, and social justice. In the sixth *Letter* de Grouchy speaks of natural equality and freedom, but she also provides a Lockean version of property rights. Regarding her feminism in general, she and the Marquis de Condorcet argued for equal rights between the sexes, thus drawing on liberal values to improve the status of women. A differential approach towards liberalism is found in modern feminism as well. Attitudes toward liberal ideals in feminism vary from Nel Noddings, for instance, who claims that liberalism in inadequate, to Martha Nussbaum, who is a liberal feminist. Most feminists acknowledge their debt to the liberal tradition for the ideology it provided for the feminist and civil rights movements, but view liberal ideals as insufficient and, as seen above, leading to selfishness or a politics based on considerations of self-interest.

---

18. Held, "The Ethics of Care," p. 9.

5. Sophie de Grouchy and Feminist Ethics 75

De Grouchy again offers a valuable insight into moral theory. She disjoins liberal ideals and individualism, endorsing the former while rejecting the latter, thus avoiding the charge of selfishness. Traditionally, the arguments for civil and human rights are based on the conception of people as initially autonomous and free, arguments that thus privilege these characteristics. De Grouchy would be puzzled by the insistence that liberal values need to stem from an individualistic conception of persons. Instead of the traditional link between the value we place on autonomous individuals and the rights and equality they deserve, in the *Letters* de Grouchy traces respect for equality back to sentiments:

> Amid the shock of so many passions that oppress the weak or marginalize the unfortunate, from the bottom of its heart humanity secretly pleads the cause of sympathy and avenges it from the injustice of fate by arousing the sentiment of natural equality (*Letters*, 369/113).

For de Grouchy, viewing people as separate and independent first is not a necessary step in the argument that they deserve respect as individuals. Moreover, separateness is not as efficient a starting point because sentiments (developed in a relationship) provide the basis and motivation for just legislation:

> It is this desire [to relieve suffering] which, on seeing someone struggling in floodwaters and on the verge of drowning, leads bystanders on the riverbank to frantically stretch their arms towards him. This is a movement of a sublime nature that unveils in an instant the full power of humanity over our hearts and all the effects which the legislator could derive from this sentiment that unfortunately is more often weakened than fortified by our institutions (*Letters*, 380/119).

According to de Grouchy, we have already developed a sense of right and wrong so that violating people feels wrong, whereas respecting them feels right. The concept of rights is a construct of reason; de Grouchy labels it the "preference of reason," but she reminds us that rights are also grounded in sentiments because the effects of injustice are harmful. Thus, according to de Grouchy liberal ideals, rather than being grounded in seeing individuals as the basic social unit (as in social contract theory), are grounded in the sympathy that arises in the context of relations and dependency. Endorsing both a relational and dependent origin of morality and liberal ideals works in the *Letters* because of de Grouchy's insistence that ideas of good and evil are only begotten when reflecting on sentiments. If there is no sympathy, then morality, including social justice and civil rights, is compromised. We respect individuals because we care, and in the end liberal values would be better implemented with sympathy as an underlying motivation. Virginia Held echoes this point in noting that liberals speak of autonomous adults without paying attention to how we got there; for her and for de Grouchy becoming aware of how we become free individuals can teach us how to get better at making sure the poor, the hungry, and the disadvantaged become free as well.

Integrating Reason and Emotions

The seventeenth- and eighteenth-century debate over whether morality is embedded in reason or sentiments resurfaced with feminist criticism of theories of justice, particularly in the debate over justice and care. Contemporary debate over justice and care extends to the effect of combining the two to ameliorate personal, social, and political issues. The majority of the work in ethics of care pertaining to this dichotomy is geared towards integrating justice and care. What is striking in both de Grouchy and feminist ethics in comparison to social contract theories is their willingness to articulate the complexity and depth of human morality. Neither seeks clean, simple explanations. In a tradition where most (but not all) philosophers values rationality above all and that defines rationality basically as computation, it is no surprise that the dominant moral theories put forth a rather simple calculation to chart the moral course. Both de Grouchy and contemporary feminists argue that morality cannot and should not be reduced to rationality. They also offer a different view of the nature of reason and emotions.

Allison Jaggar writes against a long tradition in philosophy that contrasts reason with emotions. In her article, "Love and Knowledge: Emotion in Feminist Epistemology," she argues against the modern view of emotions as non-rational or irrational, asserting that emotions are intentional, and that they are about something. Rather than viewing emotions as blind, involuntary responses, Jaggar indicates that emotions are socially constructed, i.e., we are taught what to fear or value. Emotions both presuppose and indicate values; for example, we may feel angry because of something we already think is wrong, or our feeling of indignation can be an indication that something is wrong. Jaggar writes: "Just as values presuppose emotions, so emotions presuppose values."[19] Similarly, as previously quoted, de Grouchy claims: "...reason's judgment is nearly always preceded and followed by a sentiment that indicates and confirms it" (*Letters*, 464/162). For Jaggar our reaction to different situations, such as racism or sexism, is determined by the values and standards already embedded in our emotional constitution. Since emotions are so deeply rooted in us, not only do they affect observation and evaluation prior to intellectual understanding, but they also color it. Understanding emotions, then, is indispensable to our understanding of our values and our morality. In her book, *Feminist Morality: Transforming Culture, Society, and Politics*, Virginia Held similarly argues that emotions form a necessary part of moral understanding.

> The "care" of the alternative feminist approach to morality appreciates rather than rejects emotions, and such caring relationships cannot be understood in terms of abstract rules or moral reasoning. And the "weighing" so often needed between the conflicting claims of some relationships and others cannot be settled by deduction or rational calculation. A feminist ethic...will embrace emotion as providing at least a partial basis for morality itself and certainly for moral understanding.[20]

For Held, emotions play a vital role in forming our moral dispositions: "Such emotions as empathy, concern for others, hopefulness, and indignation in the face of cruelty—all these may be crucial in developing appropriate moral positions."[21] De Grouchy well understood the epistemological values of emotions, as expressed in the fifth *Letter* where she argues that emotions serve as an indication of right and wrong prior to any rational judgment. There is a certain intelligence to emotions based on pleasure and pain such that:

> We thus have motives, not only to do good to others, but of preferring good actions to bad as well as those that

---
19. Jaggar, "Love and Knowledge: Emotion in Feminist Epistemology," p. 137.
20. Held, *Feminist Morality: Transforming Culture, Society, and Politics*, p. 52.
21. Ibid,, p. 30.

are just to those that are unjust. These motivations are based on our natural sympathy, itself a consequence of our sensibility (*Letters*, 462–3/161–2).

Other than their epistemological value, emotions are also viewed as a moving force. Nel Noddings claims, "I am suggesting that our inclination toward and interest in morality derives from caring."[22] Although Noddings is careful to distinguish her theory from emotion- or empathy-based ethics and continues to develop a phenomenology of caring, at the foundation, for Noddings as for de Grouchy, morality begins with feelings. Altogether, de Grouchy describes moral sentiments as a powerful moving force:

> After having shown you, my dear C***, the origin and nature of these sentiments, by applying what you have read in the preceding letters concerning particular sympathy, the effects of enthusiasm, and the power of habit, you will easily understand that these sentiments can become active and permanent and can acquire, according to circumstances, an overpowering force and even an irresistible power (*Letters*, 438–9/150).

In addition to the power of emotions one has to keep in mind the attention to reflection in feminism. Recall that in the beginning of the second *Letter* de Grouchy claims that reflection is needed to sustain what could be a too-brief impression of suffering. Similarly, Nel Noddings writes: "Thus, at the foundation of moral behavior—as has already been pointed out—is feeling or sentiments. But, further, there is commitment to remain open to that feeling, to remember it, and to put one's thinking in its service."[23] Reflection, as opposed to using the term reason, specifically means thinking about the material emotions provide. Rita Manning also argues that mere awareness of suffering, especially in a distant place, is not sufficient for action. Manning argues that in order to increase our empathic response one needs to reflect on the victims' humanity and common characteristics they share with us: "Here what we see is sentiment, colored by reflection."[24]

Given a different and a more sophisticated view of emotions, a theory that values both reason and emotions only follows.

---

22. Noddings, *Caring*, p. 83.
23. Ibid., p. 92.
24. Manning, *Speaking from the Heart*, p. 68.

Alison Jaggar claims: "There is a continuous feedback loop between our emotional constitution and our theorizing such that each continually modifies the other and is in principle inseparable from it."[25] We previously saw de Grouchy's arguments concerning the essential role of reason and sentiments, her claim that both are indispensable to morality, and that alone neither is sufficient. De Grouchy also argues for a reciprocal relation between reason and emotions, as previously mentioned: "One must first seek in their passions the forces that can extend and renew their intelligence weakened by inaction or degraded by error. One can then have them adopt the truth...by gently captivating reason through a logic...." (*Letters*, 449–50/155). Both reason and feelings ought to be constantly revised in light of the dictates of each. It is worth repeating the point here: de Grouchy concludes that "One of the primary goals of education should thus be to provide the ability to acquire general ideas and to experience these abstract and general sentiments I have discussed" (Ibid., 450/155).

The issue of the respective values of justice and care occupies a significant place in the literature in feminist ethics, although views greatly vary regarding the manner of combining both those elements and their importance. Most feminists value both justice and care but disagree regarding what they take to be a primary value and the way in which justice and care are integrated. The strength of this view is its dynamic, rather than rigid, concept of morality that can integrate many factors. In such a philosophy, it is never the case that we make up our minds concerning a certain issue and can never develop it further.

Experience and Impartiality

Further insight into the differences between Smith and de Grouchy and feminist ethics can be gained from the work of Nona Plessner Lyons and her article, "Two Perspectives: On Self, Relationships, and Morality." Lyons' thesis is that understanding the way people see themselves in relation to others is crucial to understanding their conception of morality. (We already saw this point above in Chapter Three with regard to self-interest.) Lyons' work is an outcome of empirical research showing that females tend to describe the self in relation to others as con-

---

25. Jaggar, "Love and Knowledge," p. 147.

nected and interdependent, whereas males tend to describe the self in relation to others as separate and independent. (The positions of Smith and de Grouchy certainly fit this description.) Lyons reports that "the data revealed that separate/objective individuals tend to use a morality of 'justice,' while connected individuals use a morality of 'care'."[26]

In her analysis Lyons speaks of two perspectives. The perspective of a separate, independent self is based on seeing oneself as distant and impartial and leads to seeing moral relations in terms of "reciprocity." Reciprocity entails a fair, just, and equal exchange. By contrast, the perspective of a connected self is based on an interdependent and related self and leads to seeing moral relations in terms of "response." Response entails concern with the well-being of others and responding to their needs.

Lyons' analysis of the perspectives of reciprocity and response shines a light on the differences between de Grouchy's and Smith's initial conception of sympathy. (Recall that his is indirect, conditional, and serves as judgment; hers is a direct and an immediate response and serves as moral motivation.) Lyons writes: "To consider others in reciprocity implies considering their situation as if one were in them oneself."[27] This is precisely what Smith instructs us to do, place ourselves in another's situation and see whether we would feel the same:

> If, upon bringing the case home to our own breast, we find that the sentiments which it gives occasion to, coincide and tally with our own, we necessarily approve of them as proportioned and suitable to their objects; if otherwise, we necessarily disapprove of them, as extravagant and out of proportion.[28]

According to Lyons, Smith's mediated concept of sympathy follows his individualism. On the other hand, Lyons claims that "to be responsive requires seeing others in their own terms, entering into the situations of others in order to know them as others do, that is, to try to understand how they see their situations."[29] Indeed, de Grouchy's very definition of sympathy is a disposition to feel "as others do." The point for de Grouchy is

---

26. Lyons, "Two Perspectives: On Self, Relationships, and Morality," p. 135.
27. Ibid., p. 134.
28. Smith, *TMS*, pp. 18–19.

5. Sophie de Grouchy and Feminist Ethics

to be responsive to others, not to analyze the propriety of their reaction: "First of all, we are obviously led to concern ourselves with the sufferings of others in order to relieve them" (*Letters*, 380). There is only one point in the *Letters* in which de Grouchy expresses reservations with regard to sympathy, and that is sympathy with hatred, envy, and revenge.

Lyons' analysis next illuminates the issue of impartiality in Smith versus general and abstract sentiments in de Grouchy (see Chapter Two.) Concerning impartiality there are two distinct points; one is impartiality in regard to the situation, and the other is impartiality in regard to our emotions. Regarding the situation, we saw that the impartial spectator for Smith serves as basis for self-judgment and judgment of others. For Smith we are initially too partial:

> So partial are the views of mankind with regard to the propriety of their own conduct, both at the same time of action and after it; and so difficult is it for them to view it in the light in which any indifferent spectator would consider it.[30]

Thus, in order to be fair, we need an impartial spectator:

> We can never survey our own sentiments and motives, we can never form any judgment concerning them; unless we remove ourselves, as it were, from our own natural station, and endeavour to view them at a certain distance from us...We endeavour to examine our own conduct as we imagine any fair and impartial spectator would examine it.[31]

We saw that impartiality is an important concept in *TMS*, and its main purpose is to overcome selfishness. Smith is very clear in his argument that without the impartial spectator, we will always think of ourselves first. When it comes to other people, particularly those with whom we have no connection, Smith claims that viewing their interests from "our station" will not restrain us from acting in our own best interest, even if our actions would be "ruinous" for them. In order to avoid this imbalance we must establish a point of moral neutrality:

---

29. Lyons, "Two Perspectives: On Self, Relationships, and Morality," p. 135.
30. Smith, *TMS*, p. 158.
31. Ibid., p. 110.

> Before we can make any proper comparison of those opposite interests, we must change our position. We must view them, neither from our own place nor yet from his, neither with our own eyes nor yet with his, but from the place and with the eyes of a third person, who has no particular connexion with either, and who judges with impartiality between us.[32]

Smith's concept of impartiality is one of distance and not lack of sentiments, since we do consider how other people would feel about our situation. But the distance is crucial for us in order to be able to see ourselves "in the light in which others see us."[33]

De Grouchy addresses the problems of selfishness and prejudice as well, but in line with all the other differences between them, her philosophy entails just the opposite of Smith's impartiality. Although de Grouchy does not see selfishness as such a natural tendency the way Smith does, she does recognize that people can be selfish. She views her own time as one in which egoism was a serious social problem, and claims that egoism weakens sentiments of good and evil, causes the oppression of entire classes, and is too lightly condemned by morality and public opinion. Selfishness for de Grouchy stems from forgetting our sentiments: "Egoism, no doubt produced by forgetting these abstract and general sentiments or by an inability to experience them, in turn ends up extinguishing them" (*Letters*, 447). Thus, it is because of the omission of actual feelings and relatedness to others that egoism becomes such a significant problem. Accordingly, in order to overcome selfishness, we need to appeal to our feelings, and feelings are most effective in particular situations and relations where distancing oneself would not make sense. In other words, overcoming self-interest follows from seeing our connection with people rather than the distance:

> Being accustomed to the ties that bind their existence to ours, at the sight of their pains or pleasures we must further experience the feeling we would have at the idea of a danger or a good happening to us personally, and this by the force of habit alone, without any specific or conscious attention to our own interest (*Letters*, 377/118).

---

32. Ibid., p. 135.
33. Ibid., p. 159.

5. Sophie de Grouchy and Feminist Ethics

Whereas for Smith the only way to correct the distorted view of self judgment is to "transport" ourselves to a distant station, for de Grouchy it is to remember our connection to others and how we feel about them. Removing or distancing ourselves from the relationship in question or situation at hand, or being impartial with regard to our sentiments, will weaken our urge to help. Smith asks us to step outside of the relationship to judge; de Grouchy asks us to think through our relationships, because sympathy is inherent in relationships and is a superior source for morality.

Impartiality with regard to our feelings follows for Smith. By distancing ourselves we also cool our emotions. He speaks of the cool impartial spectator, how we need to coolly reflect on our past conduct, and how our best judgment is attained during the cool hours of reflection. Smith claims that we need to wait for the effect of passion to wear off: "When the action is over, indeed, and the passions which prompted it have subsided, we can enter more coolly into the sentiments of the indifferent spectator."[34] Passion, Smith thinks, can mislead and cause us to forget rules which we agreed upon during the "cool" hours.[35] Smith does not take into account the following distinction: When it comes to passions such as hatred and revenge, cooling these emotions is a good idea. But when it comes to his philosophy of distance and self-control, Smith does not distinguish social passions from unsocial ones, and he instructs us to distance ourselves from all emotions. Why should we be cool and impartial with regard to care and sympathy? De Grouchy wants to stir up and augment our emotions (through reflection and enthusiasm, as seen in Chapter Two) so we would not become indifferent. The idea of partiality is tied to the concept of moral emotions. Emotions indicate a moral value and we need to act accordingly—not eliminate them. By the same token we should not act on destructive emotions such as envy and revenge.

Criticism of impartiality is a prevalent theme in feminist literature today as well. Instead of impartiality, feminists argue that morality ought to be contextual. The arguments are similar to the ones found in the *Letters*. While impartiality requires distance, relationships by nature are contextual, Lyons writes:

---

34. Ibid, p. 157
35. Ibid., p. 237.

"Relationships can be best maintained and sustained by considering others in their specific contexts..."[36] Care, which is more morally effective, arises in the context of relations. Rita Manning argues that the kind of attention care requires cannot be impartial:

> An Ethics of caring, as I shall defend it, includes two elements. First is a disposition to care. This is a willingness to receive others, a willingness to give the lucid attention required to appropriately fill the needs of others. In this sense, an ethics of care is contextual."[37]

Held notes that, in focusing on balancing self-interest and other's interests, standard moral theory "...neglected the sympathy and concern people actually feel for particular others."[38] Moreover, Held thinks (similar to de Grouchy) that it is because of the omission of actual feelings and relatedness in moral theory that egoism becomes such a significant problem. At this point the effect of one's stances on partiality/impartiality and on global issues becomes clearer. We saw previously the difference between Smith and de Grouchy on poverty. Instead of asking what an impartial spectator would do in a situation, Virginia Held argues that what we need to think about is particular others. Held notes that the domain of particular others is already constituted by a relation we have with them, and this relation plays an important part in our moral decision. Held reminds us that we are a part of a network of relations; for instance, we are children of some parents, parents ourselves, friends, colleagues, lovers, and so on. Thus it is better to think about real people and their real circumstances, rather than engage in hypothetical or abstract considerations. What about people who we do not know and with whom we have no relations? Held writes:

> Particular others can, I think, be actual starving children in Africa with whom one feels empathy or even the anticipated children of future generations, not just those we are close to in any traditional context of family, neighbors, or friends.... In recognizing the component of

---

36. Lyons, "Two Perspectives: On Self, Relationships, and Morality," pp. 134–135.
37. Manning, *Speaking from the Heart*, p. 61.
38. Held, "Feminism and Moral Theory," p. 117.

feeling and relatedness between self and particular others, motivation is addressed as an inherent part of moral inquiry.[39]

De Grouchy and feminist philosophy provide a better ideology to deal with famine relief and other global issues than do variants of Smith's cold impartiality. Feminists realize that people are more likely to help others or to sacrifice their own interests when they care. People come to care through relations and connections. It is very hard to care in the abstract while distancing oneself from a particular situation. Hence the insistence on thinking about others in concrete terms.

We saw that Smith's main weakness in *TMS* is his inability to adequately address poverty and other issues on a global scale. This weakness is rooted in his ideas concerning the problem of selfishness and its solution in impartiality. Starting with the problem of famine relief, for instance, Smith prescribes distance, impartiality, and a consideration of the rules of morality. In the end he ends up with a very minimal solution, if any at all. Regarding rules, Rita Manning writes:

> We don't live in a caring world. By that I mean that not everybody recognizes his or her obligation to care...Rules and rights provide a minimum below which no one should fall and beyond which behavior is morally condemned. Rules provide a minimum standard of morality...But we should not fool ourselves into thinking that staying above this minimum is a sufficient condition for being a morally decent person.[40]

Further comparison between de Grouchy and feminist ethics can be gained from Virginia Held's concept of *moral experience*. In her book, *Rights and Goods: Justifying Social Action*, Held develops this concept not necessarily from a feminist perspective but against a dominant tradition that offers general, ideal, and hypothetical formulations that are not necessarily applicable to real life experiences. Ethical theory, she argues, ought to be derived from experience. But the concept of moral experience, according to Held, is not merely empirical experience as usually found in the literature.

---

39. Ibid., p. 118.
40. Manning, *Speaking from the Heart*, p. 74.

> The central category of feminist thought, at least in its contemporary phase, is experience. It is not the constricted experience of mere empirical observation. It is the lived experience of feeling as well as thought, of acting as well as receiving impressions, and of connectedness to other persons as well as of self.[41]

Moral experience is different from moral theory in that it is the theory as experienced in action and in context:

> As I understand it, moral experience is the experience of consciously choosing, of voluntarily accepting or rejecting, of willingly approving or disapproving, of living with these choices, and above all of acting and of living with these actions and their outcomes.[42]

De Grouchy's empiricism is also distinguishable from empiricism in general. In comparison to Locke, for example, her account is more complex because she adds the human interaction taking place to the mere sensations of pleasure and pain. Throughout the *Letters*, de Grouchy gives us an in-depth study of the way we experience morality through sensations, emotions, and connection to others. Whenever we make a moral decision she wants us to refer and connect to our own experiences. We learn from both de Grouchy and Held that a theory that is derived from hypothetical, ideal situations, also gives us hypothetical ideal answers, whereas a theory derived from experience is also applicable to experience. Held writes:

> The difficulty with ideal theory is that it suggests only what we ought to do in an ideal society, not what we ought to do here and how, given the very unideal societies in which we live…Actual societies are the results of war, imperialism, exploitation, racism, patriarchy—the imposition of the will of the strong on those who have been overcome.[43]

Held suggests that not only ought moral theories be based on experience, but they also need to be tested in experience. The results are first a theory that is relevant to actual rather than hypothetical experience, that is, to real situations, relationships,

---

41. Held, *Feminist Morality*, p. 24.
42. Held, *Rights and Goods: Justifying Social Action*, p. 272.
43. Ibid., p. 2.

and dilemmas, and these results then lead to an ever-improving moral stance. Held offers a method akin to Rawls' "reflective equilibrium," only in her view we should seek coherence between general principles and particular judgments arrived at in actual rather than merely hypothetical situations.[44] Moral theories that are not able to address actual problems in particular situations, Held insists, would be mere intellectual exercises and thus not effective enough.

In her book, *Feminist Morality,* Held further develops her concept of moral experience to include women's experiences in the formation of moral theory, and this inclusion thereby enriches and transforms morality. If we take moral experience into account, then what we have to date in moral theory are theories based on the experience of the *men* who wrote them, and thus, says Held, we have only half of the story:

> As feminists repeatedly show, if the concept of "human" were built on what we think about "woman" rather than what we think about "man," it would be a very different concept. Ethics, thus, has not been a search for universal, or truly human guidance, but a gender-biased enterprise.[45]

Held uses the concept of transforming culture to indicate that she does not mean to merely include women in traditional theories and existing social structures. Such a view does not go far enough or in effect is not conducive to any kind of transformation. To simply include women among the rational will leave emotions out, and to include women in the public domain will leave the household outside of the domain of morality.

> Far from merely providing additional insights that can be incorporated into traditional theory, feminist explorations often require radical transformations of existing fields of inquiry and theory. From a feminist point of view, moral theory, along with almost all theory, will have to be transformed to take adequate account of the experience of women.[46]

---

44. See Held, *Feminist Morality*, p. 28.
45. Held, "Feminist Transformations of Moral Theory," p. 5.
46. Held, *Feminist Morality,* p. 43.

Held continues to develop the way in which women's experiences transform moral and political concepts and cultural beliefs and practices. In addition, including women's experiences will blur the dichotomies prevalent in traditional moral theory: reason and emotion, moral and natural, public and private. Traditionally, these dichotomies divide along gender lines, identifying the male with the former and the female with the latter. We can see the two aspects of feminist ethics mentioned above: Apart from compromising moral theory, these divisions also serve as elements of an ideology of oppression as reason, the moral, and the public are thought to supersede and dominate the emotions, the natural, and the private.

Although de Grouchy does not address the transformation of culture the way Virginia Held does, her experience of motherhood is reflected in the second *Letter*, and repudiation of all three of the above dichotomies and similar implications for moral and political theory are found throughout the *Letters*. In her *Letters* addressing social and political philosophy, we see de Grouchy argue that the application of sympathy to the public domain will enable social justice and respect of rights to flourish. The aforementioned dichotomies and the inclusion of women's experiences and their political implications deserve separate consideration next.

Effect on Political Theory: The Private-Public Dichotomy and Social Reform

According to traditional moral theories, morality functions in the public domain with government, law, and other social institutions. The household, on the other hand, where women perform their biological functions of reproducing and rearing children, is seen as the domain of the natural. In the family, women give birth and rear children, while also traditionally serving men's needs in a domestic context. Taking care of basic, biological functions is not seen as distinctively human or moral. Consequently, caring is viewed as woman's work and as natural, but not as a good candidate for the basis of moral theory that needs either to advance beyond the mere natural or to overcome it. (This is the case with theories that view emotions as in need of control by reason.)

Collapsing the private-public dichotomy goes hand in hand with incorporating care or sympathy to political theory, thus extending these dispositions to the public domain. Looking again at Virginia Held's philosophy, there are roughly three stages to the argument, all of which are presaged in de Grouchy's work. First, Held argues that mothering is a moral activity and not merely a natural one. "Human mothering teaches consideration for others based on moral concern; it does not merely follow and bring the child to follow instinctive tendency."[47] It is through human mothering that society is created: "Human mothering shapes language and culture, it forms human social personhood, it develops morality. Animal behavior can be highly impressive and complex, but it does not have built into it any of the consciously chosen aims of morality."[48] Of course, there are biological aspects to mothering, such as nursing a baby, but Held reminds us that businessmen have to eat lunch as well, and we do not reduce their activity to a biological function. For her part, de Grouchy credits her own mother for teaching her the workings of sympathy:

> You have taught this to me, venerable mother, whose footsteps I have so often followed under the dilapidated roof of the unfortunate, fighting poverty and woe! Receive the life-long homage I owe you, every time I do good and every time I have the happy inspiration and the gentle joy of so doing. Yes, my heart came alive in seeing your hands relieve both misery and illness and in seeing the suffering gaze of the poor turn toward you and become tender in blessing you, and that the true good of social life manifested before my eyes appeared to me in the joyfulness of loving humanity serving it (*Letters*, 367/112).

The second point about mothering is Held's view that the mother-child relation constitutes the most basic social relation. She writes: "The most central and fundamental social relationship seems to be that between mother or mothering person and child. It is this relationship that creates and recreates society. It is the activity of mothering which transforms biological entities into human social beings."[49] For Held, a mothering relation is prior to the concept of human relations found in liberal theory:

---

47. Held, "Non Contractual Society," p. 119.
48. Held, "Feminist Transformations of Moral Theory," p. 17.
49. Held, "Feminism and Moral Theory," p. 114.

> On the face of it, it seems plausible to take the relation between mother and child as *the* primary social relation, since before there could have been any self-sufficient, independent men in a hypothetical state of nature, there would have had to have been mothers, and the children these men would have had to have been. And the argument could be developed in terms of a conceptual as well as a causal primacy.[50]

The causal primacy of mothering relations is a fundamental fact about people. De Grouchy knew this fact, and she pointed out that Smith regrettably omits it. Held argues that the mother-child relation should become the paradigm for various other social relations. In her discussion of mothering and markets, Held argues that the relationship between a mother and child is a much better paradigm for many social relations than the self-interested, competitive individual. "Perhaps morality should make room first for the human experience reflected in the social bond between mothering person and a child, and for the human projects of nurturing and growth apparent for both persons in the relationship."[51]

Currently, the dominant paradigm of social relations is of contractual relations between self-interested individuals, mainly for economic reasons. Held argues that on the contractual model of human relations people are not viewed as related to others in fundamental ways, and because of that individuals are primarily motivated by the pursuit of their own interests. On the other hand, what ties a mother and a child are emotional ties, or for de Grouchy ties of sympathy. The practice of mothering entails becoming sensitive to the needs of the helpless. Held argues that one cannot analyze mother-child relations in terms of contractual agreements, losses and benefits, or buying and selling:

> If we look, for instance, at the realities of the relation between mothering person (who can be female or male) and child, we can see that what we value in the relation cannot be broken down into individual gains and losses for the individual members in the relation.[52]

---

50. Held, "Non Contractual Society," p. 114.
51. Held, "Feminism and Moral theory," p. 115–116.
52. Held, "Feminist Transformations of Moral Theory," p. 20.

5. Sophie de Grouchy and Feminist Ethics

Thus a politics based entirely on self-interest cannot follow from a feminist foundation. De Grouchy, Held, and other feminists wish to change the current conception of social relations and our ties to others. Held writes: "Perhaps what are needed for even adequate levels of social cohesion are persons tied together by relations of concern and caring and empathy and trust rather than merely by contracts it may be in their interests to disregard."[53]

The third point follows from envisioning what the effects would be of applying women's experience and expanding the mother-child paradigm to encompass political and social issues. In *Maternal Thinking: Towards A Politics of Peace* (1989), Sara Ruddick first argued that the practice of mothering denotes a desire for preservation, for growth, and for the well-being of children and is conducive to non-violence. Maternal thinking (not related to gender but to practice) applied to politics, particularly to war, would create a politics of resistance and peace. In her article, "Care and the Extension of Markets," Held argues that as more public services, such as health care, child care, and education are privatized, more areas of our lives are controlled by the norms of the market. Decisions concerning people's lives and human needs are driven by economic considerations of corporations and their quest for profits. Held argues that there should be boundaries to the market, and markets should not expand into areas that affect health and well-being. The problem, Held notes, is that liberal individualism cannot provide an adequate ideology to counteract the expansion of markets because liberal values such as freedom, equality, and rights pertain to the individual only and not to social relations. An ethics of care views people as relational, and hence the primary values such as sensitivity, care, and sympathy are always found in relation to others. Held writes: "With an ethics of care and an understanding of its intertwined values, such as those of sensitivity, empathy, responsiveness, and taking responsibility, we could perhaps more adequately judge where the boundaries of the market should be."[54] Politically, the ethics of care dictates that we should care about one another in local and global communities. Virginia Held describes a caring society:

---

53. Held, "Non Contractual Society," p. 125.
54. See Held, "Care and the Extension of Markets."

> Instead of seeing the corporate sector, and military strength, and government and law as the most important segments of society deserving the highest levels of wealth and power, a caring society might see the tasks of bringing up children, educating its members, meeting the needs of all, achieving peace and treasuring the environment, and doing these in the best ways possible, to be that to which the greatest social efforts of all should be devoted.[55]

Joan Tronto in her 1993 book, *Moral Boundaries: A Political Argument for an Ethic of Care*, takes the same approach. She argues that if care is viewed as a political idea, then meeting the needs of care would take precedence over pursuing profits.

De Grouchy recognizes that early family ties constitute a moralrelation to be replicated and enhanced throughout one's life. Sympathy, she argues, is initially created between infants and their caretakers. Feeling for others is what is missing in the public sphere, and de Grouchy attributes social injustice to the absence of sympathy. She also faults her current social structure for stifling, rather than simulating and encouraging our natural moral tendencies. De Grouchy expects sympathy to carry over to society and social issues as well. Held argues that care is suited for civil society as well as for the personal, a sentiment evident in the *Letters* where de Grouchy writes:

> Civilization, such as it still exists in half the nations of Europe, is thus the enemy of goodness in man, as well as his happiness. What an immense labor remains for education, not to develop or direct nature, but only to preserve nature's beneficent inclinations, to prevent them from being stifled by prejudices that are so well accepted and common and that totally corrupt any sense of humanity and equality. These sentiments are as necessary to the moral happiness of each individual as they are for maintaining fairness and security in all relations of social order! (*Letters*, 425/137)

In his *Lectures on Jurisprudence* and discussion of property rights and crime, Smith uses sympathy as the basis for moral

---

55. Held, "The Ethics of Care," pp. 23–24.

judgment as established in *TMS*. One can claim that he does apply sympathy to the public realm, and in this sense one might claim that he overcomes the private-public dichotomy. But Smith does not start from the private, and his concept of sympathy does not replicate or capture the moral relations and characteristics of early relations of family ties. Again, comparison to feminist ethics highlights differences between Adam Smith's and de Grouchy's concepts of sympathy. Hers is an extension of the moral interaction found in the private sphere; his is an independently existing disposition. What is found in de Grouchy and feminist ethics is the desire to continue and extend the moral relations, or the kind of sympathy found in the family, to the public arena in order to obtain social reform. We saw in Chapter Three that de Grouchy argued that sympathy is necessary for justice and rights to be respected, and therefore sympathy is necessary for political purposes. Held expressed a similar view:

> Gradually, we can hope, feelings of solidarity will be extended to all persons everywhere, sufficiently to see their rights respected and their needs addressed. But it may be the value of care as much as the value of justice that can help this happen. Unless the presumption of care is met, people seem not to be concerned enough about others to care whether their rights are respected or even recognized.[56]

In her article, "The Need for More Than Justice," Annette Baier argues that justice should not be the only social virtue because in and of itself it is insufficient. She reminds us: "For the moral tradition which developed the concept of rights, autonomy and justice is the same tradition that provided 'justifications' of the oppression of those whom the primary right-holders depended on to do the sort of work they themselves preferred not to do."[57]

De Grouchy opened the *Letters* by faulting Smith for neglecting to address the causes of morality. In the end her approach to social progress addresses the causes of oppression which she finds in lack of connection and sympathy. In de Grouchy's, Virginia Held's, and other feminists' work one finds the insight

---

56. Ibid., p. 132.
57. Annette Baier, "The Need for More Than Justice," in Held (1995), p. 53.

that a very fundamental change has to occur in our perception of what it means to be human in relation to others before we will witness real social and political transformations. From this perspective, trying to amend the legal system is only tinkering, and without addressing the root problem we will only have a superficial and temporary solution. De Grouchy and contemporary feminists wish to reform our social consciousness; when the right intention is present, the spirit of the law will be respected as well.

Sympathy and Feminism

Generally speaking, feminist ethics shares many features with related, more traditional male-oriented theories, such as virtue ethics, moral emotions, and communitarian ideas. Rita Manning, for instance, acknowledges her debt to Hume, and contemporary feminists embrace emotional motivation and Hume's criticism of rationalism. Also, both Hume and Smith wrote a moral theory based on sympathy. The question then arises: in what way, if any, does feminist ethics encode a distinct women's morality? There is a certain tension surrounding this question. On the one hand it is important to value and acknowledge women's contributions to moral theory; on the other hand classifying morality along gender lines seems counterproductive to feminist goals. Rosemarie Tong notes that part of the criticism of feminist ethics is that it is sexist and that it is just as wrong to use the term "female values" as it is to use "male values."[58] Cheshire Calhoun argues that gender essentialism, the view that all women, by virtue of being women, share a common gender subjectivity, is a mistake since "feminist ethics comprises a complex and theoretically *disunified* body of work."[59] She also claims that because of the diversity in the literature, identifying feminist ethics with an ethics of care is a mistake. She, too, expresses reservations with regard to grouping a body of work as women's philosophy because "it thus risks perpetuating the very style of thinking that sustains gender inequality in the discipline."[60]

---

58. Tong, *Feminine and Feminist Ethics*, pp. 179–184.
59. Calhoun, *Setting the Moral Compass*, p. 8.
60. Ibid., p. 9.

Feminist philosophers today unpack this issue by explaining that a caring attitude is the result of practice and experience. Although traditionally the domain of women, men who engage in this type of work will be socialized in the same way. For Sara Ruddick, "Whatever difference might exist between female and male mothers, there is no reason to believe that one sex rather than the other is more capable of doing maternal work."[61] For Virginia Held, "'Mothering' suggests this activity must be done by woman, whereas, except for lactation, there is no part of it that cannot be done by men as well."[62] Held uses the term "mothering person" to emphasize the possibility of gender neutrality. In fact, the whole point of paying attention to caring and maternal thinking is to achieve social change by extending these dispositions to men and the public sphere. Women's morality, then, is thought to be an outcome of practice and not necessarily gender related. Held cautions not to glamorize parental care as parents can neglect and even harm their children.[63] Elizabeth Spelman directs our attention to the fact that historically, women are not free of violence and mistreatment of others.[64] If we idealize mothers we would not be able to explain violent mothers or mothers in favor of war. Furthermore, it is obvious that one can be loving and devoted to one's children, but indifferent to others. In order to fully understand the feminist claim, one has to understand the element of conscious choice in extending these experiences. What we can say about mothering, care, and sympathy is that they can transform morality if applied. Held addresses this issue with her arguments that care is both a practice and a value, and Rita Manning argues that there is an obligation to care. In the *Letters* de Grouchy argues that sentiments need to be exercised because otherwise they will diminish. She also thinks that feelings for others, once developed, should become a matter of regular practice and habit. Seeing emotions the way Smith defines them leaves us with little room for change. Seeing emotions as a social construct, as subject to change and development, leaves us with the ability to make demands on people's emotional and moral capacity.

---

61. Ruddick, *Maternal Thinking*, p. 41.
62. Held, "Taking Care: Care as Practice and Value," p. 65.
63. Held, "Feminism and Moral Theory," p. 118.
64. Spelman, "The Virtue of Feeling and the Feeling of Virtue."

When looking at the *Letters* one sees that de Grouchy placed a heavy emphasis on education. In addition, we know from her biography that she wrote an unpublished work on education for her daughter. I have already suggested that the differences between de Grouchy and Smith are embedded in her criticism of the causes of morality. It is reasonable to conclude that de Grouchy's *Letters*, particularly her ideas concerning the origin of morality in ties formed "in the crib," were influenced by the practicing of mothering and the relationship she had with her daughter. One cannot claim that de Grouchy's ideas arose because she was a mother—such a claim does entail sexism. But one can claim that the ideas in the *Letters* were influenced by her decision to apply her experience to her philosophy. Linking de Grouchy's role as a mother and some of her ideas in the *Letters* supports the emphasis on practice in feminist ethics and the connection between practice and morality. This link supports the view that engaging in caring work develops certain sensitivities and concerns. From this perspective, feminist morality is not women's morality but a morality of practicing care.

De Grouchy's emphasis is on education. Her hopes for the future and for social change are wrapped up in the education of the next generation. Interestingly, she holds everyone responsible, and thus one can claim her writing is gender neutral:

> Of what great importance it is, therefore, to train the sensibility of children so that it may develop to its fullest capacity in them. Their sensibility needs to reach that point where it can no longer be dulled by things that in the course of life tend to lead it astray, to carry us far from nature and from ourselves, and to concentrate our sensibility in all the passions of egoism or vanity. It should not take us away from simple things, from a reasonable life, and from natural inclinations in which the true happiness of each individual resides, happiness that does not reduce another's and that tends toward the good of all. Fathers, mothers, teachers, you have virtually in your hands alone the destiny of the next generation! Ah! How guilty you are if you allow to wither away in your children these precious seeds of sensibility… (*Letters*, 365/111–2)

* * *

In spite of the fact that de Grouchy's ideas and ideas in feminist ethics today emerged out of very different historical and philosophical backgrounds, the fundamental common denominators are striking. In addition, both the Enlightenment and the feminist movement were and are revolutionary movements that were and are intensely interested in social reform. De Grouchy was deeply affected by late-Enlightenment thought, and she incorporated her unique conceptions, which are now presented in a feminist light, to the theories of progress of her time. Perhaps after considering these points of comparison the reader can view the *Letters* as a feminist Enlightenment text, and a rare one at that.

Part II

Letters on Sympathy

Translator's Preface

This project came to me more or less by accident, and the effort to render Sophie de Grouchy's *Lettres sur la sympathie* into English was already advanced when I assumed the role of translator. I first learned about Sophie de Grouchy and her *Letters* from Karin Brown, whose analytical treatment of the *Letters* heads this volume. This introduction took place when Professor Brown was briefly a colleague of mine at Stevens Institute of Technology. That my own historical interests and period of expertise overlap with Sophie de Grouchy and her era of Enlightenment and Revolution aroused my interest and led me to keep up with the project. I was thus ready and pleased to accept Professor Brown's invitation when it came to assume charge of the translation. I did so hoping that my expertise as an historian conversant with the language and period of Sophie de Grouchy might spill over and so also shape the translation.

The translation I have effected has benefited from the work of others who have had a hand in it. Working with Professor Brown, Dr. Olivier Serafinowicz, and Dr. Alice Craven produced a more than serviceable complete draft translation that they did not intend for publication; this document has saved me countless hours, and I have preserved many of their stylistic turns. Dr. Julie Zilberberg contributed a publishable-quality translation of Letter 1; at another stage Dr. Bernard Roy produced a graceful translation of Letter 3. I hope to have melded all of this material into an accurate and seamless version in English of Sophie de Grouchy's 1798 work in French. Errors of style or accuracy remain mine alone, however unfortunately.

In preparing this translation, I have wrestled with art to balance accuracy with readability, and I have tried to attend to the nuances of the craft. In grappling with these matters abstractly and conceptually, I have benefited from several discussions with more experienced translators, and for their help and insights I am grateful to Ed Foster, Annie Regourd, Chris Sawyer-Lauçanno, and Mme Huang Do. In retrospect I see what great profit I gained in attending three international conferences on translation held at Stevens Institute of Technology in 1998, 2000, and 2002. I hope the sum of this critical thought and experience likewise informs the text that follows in good ways.

The consensus among translators is that a readable English text trumps any literal translation, however defined. The translator has an obvious duty somehow to be faithful to an original text, but what constitutes such fidelity exactly? Let us sidestep the point that a translation is, of course, a new text with a new author, but how literal does it have to be? No word-for-word translation would be acceptable, but neither would one that was accurate and simply grammatically correct in English if it did not somehow seek to capture the spirit of the text and the style of its original author. After all, if a translation does not succeed in this, or if no one wants to read a translation or has trouble reading it, then why bother? It is in stretching for these goals I have toyed around the edges with Sophie de Grouchy's prose to effect a document that I hope can stand on its own in its new language. One way or another, for *Feinschmeckers* there's always the original. I therefore excuse myself my liberties in crafting this translation into English that I hope does the required justice to the original text and its author.

Although the translation from Sophie de Grouchy's French has proven to be straightforward and without significant problems, a few further points regarding the translation may be mentioned. One concerns her prose style. She is a typical late eighteenth-century French stylist. Her models are Voltaire, Rousseau, Smith (for a similar English), and contemporary high literary language. Her sentences are unusually long, going on in clause piled upon clause, with verbs surrounded by fences of subordination, and objects of verbs and reflexive references buried beneath the weight of the words ahead of them.[1] There's a pace and weight to each *Letter* that cascades in emotive crescendos. Her meaning is (almost) always plain, but she expresses herself in elaborate sentences that are typical of her day and also, be it noted, entirely characteristic of the nominally epistolary form of writing then common. These are eighteenth-century letters, after all. But her constructions are not per se always worthwhile to preserve.[2] I have stayed very close to Sophie de Grouchy's order and organization throughout, and where possible her grand sentences survive in this translation. But I have also not hesitated to smooth and polish, to repunctuate and to restate de Grouchy's French in the interests, again, of clarity and readability in English.

That the *Lettres sur la sympathie* appeared in 1798 complicates the translation somewhat in that the translator is faced with choices about how modern or how eighteenth-century-like the translation should read. In general the approach I have adopted in consultation with Professor Brown is to reach for both, that is, to maintain the flavor and authenticity of the eighteenth-century document that Sophie de Grouchy published while at the same time modernizing her language somewhat for a contemporary reader in 2008. The rationale for attempting this stylistic compromise is to vivify her points while trying to avoid stilted pseudo-eighteenth-century language.

This consideration of, so to speak, the contemporaneity versus historicity of the translation became particularly pointed for the translator in dealing with Sophie de Grouchy's own sexist language. Despite her deep and genuine feminist thinking and despite other feminist thought around her, Sophie de Grouchy wrote unselfconsciously in the patriarchcal patois of the public arena of Old-Regime and Napoleonic-era France inhabited by men. Thus, her references are regularly to "man," "a man," "men," "mankind," and the like. Women (as persons) are nominally subsumed in these categories (but actually not); Sophie de Grouchy's explicit references to women are generally to their gender collectively or to their private, domestic existences as wives and mothers. Somewhat reluctantly, I have

---

1. The complexity of Sophie de Grouchy's prose is a point is made independently by the team responsible for the recent re-translation (into French) of Smith's *Theory of Moral Sentiments*; see Smith (2003), pp. 12–13.
2. For example, her use of the conditional tense translates best in the present in English.

been persuaded by Professor Brown that for the most part the translator has to maintain Sophie de Grouchy's explicit terminology and male-dominated language. For one thing, Sophie de Grouchy does criticize men collectively and in subgroups, and a critique of gender relations figures in the *Letters*. Furthermore, to time after time rewrite her "men" into our "humankind" would be too much of an injustice to the imprint of society on her, on her language, and on her *Letters*. By the same token, it is equally plain, given the language of her day, that she can refer to "a man," for example, when she means "someone" or "that person," or "all men" for "everyone," and like formulations. Wherever possible, therefore, I have chosen to temper her usage in order to highlight the sexist language of her day yet bringing it a little closer to what Sophie de Grouchy probably intended and could she have expressed herself in a liberated voice more familiar to the modern ear.

As free as the translator has felt in bringing a new text to life, a handful of words ring throughout the *Lettres* that need to be treated essentially as technical terms pertaining to contemporary sensationalist psychology and especially Sophie de Grouchy's sentimentalist version of it involving sensibility and sympathy. Here as much as possible stylistic variations are eschewed in favor of analytical clarity and consistency over the course of the text. *Sensibilité* is the main one of these terms. *Sensibilité* is generally given as sensitivity to highlight the physiological nature of what Sophie de Grouchy has in mind. It is also translated as sensibility, but not in English sense of being sober about things, or of good taste(s), but being a degree of sensitivity or receptiveness to outside impressions, notably affective sentiments.[3] For these reasons *sentiment* is largely preserved as 'sentiment', but sometimes also as 'feeling' and 'sensation'. She sometimes uses *sensitivité*, which is likewise rendered as sensitivity; sensible (as in 'être sensible') is rendered as sensitive, sensation likewise preserved as such, etc.

Other standard Enlightenment vocabulary (reason, imagination, reflection, liberty) has been straightforwardly brought over into English. *Intérêt* is another of these words of note, being a technical term in moral theory concerning someone's interest somehow defined. In other cases, however, such as her repeated use of the French words 'mal', 'peines', 'douleur',

---

3. On this point see Jessica Riskin.

'motif', etc., some effort has been made to vary her usage. Problem words included especially 'jouissance' (pleasure, enjoyment, possession, entitlement) and the ever troublesome 'convenances'. I broke up two of her pages-long paragraphs, but otherwise retained her paragraphing and italics. One or two other points re translation appear in notes. There are no footnotes in the original; all notes are editorial additions by Professor Brown and myself.

The translator has come to know the author through her prose. She is courageous in setting out her ideas. She is serious and makes real, original contributions to the philosophical subjects under discussion. She is intelligent and a sensitive observer of the world around her, from the nursery to the legislature, and she is highly knowledgeable of contemporary politics, society, friendships, and social and family relations. A personality comes through as a smart and vivacious woman of her day, to whom love and loving (child, missing husband, unfaithful lovers) is central. Sophie de Grouchy reveals her obviously upper-class background of pre-Revolutionary French nobility and salon culture, and she shows herself attentive to beauty, flirtation, gallantry, and the importance of *charme*.

By the same token, her strong and avant-garde political stance comes through strongly in the *Letters*. Her radical notions of social justice, of obligations of the rich to the poor, of reforming social institutions (and notably the laws), and of social relations and gender relations, had their roots in her pre-Revolutionary upbringing. It was refined in the fires of the Revolution, wherein she was on the forefront of radical republican debates and action. That she carried over this political stance and further refined it in France after Thermidor and restated it so strongly is testimony to her strength of character and the depths of her convictions.

Letter I

Man does not appear to me to have any more interesting object of meditation than man himself, my dear C***.[1] Is there, in effect, an activity any more satisfying and agreeable than to turn the soul's gaze upon itself, to study its operations, to trace its movements, to use our faculties alternatively to observe and to probe, and to seek to identify and grasp the hidden and furtive laws that guide our intelligence and our sensibility? Furthermore, to be often with oneself seems to me the most pleasant and wise life possible. It can blend the pleasures of wisdom and philosophy with those afforded by strong and profound emotions. This contemplative life puts the soul in a state of well being that is the first element of happiness and the disposition most favorable to virtue. Many people never achieve the recognition and happiness they might attain because they ignore, hate, or fear this life that, in simultaneously perfecting reason and sensibility, improves conditions for oneself and for others. You know if I live it myself. After all, after works that treat the primary means of assuring human happiness in society, I rank first those that lead us back to ourselves and make us dwell within our souls.

---

1. Cf. Alexander Pope line, "The proper study of mankind is man," *An Essay on Man* (1732)

However, I had not yet read Smith's *Theory of Moral Sentiments*. I had heard bad things said about the French translation of this famous work, and I did not understand enough English to read the original. I finally dared to undertake this task, but instead of following the ideas of the Edinburgh philosopher, I gave my own ideas free rein. In reading his chapters on sympathy, I concocted others of my own on the same subject. I will write them out for you in turn, so that you may judge me. I do not say that you can judge us because I am far from claiming to be on par with Smith.

You know that the subject of the opening chapters of Smith's book is sympathy. Smith limited himself to noting its existence and to showing its principal effects. I regretted that he did not dare go further, to penetrate its first cause, and ultimately to show to how sympathy must belong to every sensible being capable of reflection. You will see how I had the temerity to fill in these omissions.

Sympathy is the disposition we have to feel as others do.

Before examining the causes of the sympathy we experience when faced with a moral evil, we must examine the causes of the sympathy we experience when faced with physical afflictions.

Every physical pain produces a compound sensation in the person who experiences it.

It first produces a local pain in that part upon which the cause of pain acts initially.

Beyond that, it produces a painful general impression in all our organs, an impression very distinct from the local pain and that always accompanies the latter, but that can continue to exist without it.

One will gather just how distinct this latter sensation is from local pain, if one is willing to observe what one feels the moment local pain ceases. Often in such circumstances one experiences both the pleasure caused by the cessation of the local pain and at the same time a general feeling of malaise. Now this feeling of malaise is sometimes very painful. It can even, if particular causes prolong it, become more intolerable than the more intense, though short-lived local pains because the organs that are the principal seat of that general impression are the most essential for vital functions as well as for the faculties that make us sensitive and intelligent.

This general sensation renews itself when we remember injuries we have suffered. This is the sensation that makes the memory distressing, and it always accompanies this memory to varying degrees.

We should observe that, although this systematic impression is doubtless capable of some variation, it is nonetheless the same for many otherwise very different local pains, at least when these pains share certain analogies among themselves, either in intensity or in their character. But should this impression be different for different types of pain—for a broken bone, for example, and for an internal lesion on some organ, it can happen that the person who has felt them both experiences the same impression in recalling them, if time has weakened the memory he has of them or if he pays insufficient attention to them to allow his imagination and his memory to transmit to him the different sensations attached to these different impressions.

In the same way as the memory of an injury we have felt reproduces the painful impression that affected all our organs and that formed part of the local pain this injury caused us, so, too, we feel this painful impression again when, being in a position to notice the signs of pain, we see an impressionable being suffer or whom we know suffers.

In effect, as soon as the development of our faculties and the repeated experience of pain permit us to have an abstract idea of it, that idea alone renews in us the general impression made by pain on all our organs.

Here, then, is an effect of pain that follows equally from both its physical presence and its moral presence.

One understands here by its moral presence either the idea that our memories give us of pain or that which we can have of it by the sight or knowledge of another's pain.

The cause of sympathy for physical pains, therefore, comes from the fact that the sensation physical pain produces in us is a compound sensation, a part of which can renew itself simply by the idea of pain.

One can now see how a child, as soon as he has enough intelligence to discern the signs of pain, sympathizes with the suffering being who manifests them. One sees how witnessing pain can affect the child to the point where he cries out and flees the scene and where he is more or less moved by the sight, depending on whether he has more or less knowledge of the signs of pain and more or less sensitivity, imagination, and memory.

The reproduction of the general impression of pain on our organs depends on sensibility and above all on the imagination.

This impression is all the more intense as our sensitivity is stronger, and its replication is commensurately easier as the impression was more intense and as our imagination is more capable of receiving and conserving all the ideas that can reignite it.

Not only does the general impression of pain on all our organs reproduce itself at the very idea of it, but also its local impression sometimes repeats itself when the memory or the idea of the pain strikes us vividly. That is how someone who has suffered a major operation, in recalling it in full detail, believes he feels a portion of the local pain it caused him. Similarly, someone who sees a wounded man, besides the unpleasant impression felt at the sight of pain, if his imagination is strong or easily moved, believes he experiences a local pain in the corresponding part of his body where the wound was inflicted and sometimes also in the neighboring part traversed by the same nerves. I knew a woman who read a very detailed passage on lung diseases in a medical work and whose imagination became so frightened by the many causes capable of afflicting this vital organ that she believed herself to be experiencing some of the pains characteristic of lung congestion, and she had trouble ridding herself of this idea. Similar examples are not rare, especially in that class of individuals whose soft and idle lives leave them few ways to protect themselves from being mislead by an overactive imagination.

One easily gathers that the general impression produced by seeing physical pain renews itself more easily when we witness afflictions we ourselves have suffered because that impression is then aroused both by our memories and by seeing the effects. It is for this reason that pain and adversity are such effective schools for making men more compassionate and more human. How necessary this school is for you, the rich and powerful, who are distanced from the very idea of misery and misfortune by the almost insurmountable barriers of wealth, egoism, and familiarity with power!

Elderly people who have ordinarily lost some of their sensibility experience sympathetic reactions to physical pain with greater difficulty. If one sees that some of them wilt easily and shed tears often, this is not due to the strength of their sympathy but to the weakening of their organs that augments the power of pain over them. Also, the sight of pain is dangerous to them and can even shorten their lives.

Here, one will wonder, perhaps, why surgeons, physicians, and all those who provide care to suffering beings are usually less affected than other men by the sight of pain? How, for example, do surgeons remain cool enough to probe a wound, to apply iron and fire to it, and to penetrate inside delicate organs amid bloody and torn flesh without the sight and sound of pain affecting their own organs enough to make their hands tremble, to distract their gaze, and to sway their attention and judgment? Upon reflection, one will see that this is not only because the necessity of protecting oneself from a pain, repeated exposure to which becomes unbearable, has toughened them against the impression of pain. (This is a rare insensitivity, which fortunately the human heart cannot develop except by long and arduous efforts.) But rather, their self control develops because surgeons anticipate and block painful impressions through the habit they have acquired with the aim of preserving their patients and because in their eyes and to their ears the idea of preventing the sufferer's demise constantly mitigates the usually awful aspect of his disorders and the acuteness of his groans and pleas. The interest that is so touching and so imperative to save his fellow man and the focus necessary for figuring out ways to do so suspends, for the preservation of his patient, the impression the surgeon receives of the pain. And beneficent nature protects the surgeon from this impression that might prevent him from being useful.

It seems that there is no need to prove that the more sensibility is exercised, the more it intensifies, excepting that by overstimulation one carries it to a point that makes it tiresome and unpleasant and that leads one to seek relief from it. A sensibility that is not exercised at all tends to weaken and can no longer be stimulated except by very strong impressions.

The soul is a fire that must be nourished
And that extinguishes itself if it does not grow.
Voltaire.[2]

Of what great importance it is, therefore, to train the sensibility of children so that it may develop to its fullest capacity in them. Their sensibility needs to reach that point where it can no longer be dulled by things that in the course of life tend to

---

2. Lagrave, *Sophie de Grouchy*, p. 75 cites: *Oeuvres Complètes de Voltaire* [Louis Moland, éd.], tome XIX, Paris, Garnier, 1877–1882, p. 345.

lead it astray, to carry us far from nature and from ourselves, and to concentrate our sensibility in all the passions of egoism or vanity. It should not take us away from simple things, from a reasonable life, and from natural inclinations in which the true happiness of each individual resides, happiness that does not reduce another's and that tends toward the good of all. Fathers, mothers, teachers, you have virtually in your hands alone the destiny of the next generation! Ah! How guilty you are if you allow to wither away in your children these precious seeds of sensibility that need nothing more to develop than the sight of suffering, the example of compassion, tears of recognition, and an enlightened hand that warms and coddles them! How guilty you are, if you are more concerned with the outward success of your children than with their virtues, or if you are more impatient to see them please a social circle than to see their hearts roil with indignation in the face of injustice, their foreheads pale before sorrow, and their hearts treat all men as brothers! Think less of their graces, their talents, and their occupations. Draw out all the feelings that nature has placed in their souls. Render them easily remorseful and sensitive to the voice of honor and integrity so that they are unable to see suffering without being compelled to relieve it. Amid this host of oppressive barriers raised between man and man by need, power, and vanity, it is no less necessary that they hesitate at each step before harming the rights of others or to failing to redress old affronts! Let the gentle habit of doing good teach them that it is by means of their hearts that they can be happy, and not by their titles, luxury, high rank, or riches!

You have taught this to me, venerable mother, whose footsteps I have so often followed under the dilapidated roof of the unfortunate, fighting poverty and woe! Receive the life-long homage I owe you, every time I do good and every time I have the happy inspiration and the gentle joy of so doing. Yes, my heart came alive in seeing your hands relieve both misery and illness and in seeing the suffering gaze of the poor turn toward you and become tender in blessing you, and the true good of social life manifested before my eyes appeared to me in the joyfulness of loving humanity and serving it.

As we receive the impressions of pleasure with the same organs that receive the impressions of pain, both these impressions follow the same laws. All physical pleasure, like all physical ailments, produces in us a sensation composed of a particular sensation of pleasure in the organ that first receives it and a general feeling of well-being. And this latter sensation can renew itself at the sight of pleasure, just like the general impression of pain on our organs repeats itself at the sight of pain.

We are thus capable of sympathy towards the physical pleasures which others experience as well as their afflictions. Only this sympathy is more difficult to arouse and consequently more rare. In the first instance, because the intensity of pleasure is less than that of pain, this general impression of pleasure on our organs is less easily awakened. Then, because nearly all physical pleasures have something particular about them that, in giving us the idea and the feeling of deprivation, balances and can end up destroying the agreeable impression that the idea of the pleasure of others must arouse in us.

Sympathy, which the sight of physical pleasure makes us re-experience, is thus a feeling with less power over our soul than the one inspired in us by the sight of pain. But it was important to recognize its existence because it serves to explain several phenomena of moral sympathy.

You see, my dear C***, that the first causes of sympathy derive from the nature of the sensations that pleasure and pain cause us to experience, and it is first and foremost as sentient beings that we are capable of sympathy for physical ailments, the most common afflictions among men. You will see in the next letter how this sympathy born of our sensibility completes itself by reflection. What do we not owe to sympathy, even in its faintest glimmerings, since from that moment sympathy is the first cause of the feeling of humanity, the effects of which are so precious. It compensates for a portion of the evils issuing from personal interests in large societies, and it struggles against the coercive force that we encounter everywhere we go and that centuries of Enlightenment alone can destroy by attacking the vices that have produced it! Amid the shock of so many passions that oppress the weak or marginalize the unfortunate, from the bottom of its heart humanity secretly pleads the cause of sympathy and avenges it from the injustice of fate by arousing the sentiment of natural equality.

Letter II

The sympathy of which we are capable for physical pains and that is one part of what we understand by the name of *humanity*, my dear C***, would be too transient a sentiment to be often useful were we not as capable of reflection as we are of sensitivity. And just as reflection prolongs ideas which the senses bring to us, so it extends and preserves in us the effects of the sight of pain, and one can say that it alone makes us truly human. Indeed, reflection fixes in our soul the presence of an injury which our eyes have only seen for a brief moment, and reflection leads us to try to relieve misfortune in order to efface the painful and unwelcomed idea of it. Reflection comes to the rescue of our natural volatility and activates our compassion by offering anew a scene that had made a merely momentary impression. At the sight of pain reflection reminds us that we, like the downtrodden being we perceive, are subject to the tyranny of death, and so reflection draws us closer to the sufferer by means of an inward emotional and affective turn that leads us to be concerned with his pains, even when they might repel rather than attract our sensitivity. And finally, reflection conditions our sensibility by prolonging its activity and so installs humanity in our souls as an active and permanent sentiment that, eager to apply itself, spontaneously seeks the happiness of men through works of science and meditations on nature, experience, and philosophy. This sentiment attaches itself to suffering and misfortune, pursues them everywhere, and becomes humanity's comforter, its god. The feeling for humanity is thus in some way a seed lodged in the interior of man's heart by nature and which the faculty of reflection will nurture and develop.

But, as it might be asked, are some animals capable of pity but not of reflection?

One can answer, first of all, that they are sentient, and this quality suffices, as we have seen, to make animals capable of sympathizing with pain. In the second place, we do not know the nature and extent of ideas that animals might have. Consequently, we cannot affirm or deny that the degree of compassion of which they are capable is or is not the effect of some degree of reflection. One of the animals upon whom the sight of pain has the most power, namely the dog, is also one of those that seems closest to human intelligence.

But it is in observing man himself that one grasps even more easily how he owes the greatest part of his humanity to the faculty of reflection. Indeed, man is human insofar as he is sensitive and reflective. Country folks and, in general, those whose occupations are closest to material concerns that do not allow for reflection are less capable of compassion than are other people. One of the primary goals of the laws should thus be to establish and maintain an equality of wealth among citizens. The result would be for each and every citizen a degree of wealth such that preoccupation with the necessities of life and the worry of providing them would not deny citizens the degree of reflection necessary for the perfection of all natural sentiments, and particularly for that of humanity.

In a less constrained and wealthier class of higher rank, do we not also see that men are more or less human, depending on whether they are more or less capable of sensitivity and especially reflection? Beings preoccupied by unbridled passions born of egoism or vanity, attentive only to their own ends, and their reflection limited to calculating how to obtain their desires, are they not always devoid of humanity as well as compassion?

As the general impression of pain upon our organs repeats itself at the sight or just the recollection of pain, our abstract idea of pain can also reproduce it, and consequently so can the after-effects and situations where pain is inevitable. In this case, although this impression usually reproduces itself in a more vague and indeterminate manner (because the abstract idea of pain brings it home to us only in a weak way), nonetheless, if this idea offers us a new and extraordinary combination of pains, its effect can equal an existing pain. Such is the cause of the disquieting sensation we experience when, without thinking precisely of such and such an individual, we turn our thoughts to the class of men doomed to both the harshest labors and to poverty, or at least to dreading poverty; or when (without stopping to consider any particular pain or hardship), we are powerfully moved on hearing that someone has been reduced to poverty by an unexpected reversal of fortunes or even if he is only threatened with that possibility.

The most abstract idea of physical pains, i.e., their possibility for an individual who is a stranger to us, thus more or less strongly renews the general impression of pain on our organs. The idea of moral pain also produces the same effect. But to explain our sympathy with respect to moral suffering shared by all beings of our species, one must go back to the causes of our particular sympathies that form the basis of such sympathy.

Let us see, first of all, how we are inclined to sympathize with the distress of certain individuals rather than others who experience similar or equal travails.

Independent of the moral conventions that constitute the greater part of the happiness and existence of those whose souls have been developed and exercised, and independent of everything that renders civilized man happy, each individual finds himself depending upon many others for the necessities of life, for his well being, and for life's conveniences. This dependency, in truth more extensive and more marked in childhood, continues to a certain degree into later years and remains more or less strong insofar as moral development sets it aside or lets it subsist. But, because the extreme inequality of wealth reduces most men socially to providing for their own physical needs, the vast majority of the human species is condemned to a strict dependence on everyone who can help in satisfying its needs. It follows that each individual soon recognizes those whom he owes the better part of his existence and who are the proximate and permanent causes of his hardships or his joys. He cannot be indifferent to their presence or to the very idea of them. These people unfailingly make him feel pain or pleasure.

The specific dependency on some individuals begins in the crib. It is the first tie that attaches us to our fellows. It causes the first smiles, and the most regular smiles of a child are for his wet-nurse; he cries when he is not in her arms and for a long time he loves to throw himself upon this breast that satisfied his first needs, that made him feel the first sensations of pleasure, and where at long last he began to mature and to form his initial life habits.

The force of our sensitivity, depending on the state we happen to be in, and the idea of the persons to whom we owe the better part of our welfare are alone sufficient for us to experience a feeling, and we are thus emotionally predisposed to care about everything that could happen to them. Their pleasures or pains must therefore affect us more intensely than the pleasures and pains of other people.

In essence, their suffering must move us more than anyone else's because we regard these people as connected to us. And because we see them and think about them more often, when they suffer we must be simultaneously moved both by the idea of their current pain and by its after effects, that is, ailments more or less long lasting and grievous to which their present state exposes them.

Being accustomed to the ties that bind their existence to ours, at the sight of their pains or pleasures we must further experience the feeling we would have at the idea of a danger or a good happening to us personally, and this by the force of habit alone, without any specific or conscious attention to our own interest.

When civilization has attained a certain degree, what we have just said concerning the sympathy towards people who contribute directly to our happiness or who help us to satisfy our needs, extends to two other classes of individuals. First of all, are those whom we can regard as a resource or support in the face of calamities that may threaten us. This involves an apparently vague, less direct connection, less physical as it were, but one which can become very close in certain social strata where one is more concerned with one's fears and hopes than with one's needs and where one is especially future-oriented. A specific sympathy can also be established between those who are brought together by their tastes and habits and who mutually find more affinity and enjoyment in each other's company. This sympathy is stronger or less strong, accordingly as propriety and social graces constitute a larger or smaller portion of one's happiness.

One now sees how we are capable of a particular sympathy towards individuals we value because of the utility or pleasure they bring us. One sees that the cause of this sympathy, like sympathy for physical pains and pleasures common to all men, derives from the general impression of pain and pleasure upon our organs, an impression itself awakened solely by the abstract idea of pleasure and pain, and modified by all the circumstances that can affect our sensibility.

Perhaps you have asked yourself, my dear C***, why, despite the disagreeable impression the sight or idea of pain spreads through all of our organs, we like to recall the troubles we have undergone and those which we have witnessed, and why, not satisfied with the emotions provided by real woes, we seek out new ones in accounts of the most frightful misfortunes and the most heartrending circumstances born only of the imagination? Why do all vibrant and tender souls, upon whom the impression of pain is stronger and more unfailing, enjoy renewing it by reading novels and tragedies and by identifying with unhappy beings and devouring every detail of their misfortunes? Why do they every day seem to need to expend the full power of their sensitivity in order to partake of it?

Several reasons explain this need.

First of all, we are obviously led to concern ourselves with the sufferings of others in order to relieve them. This desire acts in us without any reflection over the possibility of doing so and even before we have had time to discern whether or not this possibility might ever exist. It is this desire which, on seeing someone struggling in floodwaters and on the verge of drowning, leads bystanders on the riverbank to frantically stretch their arms towards him. This is a movement of a sublime nature that unveils in an instant the full power of humanity over our hearts and all the effects which the legislator could derive from this sentiment that unfortunately is more often weakened than fortified by our institutions.

Experience has shown how exact knowledge of objects is often useful to us and how important it is for us not to deceive ourselves concerning their reality. From there a sentiment arises in us which habit makes natural and almost mechanical. Its existence often escapes us, but should a mix of confused ideas present itself to our minds or a vague picture of some event to our imagination, we experience as an effect of this sentiment a disagreeable impression that compels us to clarify whatever this mix or picture was and to delve into all its details. This is the same type of impression which we feel at the sight of pain. It starts from the same principle. It is produced by the vague idea that a harm can result from this real state of affairs of which we are not fully cognizant. Thus a hidden inner impulsion leads us to recognize the sufferings of others as soon as we suspect their existence and in general to probe every combination of ideas and every fact of which we only have an incomplete notion. And this motive of concealed personal interest, if we are involved, or of comparison, if others are involved, is not the least cause of natural human curiosity. As soon as our physical needs are satisfied, moral needs torment us, and we become liable to depression.[1] Some people (and especially those whose souls are subject to whims, calculation, and the empty pleasures of vanity) experience depression alone because the desire for a more advantageous position than the one they have and the mere possibility of such a position disgusts them with all that they do possess and leaves them wanting only what they do not have. For the human heart, although difficult to satisfy, even by things that can bring it true contentment, is even more voracious and insatiable when one can only barely satisfy one's needs. Other people have no new ideas and are unable to come up with any because the weakness of their spirits or their health will not allow it. These people remain enthralled to the dis-ease which the state of their physical constitution, their fears, and the recollection or idea of their burdens force them to experience. Many are tormented by depression only because they lack reason enough, courage enough to exercise their intelligence, or experience and insight enough to recognize that the mind is like an instrument that overburdens and fatigues the hand that carries it if it is not utilized. Depression is thus one of the most cruel ailments of the human heart. It is such an unbearable state that in order to avoid it we do not fear giving ourselves over to painful sensations, and the desire to avoid it is one of the causes that leads us to familiarize ourselves with the idea of pain.

But there is yet another more powerful, active and continuous cause. It is the need we have of being moved, even given

---

1. The word she uses, *ennui*, usually translates as boredom or tiresome, but here Sophie de Grouchy clearly means depression. See Part I, above.

that, the causes of pain being far more numerous than those of pleasure and their intensity stronger, we cannot hope for as many agreeable sensations as disagreeable ones. This need to be moved is found not only among souls whose sensitivity and natural activity have acquired the greatest possible development through education, thinking, and experiencing passion; it is even easy to observe in the almost habitually insensitive multitude. Is this not in essence the kind of attraction tied to all emotions, even painful ones, that leads the multitude to always encircle the scaffold and sometimes to see tortures in all their horror that nearly always melt the masses and make it shed tears. The human heart in some fashion is drawn to what agitates it and stirs it up. It senses that these exotic emotions distract it from habitual impressions it often finds disagreeable or insipid. These emotions, it feels, will save it from 'ennui'; they will augment its strength, and, in making the heart more pliant, they open it up to receiving new impressions and thereby enhance one of its richest sources of enjoyment. Emotion thus seems fitting for the soul, just as exercise is fitting for the body. And the calm that follows appears as the only one the soul can genuinely appreciate.

One must observe, however, that with only a few exceptions, the unpleasant emotions we seek are always admixed with some pleasure, and the impression produced by these pleasures overcomes or at least effaces the idea of pain. We know, for example, that at a play when we surrender our soul to the grand sweep of tragedy, to the charm of poetry, to the novelty of situations, to the grandeur and originality of the characters, and to the skill with which the play unfolds, the pleasure of enjoying both the creation of art and the effect art produces, that is, of enriching our imagination and memory with images and new ideas and of feeling ourselves moved in new ways that can ennoble us,…that pleasure elevates us in our own eyes, instantly balances out the painful sensations mixed with these pleasures, eradicates them, and remains afterwards. This is so true that we rarely seek these kinds of disagreeable emotions when we are not sustained by the hope of experiencing agreeable ones later. Indeed one rarely rereads novels and tragedies that end in a sinister catastrophe except when the beauties of the art and the dramatic settings, constantly taking us from fear to hope and from tears of pain to tears of joy, make us forget at each moment as the drama unfolds, the tragic and unhappy ending.

You see, my dear C***, that if nature has surrounded us with a crown of troubles, it has in some way compensated for them in sometimes turning our very pains into the most profound source of pleasures for us. Let us bless this sublime relation found between the moral needs of some men and the physical needs of others, between the misfortunes to which nature and our vices subject us, and the penchants of virtue which receive satisfaction only in assuaging misfortune.

Letter III

Today, my dear C***, I wish to speak to you about particular sympathy,[1] the one that establishes intimate bonds between men that are necessary for their perfection and happiness. It draws hearts together and entwines them with the most tender affections. And, grounded in more direct relations than general sympathy,[2] it more readily pertains to all men and could, were it attended to more, make this mass of men who have become almost insensitive to everything but their own circumstances and happiness more attuned to the ills and needs of all humanity. Indeed, all parts of our sensibility are connected. As soon as one is exercised, the others become increasingly refined and more likely to be stimulated.

The first manifestations of particular sympathy arise at the very instant objects capable of stimulating it present themselves to us. When we see someone for the first time, we look at his features, and we seek the person behind the face. Should his face be the least graceful or beautiful or should some particular mark distinguish it, we scrutinize it closely, and we attempt to grasp the impressions it receives and to untangle those that

---

1. Here the French reads: *sympathie individuelle*; elsewhere she uses synonymously *sympathie particulière*.
2. The French reads: *sympathie générale*.

most often affect it. There is not anyone whose looks, even at first glance, do not give us some idea of his character or force us to presume, favorably or not, something of his mind. Impressions from physiognomy are soon increased, changed, or erased by the way the individual moves, by his mannerisms, by his speech, and by any contrast between what he says and what he does. For it is through the gaze that the moral character seeks to emerge; it is through speech that the movements of the soul unfold; it is in the features that habits are disclosed and betrayed by gestures. When, through all these, we believe we have found the characteristics and marks of some qualities of particular interest to us, variously on account of their connection to our own, because we hold them in high esteem, or because their combination appears to us as striking and out of the ordinary, then a wave of goodwill rises within us directed at the person who appears to be endowed with these qualities. We feel drawn toward him. We take pleasure in attending to him. We intuit something that triggers a redoubling of our observations and that makes them more and more penetrating. Sometimes, however, this first impression is strong enough to confuse us, so much so that we lose our ability to observe. For those endowed with a lively soul, the effect of this first impression is the fundamental source of the prejudices that blind them and that make them incapable of discerning reliably or even of judging reasonably.

This particular sympathy, so long considered inexplicable, is nevertheless nothing but a very natural effect of our moral sensibility. When someone's demeanor hints at qualities which we like, we feel drawn towards him because, by awakening in us the idea of these qualities, he leads us to expect all the advantages we tacitly associate with their reality. Thus, because their opinions concur with ours it necessarily follows from the most primitive self-love that we like people who enhance the value we attach in our own eyes to our own judgments and who assuage any fear we might harbor of being mislead. And so it is that we show interest in people who are praiseworthy for their virtues, their humanity, and their benevolence. This, either because our memory of them provides a resource for our own planning and projects, or because the mere idea of the good they have done and can do renews in us the memorable impression usually caused by the promise or reality of some public happiness or by the relief of a particular misfortune.

You may perhaps think here, my dear C***, that the effect is disproportionate to the cause, and you will surely ask me why particular sympathy is sometimes so strong, yet its bases remain so weak and vague. Why? The answer is that enthusiasm gets mixed in with the first impressions we forge, and enthusiasm extends them beyond the point where our knowledge of the facts would normally lead.[3] Consider this moral phenomenon, and you will see how much strong and unexpected particular sympathies pertain to it and how perfectly it explains them.

Enthusiasm derives from the ability the soul more or less possesses to represent to itself simultaneously, but also in a rather confused manner, all the pleasures and pains that might arise in a certain situation or from the existence of a particular person and our relationship to him or her. This representation unites in a single instant what in real life should take months, years, or even a lifetime to gather. Thus, enthusiasm sees its subject in an exaggerated fashion, and this representation, too complex for the mind to grasp its parts distinctly, in some respects always remains uncertain. Whence in the realm of sentiment, another kind of exaggeration results, arising out of the proliferation of pains and pleasures we picture for ourselves. A real error even results, since often, when we are emotionally upset by irrational fears and desires, we are unable to discern their impossibility amidst the agitation of the soul. Habit has an odd influence on this disposition. Should an event or an individual stir it up in us several times over, habit retains the power to stimulate it again, even independently of all reflection, and thus we can consider enthusiasm an emotion of the soul. The fear of being dishonored, for example, feels real only because we can vividly and immediately conjure up all the ills of a blameworthy life. But once this horrible feeling has taken hold, the idea of disgrace can stimulate the feeling of disgrace without reviving the ideas that brought it forth in the first place. Likewise, the enthusiasm we have for certain qualities disposes us to a sudden and unreflective sympathy toward individuals in whom we think we perceive these traits.

The ability to experience these sudden and vivid sympathies therefore depends, as does enthusiasm, on the following:

1. The strength of the imagination that with greater or lesser alacrity embraces vast panoramas of sensations and events.

---

3. On the concept of enthusiasm see above, Part I.

2. The strength of sensibility that is variously affected by these imaginings and that maintains them more or less entire.

3. We could also add some more or less deep reflections which we have made on the object of these sympathies. For, if some kind of instinct or some distinct circumstances caused us to reflect on a situation, an opinion, or a personality trait, then our ideas, having had a chance to consider the respective advantages or disadvantages, have in some way readied within our hearts an inclination toward individuals who find themselves in this or that situation, who share this or that opinion, or who possess this or that trait. And, the need or desire to find a focus for that affection and to let go of an emotion we have long carried in our soul without giving it an outlet produces in us these sudden sympathies that often appear to have no other cause than chance or caprice.

The nature and duration of particular sympathies thus depend on the strength of both the imagination and sensibility, as well as on how much we reflect on their causes.

These sympathies come about all the more readily and they seem all the more intense in those individuals who perceive with their imagination, who feel according to first impressions, and who are governed more by the swirl of ideas than warmth of feeling.

Particular sympathies occur even more often between people who have a highly developed moral sense. Such sympathies are all the more gentle as the other person is more delicate and more pure. This, because to better link us one to another, nature has willed that virtuous sentiments be nearly as sweet as virtue's deeds.

They are longer lasting between those whose sensitivity is more deep than lively, more gentle and delicate than impassioned. They are more steadfast between those who love with a truth and a purity of heart that are as necessary for personal charm as for enduring attachments.

They are more intimate between melancholic and reflective souls who delight in feeding on their own feelings and savoring them in meditation, who see in life only that which binds them to it, and who remain focused on their feelings, being incapable of desiring more. For no matter how insatiable the human heart may be, it never exhausts true happiness when it wants to stop there.

It has often been said that esteem was the strongest foundation of particular sympathies, but not enough has been said about the appeal of this feeling itself, and in these previous accounts the human heart was not made delicate enough. Esteem, nevertheless, is necessary in order to acquire the trust and freedom that represent the first stages of well-being which our soul is capable of attaining. Only with esteem can we love with the full force of sensibility. Esteem is in some sense the single medium where our affections develop, where the heart can let go, and where, as a result, the heart can fully flourish. In honest souls, esteem is always the tacit companion of particular sympathies. Esteem can even cause these sympathies, as when it focuses on some extraordinary qualities and in so doing becomes a source of enjoyment.

The man worthy of esteem is happy to esteem. His heart, easily moved by the mere thought of a good deed, finds itself tied and attached to the heart he thinks capable of performing a good deed. He feels good in this company, and this brotherhood of virtue establishes between two people a freedom and an equality, the feeling of which may be as tender as that of the closest blood and natural ties.

If the first movements of sympathy convey a feeling for an individual we barely know only because of his looks, his mannerisms, and the few words we exchange are enough to make his presence a pleasure, and if mere esteem engenders in us a sentiment of goodwill and freedom—the preeminent positive feeling that enables us to experience them all—we are led to grasp the import of a more deeply rooted and deeply felt sympathy and what the attraction of friendship can be. We can say that the appeal of friendship begins before friendship is in place and in some sense as soon as we can imagine its existence. As a matter of fact, as soon as we can conceive of the idea of someone who might befriend us and who is uniquely capable of deep and delicate affections, we experience a delightful feeling because we fashion in our soul an idea of all the tenderness that friendship has in store for us. This feeling is already a joy, and here is why: given that we consider ourselves beings sensitive to physical pain and pleasure, the exclusive pleasure of loving and being loved is happiness for us.

In part, the pleasure of loving is also born from the enjoyment we take from the idea, the recollection, or the anticipation of the happiness that our affection brings to another sensitive being. If we find ourselves in the regular company of this individual, if particular sympathy strengthens our connections, and if enthusiasm vividly represents for us all the happiness our friendship can bring to him or her, as well as the happiness we ourselves can expect out of this friendship, then the pleasure we find in caring for another increases. And by the time this pleasure has been repeated enough for our sensibility to sense its attraction and to develop a need for it, the person through whom we experience this feeling becomes dearer to us, and the feeling he inspires in us becomes a necessary part of our existence.

It is so true (at least in the case of friendship) that the pleasure we take in making other people happy by being affectionate is, in large measure, the cause of the pleasure we find in loving, and that only generous souls are capable of loving. All those souls lacking magnanimity or nobility or that have been corrupted by selfishness may very well wish to be loved, and thus may seek both the delight and fruits of love, but only generous hearts capable of being touched by the happiness of others really know how to love. All the reasons behind particular sympathy, including having the same views, the same tastes, and the same moral character, can bring two people together and unite their hearts on the surface, but only the felicitous capacity of sharing the happiness of others can establish in these hearts the solid, true, and durable affections, independent of place, time, and the interests of each, and that are suitable for enchanting life or at least to temper it. When children are led to practice and carefully cultivate in their souls their natural sensitivity to the pleasures of others and especially to the satisfaction of contributing to such pleasures, they are not only disposed toward the most tender and useful virtues, but they are also assured that they will be capable of love, that they will feel all love's charm, or at least that they will be worthy of love.

The sight of beauty (and, whatever the true origin of the beautiful, by this word let us understand here that which we enjoy seeing) inspires a pleasurable feeling. A handsome individual is, to all eyes, a being endowed with the power to add to the happiness of everyone who has the least connection with him or her. We are led to attach greater weight to what they say, to their ways of being, to their feelings, and to their actions because, in effect, they are more charming. We therefore feel affection for that individual naturally. This feeling, combined with the ones that physical traits and the qualities of the soul create in us, produces a particular emotion we call *love*. It stands apart from others especially because it gives us a pleasant sensation that always recurs at the sight or even the idea of the individual who is the source of that love. This power to make us happy at every moment and to carry away, to occupy, to bind, and to fill our entire sensibility—be it just by exciting it—exercises more dominion over people than all the joys of friendship or the appeal of engaging virtuous individuals. One can hardly doubt that beauty or at least some degree of resonance and interest in appearances is necessary for love. Exceptions are fairly rare among males, the raw taste for pleasure being nearly always the cause. If there are fewer exceptions among women, it is because they harbor moral values of modesty and duty that have accustomed them since early childhood to be wary of first impressions and nearly always to prefer certain qualities and occasionally a certain moral rectitude over physical attractions. Love can have many different causes, and the more causes love has, the greater it is. Sometimes, a single enticement or a single quality touches and captures our sensibility. Often (and all too often) our sensibility gives itself up for gifts that are extraneous to the heart. In love, our sensibility becomes more fragile and aware, and it is touched only by those things that can give it satisfaction. And, by a diplomacy as commanding as reason and prudence, sensibility yields to love only when love dominates all that is worthy of love. In this case, love, even among the purest souls and those who are the least enslaved to appearances and sensuality, becomes a true passion. Then, for such a love innocent caresses can long suffice and lose nothing of their charm and their value after they are whispered. And so, the bliss being loved produces the ecstasy so greatly needed and desired. Then, all ideas of happiness and voluptuousness coalesce around that one single object, always depend on it, and are as nothing for all others.

However, for love to be such, an exquisite mutual understanding must allow two souls to join together completely, to love with boundless trust, and to appreciate everything involved in their love. Our particular friend, whatever his imperfections, his good qualities, or other features, must be the friend of all that touches our existence. In our successes and our failures, in that period of life when we need solace from having suffered humanity and its trials, as well as when we can hardly bear life, we will find in that ennobling person someone who can restore and guide our happiness. Most of all, the propitious blend of character, minds, and hearts of two individuals must allow their happiness to check the natural inconstancy and rash desires of the human heart.

Particular sympathy is reciprocated more or less according to the various causes that bring it about. It cannot help being reciprocated when it is based on a consilience of tastes, views, and, above all ways of feeling. However, even without this conformity, sympathy is often reciprocated. In this case, it springs from the force that naturally draws us to those who love us. Sympathy is no less strong even when the inducements that bring two people together are different. To love is thus a reason to be loved, unless extraordinary circumstances distort our sensibility in such a way that sympathy cannot be requited. Thus, in everyday language the word 'sympathy' contains the idea of reciprocity.

This reciprocity is harder to find in the passion of love because the first principle of love, even the purest, is an attraction that in large part is independent of the moral qualities that otherwise condition sympathy. A sweet face pleases, affects, and inspires love, but what distinguishes this love from friendship is precisely the ever rekindled pleasure we feel in seeing or remembering that face. Thus, what precipitates love for us must be reciprocated, at least to a certain extent, in order for the sentiment of love itself to be reciprocated. The causes of this reciprocity may very well be common in nature, but they are scattered about, and one can sense how rare their coming together might be and how difficult it is that these causes be absolutely the same or equally strong in the two beings brought together by them.

Let us now explore what degree of sympathy is necessary to have towards people we see regularly in order to be drawn to the pleasure of their company.

It seems to me, my dear C***, that the sympathy derived from esteem is not sufficient because what is usually understood by the word *esteem* is only the dispassionate interest we associate with the common good or the one that austere virtues or brilliant mental qualities inspire in us. Now, an interest of this kind, if it is not combined with some other, possesses only a rather weak charm (unless it be raised to the highest degree, but that is very rare). Besides, indulgence, compassion, and kindness must accompany every quality and every perfection in order not to disturb our independence or weigh on our weaknesses. The first need of the human heart is freedom. The heart must be able to attach itself to what it admires in order to be just and happy. And it is no doubt a misfortune that the virtues we most admire often are those from which we can expect the least indulgence. A sensitive man, therefore, can only love those qualities of the mind which virtue accompanies. He can only love those virtues that are more sentimental than sober, which indulgence makes likable and affecting, which seek to be imitated only by being felt, and which we cannot discern in others without feeling their effects within us even prior to acting on them.

The sympathy necessary for friendship does not always demand likeable qualities or the tender virtues that a less intimate relationship might require. Often the particular knowledge we have of some meritorious quality, very rare in itself or somehow capable of stirring our sensibility, slowly attracts and binds us and makes us forget any associated imperfections. This reason often unites two individuals with very dissimilar characters and tastes. This apparent oddity often takes place between more reticent souls who open themselves up only to the specific things that captivate them. Because these souls reserve themselves so completely for their affective life, their affections are more temperate and of that much greater value, and they do not require any other allure to be reciprocated. Even though these souls are the most capable of constancy and passion, a very broad and intimate sympathy is nevertheless necessary for their feelings to endure. Love carried to this degree is called *passion* and embodies a series of desires, needs, and hopes that ceaselessly call out for satisfaction. They are still pleasures for the soul, despite troubling it, because this very trouble becomes an habitual emotional state in which some happiness is always to be found. In the bosom of shared happiness, the harmony of hearts and minds, the union of tastes and opinions, and finally the rapture of feeling everything together as if feeling everything for each other can by themselves satisfy the demands of love and maintain its enchantments that so often cut short love's duration. Pleasures of the mind, of the arts, and of virtue, savored at the core of the heart's pleasures, deepen and intensify them. They are even necessary for their continuation, given the level of civilization we have attained. Such pleasures add a myriad of charms. They purify them, enrich them, and renew them. They extend them across all the stages of one's life.

To this point, my dear C***, I have shown how moral pains and pleasures are born in us solely from physical sympathy transmuted by particular sympathy, after various circumstances strengthen it, and after enthusiasm makes it more active and energetic. But this sympathy with another human being has an origin independent of the nature of his pains or pleasures. We suffer in watching him suffer. And, the idea of his pains likewise becomes troublesome for us because a similar pain would make us suffer, too. It is therefore evident that what we said of physical pain is also true of moral pains, as soon as we are capable of experiencing them. The sight or recollection of the moral pains of another affects us the same way as does the sight or recollection of his physical pains.

Here, then, are new bonds of sympathy that unite us with other men and that broaden our connections to them.

Not only are the sight or memory of the moral or physical pains or pleasures of others accompanied by pain and pleasure in us, but also, as we already explained, this sensitivity, once awakened and excited in our souls, renews itself solely at the abstract idea of good or evil. As a result, we have an internal and personal incentive to do good and to avoid doing evil. This incentive is an extension of our natures as both *sensory and rational beings*. In delicate souls it is capable of both monitoring our conscience and driving us towards virtue.

Letter IV

You have seen, my dear C***, that we sympathize with physical pains and pleasures in proportion to the knowledge we have from our own experience of their force and effects. Similarly, we sympathize in general with moral pains and pleasures, accordingly as we ourselves are susceptible to them. I say "in general" because no doubt there are souls sensitive enough to be touched by pains which they would not experience in the same circumstances that produce them in others—that is to say, pains which only the imagination can apprehend. And so, as with physical pains we have not experienced, sympathy is stimulated by the general idea of suffering.

This opinion is contrary to that of the illustrious Smith, and here I am again going to take issue with a few of his assertions. Perhaps you will find me overly bold, but whilst agreeing that Smith is rightly regarded as one of Europe's most important philosophers, it seems to me that on matters pertaining less to profound knowledge than to observations of oneself, all those who reflect can claim a right to the discussion.

I do not believe that Smith indicated the true reason that makes us pity dethroned kings.[1] If we feel for their misfortunes more intensely than for those of other men, it is only because kings seem to us to be saved from such misfortunes by their elevation. We judge that they must be more sensitive to misfortune, and not (as Smith thinks) because the idea of grandeur, which in most minds is tied to that of felicity, predisposes us by some sort of affection and consideration for their happiness to sympathize more particularly with them. It seems to me that this feeling is little known in the British empire, that it is unknown in the rest of Europe, and one can say with certainty that it is absolutely opposed to the sentiment of natural equality that leads us to regard everything above us with jealousy or at least harshly.

Our sympathy for physical suffering is stronger, more general, and more deeply felt than for moral sufferings. The display of physical suffering is even more heartrending and troublesome for those whose education, or rather breakdowns in their education, have distanced them from the face of pain. The reason for this circumstance obviously lies in the very nature of physical suffering that most often leads to death, the signs of which are more striking and certain, and the image of which is, finally, more distressing and affects our organs more sympathetically.

Smith establishes the contrary proposition, and believes he justifies it by saying that the imitation of corporeal pains hardly moves us; that such aping is an object of ridicule rather than compassion, whilst the imitation of moral sufferings awakens more intense impressions in the soul. Is it thus because sympathy is weaker for a man whose leg is cut off than for a man who loses his mistress, that one of these facts can be the subject of a tragedy while the other cannot?[2] One can doubt it. It is only because the imitation of physical pains necessary for theatrical success makes the illusion more difficult to achieve. And, this imitation needs also to be accompanied by moral

---

1. Smith writes: "Great King, live for ever! is the compliment, which, after the manner of eastern adulation, we should readily make them, if experience did not teach us its absurdity. Every calamity that befalls them, every injury that is done to them, excites in the breast of the spectator ten times more compassion and resentment than he would have felt, had the same thing happened to other men." TMS, Part I, sec iii, chap. 2, p. 52.

2. Smith writes: "The loss of a leg may generally be regarded as a more real calamity than the loss of a mistress." TMS, Part I, sec ii, chap. 1, p. 29.

pains in order to produce a genuine and varied interest. And it is, finally, because the appeal of tragedy largely lies in the talent that makes us sympathetic to the misfortunes of others by progressively exciting our sensibility and not in offering us a sudden and heartrending image of physical suffering, an image from which we cannot distance our thoughts if it latches onto us and that becomes ridiculous if it does not. Besides, one knows that for the common people, the public spectacle of physical pains is a genuine tragedy, a spectacle which it often seeks only by a stupid curiosity, but the sight of which sometimes awakens its sympathy to the point of turning it into a fearsome passion.

It is absolutely false that the principle of firmness and courage in the face of physical pains something that inspires only a small degree of sympathy in others (as Smith remarks).[3] The necessity of suffering, even the utility of certain sufferings, and the uselessness of complaint are the causes of resignation in run-of-the-mill hardships. Amid all-consuming pain, resoluteness comes either from the desire to be admired or from the kind of contentment that comes with great courage. This contentment can often extend our courage and can be a vivid experience for strong and elevated souls.

Smith asserts that we sympathize very little with the pleasures of love.[4] If by this he means that we witness without interest the delights that a deep and pure feeling sets in store for two young lovers and the mysterious asylum that awaits them; that we would hear without interest the details of a happiness so often the object of our own secret desires, then his opinion will be contradicted by the opinion of everyone whose imagination is alive and whose lives have been given over to this passion. Every time the sight of contented love is offered to our eyes or

---

3. Sophie de Grouchy misreads Smith on this point. Smith writes: "The little sympathy which we feel with bodily pain is the foundation of the propriety of constancy and patience in enduring it. The man, who under the severest tortures allows no weakness to escape him, vents no groan, gives way to no passion which we do not entirely enter into, commands our highest admiration." TMS, Part I, sec ii, chap. 1. This misunderstanding is particularly curious, given that in her own translation of Smith she adds the phrase "not only disposes us to be sympathetic, but commands our highest admiration." Her French translation, TMS, vol, I p. 56.

4. Smith: "Our imagination not having run in the same channel with that of the lover, we cannot enter into the eagerness of his emotions." TMS, Part I, sec ii, chap. 2, p. 31.

our imagination, exciting neither envy nor jealousy, and every time it does not offend our modesty or our principles of honesty, love pleases us and awakes visions of pleasure in us. This sight will please us even when it stimulates our regrets, because, for those who have felt this passion and inspired it, tender and even painful regrets long remain a source of pleasure. Since sympathy for the pleasures of others comes before jealousy and ideas of honesty and modesty, one must not conclude that this sympathy is unnatural if these ideas or a wave of envy prevents us from fully sympathizing with the joys of love. But, observe only that we sympathize more or less with these joys depending on whether our principles in this regard are more or less stern or complicated and depending upon how easily we empathize with pleasures that are not natural to us or of which we are currently deprived.

It is surprising that love's passion always seems to have a touch of the ridiculous to a philosopher whose work proves that he has observed without prejudice both the natural man and man in society.[5] One would think that such an opinion is shared only by frivolous youth that judges love before having loved and that believes itself to be following the path of true happiness because it wishes to obtain pleasure without paying any price.

Our sympathy for passions associated with hatred, such as envy, revenge, etc., is not general. It is usually modified by our personal relations with the person who experiences these passions, by the particular sympathy we might share that might undermine our judgment, by the righteousness of his feelings as they strike us or are known to us to a greater or lesser degree, and by the balance between what gave rise to them and our own interests, opinions, and the nature of our sensibility. When sympathy is not stimulated by any of these particular motives, it gives way to the gentler emotion of pity, and, far from sympathizing with hateful passions, we are led instead to take an interest in the person who is subject to them. The reason for this fortunately lies in nature. We sympathize with the desire to do good for someone because a sentiment in us inclines us to do good for all, and we find a personal pleasure in doing so. We do not harbor within us an

---

5. Smith: "...and love, though it is pardoned in a certain age because we know it is natural, is always laughed at, because we cannot enter into it." TMS, Part I, sec ii, chap. 2, p. 31.

inclination to do harm to all, and so we do not sympathize with hatred because a particular reason must account for sympathy towards hatred, as well as for hatred itself. If this observation be true, you will ask me, my dear C***, why are there beings who take pleasure in seeing their fellow creatures tormented, who somehow need to spoil the happiness of others, and who relish in Shafenfreunde?[6] Why, indeed? The reason is because in society a vicious system of legislation, instead of uniting the interests of individuals, has for too long separated them and set them at odds. Human greed has led men to the point where they all cannot satisfy these social fantasies at the same time, social fantasies that, turned into habits, have usurped the name of *needs*. From childhood these men tacitly acquire the habit of perceiving the misfortunes and the goods of others as a given which fortune has bestowed on them for their own enjoyment. Civilized man, if he is governed by prejudices and bad laws, is thus naturally envious and jealous—and increasingly so, as vices of social institutions separate him further from nature, corrupt his reason, and make his happiness depend on the satisfaction of a greater number of needs.

This opinion is so true that the men whom one can accuse of mistreating others and of bemoaning their happiness only feel this way toward mishaps involving vanity or luck or towards a sensibility they believe is artificial or exaggerated, and they cease to have this feeling when it is no longer the effect of personal hatred or when it is a matter of physical pains and real misfortunes. The exceptions to this observation are very rare and only concern a very small number of individuals. These are monsters whose existence can be explained by the particular circumstances of their upbringing and their situation in society. Civilization, such as it still exists in half the nations of Europe, is thus the enemy of goodness in man, as well as his happiness. What an immense labor remains for education, not to develop or direct nature, but only to preserve nature's beneficent inclinations, to prevent them from being stifled by prejudices that are so well accepted and common and that totally corrupt any sense of humanity and equality. These sentiments are as necessary for the moral happiness of each individual as they are for maintaining fairness and security in all relations in the social order!

---

6. Equally rendered "...who never learn of discouraging news without a secret joy?" for the original, "...*qui n'apprennent point ce qui trouble le bonheur des autres, sans une joie secrète?*"

The penchant we have to imitate those who amuse themselves in the flaws and foibles of others is no doubt born of sympathy. But what is the cause of laughter triggered by the sight of something ridiculous? Is it the pleasure occasioned by this sight that our pride takes in the idea of our superiority? Indulging the pride we then feel can indeed be one of the causes of this laughter, but it is not the main one. It has often been noted that a tranquil smile is the usual sign of a satisfied pride. We fear, it seems, loosing the kind of dignity we possess when this feeling is positive, if the sight of the ridiculous causes us to let go with peals of laughter. Besides, the idea of our superiority gives us a completely different pleasure than that produced by the sight of the ridiculous; and this idea makes us look ridiculous more often than it hinges on the ridiculousness of others.

One can say that the bodily movements that constitute laughter are pleasant by their very nature, even though they sometimes can be fatiguing. Those that bring tears are painful, even though in certain circumstances tears are soothing. This observation explains well, in part, the cause of our sympathy to laughter sparked by a ridiculous situation, but it does not explain why funny things elicit the movements that produce laughter and the pleasure that precedes it.

Children laugh from a very early age. They laugh as soon as they have distinct and broad enough knowledge of objects to compare them. They laugh at the same things we do, since in their games they laugh at those they make their dupes. The cause of this phenomenon thus must not be very complicated and must not depend upon elaborate ideas. Indeed, imbeciles also laugh, and do so at what surprises them, just as reasonable people laugh at what seems pleasant to them.

It is thus amongst children that one must seek the cause of laughter because, children having fewer and more limited ideas, we have both fewer possible causes to examine and more hope of finding the true one. This manner of observing the facts from the ground up (of which Locke[7] is the exemplar) is the most certain one for discovering the covering laws that govern facts.

It appears that the ordinary cause of laughter in children is the sight of an unexpected event that strikes them by offering them new images and ideas and by vigorously exercising their nascent faculties. In addition, everything that excites a feeling

---

7. "Loke" in the original French.

of pleasure or anticipation in children also produces laughter because laughter is the natural expression of everything that agreeably affects them. But, the older one gets, the more one indulges in reflection and the more laughter becomes reserved for truly unexpected things that draw our attention without necessarily inspiring great interest. The reason for this situation is simple. It is that the light spasm of laughter and the kind of pleasure that accompanies this movement cease with the mind's slightest satisfaction. Unexpected events that please us, but that are not followed by any reflection, become extremely rare after childhood.

It is for this reason that as life goes on laughter (except for imbeciles) is almost exclusively reserved for bizarre, unexpected, or contrasting things, including the ridiculous.

The first cause of laughter is thus found in the pleasure we take from a simple and unexpected exercise of our faculties and from an accompanying kind of contentment or internal joy. It is clear, therefore, that, as we grow older, laughter and mockery should join forces because the pleasure of feeling our advantages and strengths leads us to the malicious pleasure of making our superiority felt, a pleasure very analogous that comes from exercising our faculties.

You will forgive me, my dear C***, for working backwards from cause to cause in order to attain the first one. And, after having observed that the cause of laughter, generally speaking, depends largely on the pleasure attached to the exercise of our faculties, you will, like me, want to seek the ultimate origin of this pleasure.

To find it perhaps it will be enough to observe that the exercise of our faculties perfects them, that this perfection is itself a source of pleasure and avoiding pain, and that this observation is not beyond the grasp of children. It is easier for them in that their faculties are developing very rapidly and are very important for their welfare. A sentiment of pleasure thus mechanically attaches itself to any flexing of our faculties and tends to develop them.

This pleasure, which is the same as feeling our own strength, by which I mean *power* or *capacity*, seems weak at first sight because habit often conceals it from us. But it is nonetheless very intense. Children are the proof. The simple exercise of their faculties, independent of all the pleasure they may find in it, is accompanied in them by every sign of joy. This feeling of their own strength suffices for a long time to secure their happiness. The more they cultivate it, the more readily are they happy later in life. Most important initially is to restrict them to this feeling for as long as possible. Very essential afterward is not to allow them to acquire an exaggerated opinion of their own strength. If, by comparing themselves to others, the opinion they do develop is not extremely fair or accurate, their childhood self-esteem, succoured by all the blind attention they receive, becomes the source of all the defects of their minds and all the vices of their hearts. But the pleasure tied to the exercise of our faculties has yet other causes.

The exercise of our bodily faculties is not only salutary, but it nearly always produces a feeling of well-being, that is to say, the sensation accompanying *existence* in the state of health that, if not a positive pleasure, is at least the immediate and agreeable cessation of all painful feelings. Not only does this sensation exist for the totality of our organs, but with a little reflection, one can recognize that it is felt distinctly in each organ. One takes pleasure in walking after a long rest, and in recognizing this pleasure, one senses especially in the legs an agreeable sensation spread throughout the body.

Yet, this observation, true for our corporal faculties, can also be true for the organs which are affected when we think and experience feelings.

If overly applying ourselves fatigues us, it is possible that remaining too long without receiving new ideas represents a more disagreeable fatigue. If over-intense emotions, even of joy, produce a painful sensation in the *diaphragm*, why should the exclusion and absolute cessation of all sentiment not be followed in due course by a painful numbness?

It thus appears that movement and action contribute in an essential way to the well-being and even the preservation of living beings. And what completes the proof of this observation is that movement and action are necessary in childhood for the development of organs and in old age for the conservation of vitality.

Since movement and action are thus necessary to our well-being and preservation, it follows that the exercise of our faculties must be accompanied by pleasure and that it must be so accompanied even before reflection has been able to teach us how much the development of these faculties provides us with enjoyment. And the stimulus for the perfection necessary to reach this degree of reflection is the pleasure in some way tied to action, movement, and the exercise of our faculties.

But let us return to sympathy.

I cannot believe, as does Smith, that we do not sympathize with either great joys or small sorrows.[8] It seems to me, on the contrary, that we sympathize with moral pains and pleasures whatever their force and degree. This is a consequence of what we have observed to this point about our moral sensibility. Our sensitivity to the great joys of others, as for their minor troubles, is especially keen when it is a matter of persons with whom we share very strong particular sympathies. In which case, we are obedient to our nature. On the contrary, we sometimes get upset to see someone whom we don't care about making an extraordinary fortune, variously because this fortune ruptures the equality that held between us, because it destroys our rank over him, or because we aspired to the same leg up. Should someone, socially far inferior to us, enter a higher class, yet one still far from our own, then, sympathy will win out over pride, all of which proves that sympathy exists even when it is stifled by personal interest. This remark is so true that, overwhelmed by this later sentiment and capable only of being simulated, we still show sympathy as a natural and appropriate response.

The sympathy for moral suffering is stronger than for moral pleasure, and for the same reason that it is stronger for physical injuries than for physical pleasures. One can nonetheless observe that, although pains of this type are far more intense than pleasures, the difference between physical pains and physical pleasures is far less considerable and that moral pleasures have a far greater influence on our happiness.

Among the effects of sympathy, one can include the power of a large crowd to excite our emotions and the power that a few men possess to inspire us with their opinions. Here are what seem to me a few causes of these phenomena.

First of all, the mere presence of a large gathering of men acts on us through impressions awakened by their looks, their speech, and the memory of their past actions. What is more, their attention draws our attention, and their excitement alerts

---

8. Smith: "There is, however, this difference between grief and joy, that we are generally most disposed to sympathize with small joys and great sorrows." TMS, Part I, sec ii, chap. 5, p. 40.

our sensibility to the emotions it is about to receive and in so doing triggers those emotions.

There is also the pleasure of hearing said what one does not otherwise dare to say, what one has perhaps groped for in vain, or what one has glimpsed only confusedly.

There is the additional pleasure of acquiring an idea or sentiment on the spot. When it is very intense this pleasure sometimes leads us to accept an idea or sentiment without reflection, and we suddenly develop an admiration for the person who awakens them in us. Does not the person who gives you a new idea, my dear C***, seem to possess an aura of supernatural power?

The last two causes which I have just spoken of also act, though less strongly, when one is alone and reading.

Our lack of certainty in our ideas and sentiments also makes it so that we sometimes need to see them shared by others before we consent to them ourselves. An idea strikes us as true, beautiful, and touching, but we fear adopting it lightly. The applause of others reassures us, decides for us, and we give in with confidence to our first inclination. At other times, this same applause alerts us to some cautionary thought that escaped our notice. Our own contributions, in turn, produce the same effect, and everyone enjoys all the pleasures to be shared.

A lone individual who, through fear of ridicule, of compromising himself, or by mere timidity, would never dare to surrender to a violent impulse, does so dare as soon as this sentiment is shared.

Lastly, since we sympathize with the passions of others, the signs of those passions move us and suffice to make us feel them. Then, when we experience them with a certain force, the sight of these passions must augment them further, and as we reciprocally act on other people, an ever mounting rush of passion builds up to the highest degree collectively possible. Such is the cause behind the energy of crimes and of virtues in popular uprisings.

The power that certain men with great personal magnetism exercise over those who listen to them or read them and become inspired by their character of their souls also involves sympathy. This power is the result of an art, more dangerous than difficult, that ceases to be one when it is exposed.

These men know that doubt is tiresome to some. They know that there are those who find rest only on the tranquil bosom of belief, either concerning just a few topics or regarding them all. And finally, they know that for nearly all men the need to believe wins out over reason that prescribes to believe only what is proven. Thus, demagogues only have to espouse an opinion forcefully and persuasively and to artfully conceal any uncertainties. And, satisfied to be delivered from doubt, people embrace this opinion more ardently and are more struck by it in proportion as it provides them greater tranquillity.

One can also inspire belief and trust in one's person and manner of thinking by choosing certain popular opinions that are more eagerly received because they trigger a secret desire to yield to them. This approach explains the success of writers who dabble in paradoxes. The vanity attached to not holding common opinions and to seeing, even through the eyes of others, what escapes the common run of men, is a hidden appeal influential writers use to manipulate readers. On the same basis one can succeed by rejuvenating old opinions. In this case one has on one's side all the people who were forced to abandon these opinions in spite of themselves and who do not dare hold them. They take pleasure in tarnishing the reputations of those who seek to destroy prejudices and establish new truths. This project the pride of mediocre men will never accept; they always label it as foolhardy, and they seek to undermine it because it bespeaks a superiority demeaning to such men.

Another way of winning people over (and perhaps the most efficacious) is to attach to generally recognized principles, especially to opinions adopted with enthusiasm, other opinions that are in no way their consequence. The latter comes with an escort that gives them legitimacy. For the rest we are led to believe the writer who agrees with us on important matters and who professes opinions dear to us. This fact is so true that one is sometimes persuasive merely through the use of certain sacred words that inspire a kind of veneration and enthusiasm by dint of the grand ideas they evoke. The art of substituting these words in place of reason and thought produces in the souls of readers and listeners an effect that deprives them of the power to examine, and this is one of the most certain secrets of false eloquence, and in our day it has made the passing reputation of more than one political orator.[9]

---

9. These views would seem also to reflect Sophie de Grouchy's own experience during the French Revolution.

The success of genuine talent, being almost entirely the work of nature, is even easier to explain. If a writer or orator expresses himself in a passionate manner, we necessarily feel the emotion aroused by the sight of someone agitated by an intense and profound sentiment. And this emotion automatically conforms to his, and it predisposes us to share it, so long as the cause seems sufficient. The empire these men exercise over us is not limited to making us warmly embrace views we would otherwise regard coldly. It extends to our opinions as well. If one carefully examines our motives for believing something, one of the strongest and most usual motives we find is our natural and involuntary tendency to regard as constant what we have seen repeated many times, and this tendency is a consequence of our constitution. We generally regard as having always existed what we have ourselves experience as normal. And when we do not reflect on the matter, we confuse the impression of something that strikes us vividly with the sentiments that we associate with our ordinary ways and habits. And hence is born a greater ease in believing in what moves us and in adopting the opinions of mesmerizing authors.

Such is the art of Rousseau, their model. It penetrates you of its own persuasion, in a flash exciting at your core as enthralling an emotion in favor of the opinion he wishes to impart as anything that can ordinarily justify this opinion. One contemporary has perhaps had an even more striking and general influence on this century—at least if one does not limit oneself to France.[10] But their approaches, equally crowned by success, were not the same. Rousseau spoke more to conscience, Voltaire to reason. Rousseau established his views on the strength of his sensibility and his logic; Voltaire by the biting charms of his wit. The one instructed men by touching them; the other by simultaneously enlightening them and amusing them. The former, in taking a few of his principles too far, spread a taste for the exaggerated and the singular; the other, too often content with fighting the most awful abuses using only the sword of ridicule, does not sufficiently incite this salutary indignation against them that, although less efficient than scorn in castigating vice, is, nevertheless, more staunch in combating it. Rousseau's morality is appealing, though severe and carries the heart along even while

---

10. An allusion, perhaps, to Voltaire's moving to Switzerland in 1755 and his château there, *Les Délices*.

berating it; Voltaire's is more indulgent, but touches us less perhaps because, imposing fewer sacrifices, it gives us a more limited idea of our strengths and of the perfection we can attain. Rousseau spoke of virtue with as much charm as Fénelon and with the empire of virtue itself on his side.[11] Voltaire combated religious prejudices as zealously as if they were the only enemy of our felicity. The former will renew enthusiasm for freedom and virtue for ages to come; the latter will awaken every century to the sinister effects of fanaticism and credulity. Nonetheless, given that passion will last as long as men, Rousseau's empire over souls will still be at the service of mores when that of Voltaire over minds will have destroyed the prejudices opposing the happiness of societies.

---

11. François de Fénelon (1651–1715), French archbishop and author, most famous for his *Télémaque* (1699) dealing with the education of princes.

Letter V

On the Origins of Moral Ideas

It seems to me, my dear C***, that the preachers of virtue (Rousseau excepted) do not go back often enough to the origins of moral ideas. Yet, this inquiry is the only one that can lead us to understand just how intimate the relation is between these ideas and our conscience and between the sentiments we experience in following them and our happiness. Also, although moralists have often and eloquently underscored the immediate influence of vice and virtue on our felicity, they have not been sufficiently concerned with demonstrating that the principles of virtue and the internal pleasures they provide are a necessary consequence of our moral constitution and that the need to be good is an almost irresistible inclination for men subject to wise laws and raised without prejudices.

From the satisfaction we naturally feel at the sight or even the idea of another's pleasure or well-being, a selfish pleasure necessarily follows when we bring these about in others. This latter pleasure is even more intense when we are not directly involved because it is savored with more reflection, because our intention invites it, and because it is preceded by hope that always increases the activity of the soul. If the pleasure of contributing to the happiness of others is always more intense than being a passive witness, then the one we experience in comforting the ills of others must be even more intense because it is enjoyed with even more reflection and is always accompanied by the pleasant sensation one feels when one is freed from the idea of pain. Another reason redoubles the pleasure one finds in doing good: that one owes this pleasure to oneself and that consequently one holds in one's hands the power to procure it for oneself and to reproduce it at will. For if, for other reasons, the possession of something nice sometimes disgusts us, it is even more true that, the simple and natural life increases its value because such a life simultaneously unites the present and the future, our present enjoyments, and all those which a steadfast hope can provide.

We thus feel a natural pleasure in doing good. But yet another sentiment arises from this pleasure: the satisfaction of having done good. Just as in the case of physical pain, beyond the immediate, local impression, an unpleasant general sensation arises throughout our body. We thus take personal pleasure in the recollection of someone else's happiness. But, for this recollection to recur often in our memory, it must be linked to our existence and to our own trains of thought, and this is what happens when we are the cause. At this point, this memory integrates itself into the intimate awareness we have of ourselves, it becomes a part of us, it becomes as habitual as we feel ourselves to be, and it produces an agreeable sensation in us that is prolonged far beyond the particular kind of pleasure giving rise to it. When, therefore, the good we have done to others is positive, the pleasure that results for us is independent of the nature of the pleasure that results for them. But when we have freed them from some harm or evil, our pleasure, like theirs, arises from the cessation of pain, and it is even more natural that the satisfaction of having made pain stop leaves us without a detailed memory of it and even without any real focus on the nature of the pain in question.

Thus, the long-lasting satisfaction of having done good joins the pleasure of doing good. This feeling becomes, in some way, general and abstract since we feel it anew at the mere recollection of good actions without recalling their particular circumstances. In the first letter we spoke of this abstract sentiment, the most general principle of the metaphysics of the soul, just as the theory of abstract ideas is the most general principle of the metaphysics of the mind.[1] Moreover, this generalized feeling of having done good is the most delightful of our sensations, the one most analogous to our moral sensibilities. It is the one that attaches charm to the soul without impressing on it the insatiable and devouring activity of the passions. It is the only sensation capable of recompensing humanity for the ills it suffers. It is the only one constantly at our disposal, that never lets us down, that is always responsive, that calms and fills our hearts, and that is, finally, an indissoluble tie between ourselves and our fellow men. Happy is he, my dear C***, who carries this sentiment unwaveringly at the bottom of his heart and who dies feeling it! He alone has lived!

Because the sight or idea of another's misfortune makes us experience a painful reaction, the feeling is more intense when we are the voluntary or even involuntary cause of this misfortune. If we are the cause in an absolutely involuntary manner, that is, if we cannot attribute it to our intentions, thoughtlessness or frivolity, then the sentiment is strong only because, being more connected to our memories, it is more present in us, and we have more trouble freeing ourselves from it. If the misfortune of another stems from our thoughtlessness or frivolity, the pain we shall feel will be greater still since the idea that we could have spared him or her that misfortune will add to it. This idea produces in us a very painful sentiment contrasting the state in which our error has placed us and the one in which we might have been otherwise. The thought that we could have been better makes our unease all the more sharply felt for the same reason that one feels misfortune more intensely following good fortune, and, strongly represented by the imagination, a possible good is regretted as if it had been real. To this thought is joined the fear of repeating the same mistake, an unpleasant sensation that leads one to resolve avoiding events and that is the motive behind prudence. When we have done a wrong voluntarily, all of these causes act and must act even more strongly. To which is added a particular pain: that of feeling for ourselves the disagreeable sentiment stimulated by the sight or idea of someone who has wronged others.

---

1 Cf. Locke, *An Essay Concerning Human Understanding*, Book II, chapter XI.

Just as the satisfaction of having done a good integrates itself into our existence and makes us feel good, so, too, the recognition of having done something wrong attaches itself to us and upsets our existence. It produces sentiments of regret and remorse that bother us, afflict us, disturb us, and make us suffer, even when we do not retain a distinct memory of the initial impression of pain our wrong makes us feel.

The fear of remorse suffices to distance all men from evil, either because no one is entirely free of remorse at least for minor transgressions or because the imagination is sufficient to give an idea of the torments of remorse even to someone who has done nothing but good, if such a someone exists on earth! The satisfaction associated with good actions and the terror created by the memory of bad ones are two effective motivators for shaping all our actions. These two sentiments are universal. They constitute the principles and the foundation of morality for the human species.

After having shown you, my dear C***, the origin and nature of these sentiments, by applying what you have read in the preceding letters concerning particular sympathy, the effects of enthusiasm, and the power of habit, you will easily understand that these sentiments can become active and permanent and can acquire, according to circumstances, an overpowering force and even an irresistible power. Thus, for example, the remorse over a bad action or the mere fear of this remorse will be increased by the idea of its staying power when the imagination paints a picture of misfortunes spread over a whole lifetime. This faculty is one of the most deadly enemies of man's peace of mind when, more insatiable than his heart, it renders him incapable of enjoyment by constantly leading his thoughts and desires beyond what he possesses or beyond what he can attain. It is also one of the most effective causes of his happiness when it highlights the effects of vice and virtue, when it reminds him that he possesses, along with the power of doing good for others, that of always carrying in himself a joyful sentiment, a power that makes his happiness largely independent of chance and with which he can both brave death and withstand all the ills of life.

Thus, my dear C***, sentiment alone already creates a distinction among our actions since some are accompanied by pleasure and followed by an internal satisfaction, while others are accompanied by anguish and followed by an always disagreeable and often painful feeling.

But this more lasting feeling of satisfaction or pain connected to the recollection of the good or harm we have done to others is necessarily modified by reflection. And the modifications which reflection entails lead us to the idea of moral good or evil and to the first and eternal rule that judges men before the laws, a rule that so few laws have consecrated or developed, that so many others have violated, and that prejudices have so often and so absurdly stifled! When, for instance, we impart to someone a pleasure that is only momentary and that will have no effect upon his life as a whole, we will have less satisfaction, except if a particular sympathy is involved, than if we had given someone a pleasure that would remain a long lasting possession. Perhaps we will have remorse instead of satisfaction and will even repent for having allowed someone to whom we have only rendered a slight service to be exposed to real harm. Here then, we can begin to distinguish the good we do by chance and that which we do by reflection. Here we can begin to distinguish the good to which we are led by particular sympathy and the one to which we are led by general sympathy. If we follow a particular sympathy, we obey, as if by instinct, the leanings of our heart. If we follow a general sympathy, being often indifferent with respect to the choices among several good actions or undecided between the choice which our inclination inspires in us and a greater good towards which we are not so inclined, then we weigh within ourselves which of the two actions must do the greater good to others, and we decide for the one that will give us, perhaps not the greatest immediate pleasure, but the most lasting satisfaction.

Thereafter, our actions that were merely benevolent and human acquire a moral goodness and beauty. From this is born the idea of virtue, that is to say, *actions that give others a pleasure approved by reason.*

The idea of the distinction between moral pain and physical harm done to another is more difficult to conceive, but it is no less precise. When situations occur in which a slight harm done to an individual hinders a greater iniquity from happening to another, or an equal injury from happening to several others, then, if we do not perform this slight misdeed, we can suffer much more the remorse of having failed to stop the greater harm than from having committed the smaller one. On the contrary, the regret of having effected this lesser injury will be offset by the more intense satisfaction of having prevented the more serious one. The same holds true if the hurt done to another gives us some pleasure. The pleasure will be weak and cannot really compensate us for the remorse attached to the damage that gave rise to it. In these various circumstances we acquire the habit of consulting our reason as to what action we must take and the decision that will afterwards leave us with the greater satisfaction. And so, we acquire the idea of moral evil, that is to say, *of an action harmful to another which our reason repudiates.*

This definition seems to me better than that of Vauvenargues, who says that moral good or evil are what are useful or harmful to humanity taken as a whole.[2] These two definitions are, at bottom, but one, since the good or evil which reason approves or condemns is the same as that which is useful or harmful to humanity. But Vauvenargues's definition is less precise and more difficult to understand because it does not at all match the notion that the common run of men has of moral good and evil. Indeed, to be possessed of ordinary reason and conscience is not sufficient to know what is good or bad with respect to the whole universe. In defining moral things, it matters more than one might think to prefer those which the least enlightened of men can understand. When it is a question of discovering the general laws that govern the human heart, the most commonplace reason is the most certain and enlightened one.

Once the idea of moral good and evil is acquired and once the habit of differentiating one from the other has become familiar, we distinguish the pleasure and pain and the satisfaction and remorse that result from taking or abstaining from a particular action without weighing or calculating the effects that might follow. The idea that this action is *good* implies a secret satisfaction; the idea that it is *bad* suggests remorse in precisely the ways that the mere idea of physical pleasure or pain produces in the present and for the future, a painful or pleasant sensation. In some respects, what happens here is what happens in the sciences that use certain methods and certain principles that are relied on for their exactness and truth, without recalling the proofs we once worked through. Similarly, one follows general

---

2 Vauvenargues, Luc de Clapiers, Marquis de (1715–1747), (Vauvenargue in the French original), author of *Introduction à la Connaissance de l'Esprit Humain* and *Réflections et Maximes* (1746), where he argues for the primacy of passions in moral motivation and for utilitarian considerations in moral and political theory.

sentiments without thinking of the manner by which they were formed and all that justifies them.

The remorse of wrongdoing and the satisfaction of the good we have done can also exist without reimagining the details of these actions. We no longer have even the general memory of having done something good or evil, but are motivated by the more abstract and even more general feeling of having done well or not done well. Other sentiments can add to the former, depending upon circumstances, but it is not necessary that they do so for conscience to act upon our soul or to determine, judge, or reward our actions. These additional sentiments nonetheless more often serve to extend rather than to weaken the reach of conscience. Remorse for the bad and satisfaction for the good we have done increases depending, for example, on whether or not the signs of pain or pleasure induced are more expressive, more affective, and more capable of etching themselves in our imagination and thereby of speaking to our conscience. Easily moved souls more often act on these particular motives. Those whose sensitivity is deeper and more thoughtful usually comply with more abstract and more general sentiments accompanying good or evil. The one type, in doing good, acts with less self-restraint; the other acts in a more orderly fashion and with a more refined justice. The former take a more intense pleasure from the act, the others a pleasure more largely motivated by reason, but also more often mixed with vanity. The former tend to restrict and blind themselves; the latter to miss the good through their persistence in seeking the better. It is to be hoped that easily moved souls are more often found in the vast number of people who have only superiors and equals, and that those whose sensitivity is deeper be found in that overly large class of men who, either by a recognized right or a hidden power, command and govern.

What distinguishes hearts and minds even more is the greater or lesser facility we have of experiencing an abstract and general sentiment, that is, a feeling that is simply an awareness of what is common to several individual sentiments, akin to the greater or lesser ease we have in having abstract and general ideas. Hearts capable of these sentiments are the only genuinely upright ones because they alone can be guided by unwavering principles. They are the only ones whose sensitivity can be relied upon because general motives are always in place to stimulate it effectively. Conscience dies out in them only with great difficulty and is always heard to speak. Remorse is thus more surefire and effective, and their sense of obligation more complete. Above all, they know how to perform those duties demanding delicacy and honesty that morality alone imposes and recognizes, duties that, if forgotten, bring only regret and the loss of joy, and in which one finds these fair-minded virtues that can only be produced by the lofty striving to have the highest and most satisfying ideas possible about oneself.

Egoism, no doubt produced by forgetting these abstract and general sentiments or by an inability to experience them, in turn ends up extinguishing them. In effect, the shameful and base habit of considering matters with respect to oneself above all else and of judging them primarily from this point of view slowly weakens the affect attached to good and evil. Egoism is thus too lightly punished when one sticks to believing it less dangerous and condemnable than apparently more harmful passions such as hatred, vengeance, and even envy. Those passions are almost always short-lived. They are rare and ruinous to only a very small number of men, whereas egoism infects and torments entire social classes. Any excesses are nearly always repressed by the law, whereas up until now selfishness is only lightly condemned and weakly chastised by morality and public opinion. Finally, it is true that these passions sometimes lead to violent actions, but if egoism does not stop there, it is generally not for fear of retribution, and there is hardly a secret injustice or cruelty of which it is not capable. If other passions can make someone more dangerous, this one makes him more corrupt since it leaves him with no motive for virtue other than vanity and no restraint other than human respect, a paper tiger which cunning nullifies at will.

Minds lacking strength or scope to arrive at abstract and general ideas and to receive and combine their components can never attain substantial results. Neither can they consequently enlarge the sphere of important truths in any domain or assimilate those that are the fruit of calculation and broadly-based comparisons. Also, from someone who cannot even grasp them, you would seek in vain to produce assent to views that grow out of these ideas. Solely concerned with narrow and isolated issues and with particular and local views, he will label as dangerous any system he cannot understand, and, taking pride in his false discretion, he will disdainfully wrap himself up in his errors.

The greater or lesser ability to entertain abstract and general ideas represents a kind of scale against which one can measure every mind in order to ascertain its rank and station. Those who by reflection or by some sort of instinct have acquired the habit of adding to and generalizing their ideas, never stop. Those in whom the need to extend the number and reach of their ideas has been foiled or stifled by other passions (and that is most people) usually remain at a certain level and no longer change their thoughts, so to speak. This is the reason why it is so difficult to enlighten people, even with respect to their genuine interests. In some sense one must first seek in their passions the forces that can extend and renew their intelligence weakened by inaction or degraded by error. One can then have them adopt the truth, either by presenting it to them under clever or brilliant guises that prove seductive or by gently captivating reason through a logic so compelling that the last step leading to the conclusion is no more difficult to take than the first.

One of the primary goals of education should thus be to provide the ability to acquire general ideas and to experience these abstract and general sentiments I have discussed. Ordinary education usually distances itself from this goal. The study of grammar precedes all others and, it is true, begins (if children understand it) by offering them a few metaphysical ideas. But in their totality these ideas are the most mistaken or at least the most incoherent. Children then learn languages through the mechanical habit of translating authors whose thoughts they often cannot understand. One nearly always presents history to them deprived of these sweeping results that alone make it useful, for otherwise it would be too easy for them to grasp the abuses one wants them to respect. They are brought up amid all the prejudices of pride and vanity that deprive them of a feeling for the inalienable rights common to all men, that of their genuine happiness and their genuine worth, in order to instill in them the idea of pleasures and counterfeit social hierarchies, the respect and desire for which shrivel the mind, corrupt reason, and snuff out conscience. The morality they are taught almost always consists of isolated and disordered precepts, wherein the most minor duties are admixed with the most sacred responsibilities, all announced in the same way and with the same importance. Rarely does this morality lead them to seek in their own hearts the eternal and general laws that decide between good and evil or to hearken to the sentiments that reward the one and punish the other. The study of the sciences nearly always stops at the moment the mind, already accustomed to being content with vague ideas and to being occupied with words rather than things, has difficulty with the methodical and reasoned path of the sciences, gets tired in following a trail of evidence, and in the end only grasps the general principles of the sciences with difficulty or without the strength to develop new combinations from them.

Let us therefore stop, my dear C***, reproaching nature for being miserly with its supply of good men. Let us cease to be surprised that the general laws of nature are still so little known. How many times in a century does education succeed in inculcating the mental strength and rectitude necessary to arrive at abstract ideas? How many times has education perfected an instinct for truth? Has it strengthened the tendency to follow truth alone and to be ceaselessly nourished by it? How many times, on the contrary, does education mislead us in the byways of routine and convention, from prejudice to prejudice and from error to error? How many times has it not transformed, for example, the need we have of living exclusively through useful, true, and wide-ranging activities to which nature calls our minds and hearts into that of living only for the deceptive and narrow-minded pleasures of pride and vanity? Indeed! What pools of virtue, talent, and Enlightenment has this single error eliminated and every day continues to sap from the human species!

Letter **VI**

The Same Subject Continued

You have seen, my dear C***, that, when accompanied by reflection, the sentiments awakened in us when we do good or harm to others impart the abstract idea of moral good and evil. From this idea is born that of the *just* and the *unjust*. And, the latter differs from the former only in that reason's assent to a just action must be grounded on the idea of *right*, that is to say, a preference commanded by reason itself in favor of a particular individual. Whence it results that even when someone's interest appears to be weaker than another's in some particular circumstance, it must be favored nonetheless. Thus, for example, a man who, in the state of nature, has taken the trouble to cultivate a field and to oversee its harvest has a *right* to this harvest. That is to say, reason wants this harvest to belong to him preferentially because he earned it through his labor and because, in depriving him of it, in nullifying his work, and in robbing him of what he had long hoped for and the possession of which he deserved, one does him greater harm than denying him a similar harvest that might be simply at hand. This preference which reason orders be granted to him, even when he does not need all the fruits of his harvest and when someone else has a real need for them, constitutes precisely a *right*. This preference is based on *reason* and on the necessity of a general law that serves to regulate actions, that is common to all men, and that precludes considering the details of each particular case. This preference is likewise founded on sentiment since, the effect of injustice being more harmful to the party involved than the effects of a simple wrong, it must inspire a greater repugnance in us.

At first glance you will perhaps find it doubtful, my dear C***, that in the state of nature the neighbor of this man (of whom I was just speaking) with an overabundant harvest could not, without injustice, force him to share his surplus with a third party who lacks this subsistence. In thinking about it, you will see that this man's right to the surplus of his harvest comes from the work he has put in and not from his need. This right began with his self-same labor, and if a sense of humanity ought to lead him to renounce it, reason does not sanction someone else compelling him to do so. Furthermore, you will gather that this man, in refusing to share his bounty with the poor, commits a lesser evil than the powerful neighbor who would force him into this beneficent act. The first would lack humanity. The second would violate one of those very general laws that reason ordains and that lead men to follow by showing that they serve the common interest and that, except in some very rare particular circumstances, the good resulting from their infringement cannot be compared to the advantages provided by the generality and certainty of these laws. If, in the case of absolute necessity, morality excuses someone who, solely to relieve this immediate need, violates the rights of another, it does not follow that this strong *right* does not exist in general. If it ceases to exist under the hypothesis of an absolute necessity, it is because the one who withholds indispensable subsistence is in some sense an enemy attacking the life of the man he refuses to help. The definition of *right* I have given will perhaps appear incomplete to you because the word *preference* seems contrary to *natural equality* and because a part of real human rights is founded on this equality. But this contradiction is only apparent, for when equality is upset, the preference owed to someone who suffers thereby is merely a preference granted for the restoration of equality over a higher claim not acknowledged by reason. In this way, the right one thus attains over everything necessary to reenter a state of equality is an act of justice and not a favor.

A right such as the right of property is a positive right. It consists in a preference founded on reason concerning the possession of something. In some ways a right like liberty is a negative right, since it exists only on the supposition that someone wants to attack my freedom, in which case it is then reasonable to oppose this desire with the one I have of preserving my freedom because there is no reason why this someone should have a hold over me that I do not have over him. The same applies to equality. If another claims a standing over me not founded on reason, then reason would side with the concern I have to maintain equality over the one he has to obtain his claim. This, because abject submission to another's will is a greater evil than dominating someone's will and being superior to him. In evaluating moral good or evil, we submit the natural sentiment of sympathy to reason, and reason then directs sympathy toward the most pressing claim. In evaluating the just and the unjust, we submit this sentiment to reason, itself guided by general rules, notably a preference founded on general and logical grounds that aim for the greatest good, that is to say, directed by the rule of *right*.

Given this exact definition of *right*, do you not see, my dear C***, how the monstrous edifice of the pretended rights of the despot, the noble, the priest, and all holders of non-delegated power falls to pieces and instantly vanishes. Nevertheless, these prerogatives have banished liberty and natural equality from among us, and in so many nations ignorance or weakness still raise them to the rank of rights! As if reason could approve leaving to a sovereign (who, sometimes, can be a tyrant) no other restraint than his remorse, the progress of Enlightenment, or the despair of his victims. As if reason admitted that the worth of fathers was more than a prejudice favoring children! As if it authorized the minister of religion (were one really to exist) to possess obscene riches and intolerance to be a consequence of his ministry! And finally, as if reason could permit any power whatsoever originally established in the common interest to become a source of tyrannical privilege and a license for impunity for its holders! Yet, how does it happen that the sacred name of *right*, which has been used everywhere to hide and disguise the power of force, becomes a nearly impenetrable mask in the eyes of the masses, despite the interest they have in tearing it off? Doubtless for a long time now those who have governed men have calculated that they can easily control people by suppressing reason under the weight of needs, that they could distract the upper echelons by turning the people over to them and amusing noble vanity with trifles, and that they had to fear, in the one, only the excess of misfortune, and in the other, only the spread of Enlightenment.

An action in conformity with right, is just; an action contrary to right, is unjust.

Since misfortune is all the greater when it is least expected, the painful sentiment produced by injustice is stronger than one accompanying an equivalent adversity not involving an injustice. Personal interest further amplifies this sentiment, for everyone possessed of rights cannot witness another's rights being violated without immediately thinking the disagreeable thought that his own may be violated. Furthermore, injustice presupposes fraud or violence in those who commit it. It proclaims an enemy to be feared by all. It also produces unsettling feelings of mistrust and fear.

The remorse of injustice must also be greater than the remorse of having simply done wrong because, to that of having opposed the general sentiment that defends our rights, it adds the remorse of having lost trust in seeing these rights respected and that of having performed a misdeed with broader consequences because it violates an accepted rule and brings added injury to the victims of injustice.

The sentiment that leads us to be *just* is stronger than the one that directs us to do good because it is accompanied by a fear of more intense remorse. But the satisfaction we derive from justice is perhaps weaker than that of having done someone good directly. Grounded in sympathy, the satisfaction of justice, like the satisfaction doing good, is itself as strong as the latter, but appears to be of another nature. Peace enters into it more; it is less active and brings less joy.

From the idea of right and justice is born the idea of our obligations towards other people.

Spontaneously and independently of our will, but without infringing on our own rights, one is obliged to do everything which another could demand of us. Such is the strict meaning of the word *obligation* that restricts itself to things involving absolutely rigorous justice. But in speaking of actions where another could obligate us without violating our *right*, a real and physical possibility is not at issue here, so much as only an ideal one. Thus, for example, one can say that a judge is obliged to judge on the basis of what he believes to have been proven, even though it is physically impossible to force him to do so.

Thus you see, my dear C***, that our actions follow two rules, *reason* and *justice* which is nothing other than reason reduced to an inviolate rule. In the internal satisfaction of doing good to others and in the remorse of having done them wrong we have already found very powerful internal grounds for obeying these two rules. But there is yet another ground, the immediate pleasure of following reason and carrying out an obligation. And, it seems to me certain that the existence of these sentiments is independent of the opinion of other parties.

The pleasure of following reason appears to have the same source as the pleasure born in feeling our own strength. In effect, we experience a pleasant sentiment in following our reason because we tell ourselves that if we were inclined to some malicious act by an unreasonable impulse, reason provides us a resource to resist this tendency and to avoid this act. The greatest part of what I have told you in Letter IV concerning the pleasure of exercising our faculties applies here even more in that reason is one of our most wide-ranging, useful, and important faculties. What more comforting and gentle sentiment is there than recognizing through direct experience that one possesses such a guide, such oversight over our happiness, and such a guarantor of our inner peace! The pleasure we feel in following our reason is also admixed with the sentiment of our liberty and a sort of independence and supremacy over any immediate causes that might be harmful to us. This pleasure thus reassures us, elevates us in our own eyes, and satisfies the very natural reflex we all have to depend on ourselves alone. The origin of the latter comes from the greater certitude we have of our well-being when it is in our own hands.

The pleasure we take in carrying out an obligation pertains more directly to a sense of security and to the comfort of feeling oneself safe from resentment, vengeance, and hatred. The particular satisfaction of avoiding an ensuing regret is boosted by the hope of never having to experience remorse, an exquisite hope because it banishes the idea of every internal obstacle to our happiness.

We thus have motives, not only to do good to others, but of preferring good actions to bad as well as those that are just to those that are unjust. These motivations are based on our natural sympathy, itself a consequence of our sensibility, and so far, nothing foreign to our direct experience has been involved in determining them. The morality of our actions, the idea of justice, and the desire to be just are the necessary outcomes of sensibility and of reason. In this regard every reasonable and impressionable being will have the same ideas. The limits of these ideas will be the same, and these ideas can thus become the object of an exact science because they have an invariable basis. Indeed, one can express by the word *just* whatever idea one wants, but everyone who reasons well will have a common notion of justice. Given that moral ideas are not arbitrary, their definitions can vary only in the more or less clear or more or less general way of presenting them.

This first building block needed to be put in place. The origin of our moral sentiments had to be shown to lie in our natural and unreflective sympathy for the physical pains of others, and the origin of our moral ideas to lie in reflection. Assent to a moral truth especially had to be shown to differ from assent to a mathematical or physical truth in that an inner desire to harmonize our conduct accompanies it, along with the desire to see others so align theirs, as well as a fear of not doing so and a regret of having failed to do so. Yet, one cannot say that morality is founded on sentiment alone, since it is reason that shows us what is just or unjust. But, even less can one maintain that morality is founded uniquely on reason because reason's judgment is nearly always preceded and followed by a sentiment that indicates and confirms it and because reason initially acquires moral ideas from sentiments, ideas it then elevates into principles. Smith recognized that reason is indisputably the source of general rules of morality, and yet he found it impossible to deduce from reason the first ideas of the just and the unjust. So, he shows that the first intimations of the just and the unjust are the focus and fruit of an unmediated sentiment, and he claims that our knowledge of the just and the unjust and of virtue and vice derives in part from their harmony or disharmony with a kind of internal sense, which he presupposes without defining.[1]

---

1. Smith writes: "When these general rules, indeed, have been formed, when they are universally acknowledged and established, by the concurring sentiments of mankind…They are upon these occasions commonly cites as the ultimate foundations of what is just and unjust in human conduct." TMS, Part III, chap. 4, p. 160.

However, this kind of internal or inward sense is hardly one of those first causes, whose the existence can only be acknowledged but never explained. It is nothing other than the effect of sympathy which our sensibility allows us to experience. I have outlined the different phenomena of sympathy, and when sympathy becomes a general sentiment, it can be awakened simply by abstract ideas of good and evil, and it consequently must always accompany our assessment of the morality of actions. We need to reject, my dear C***, this dangerous predilection to suppose an *internal sense*, a faculty or a principle at work every time we encounter a fact we cannot explain. This philosophy is too easy on the evidence. It knows not ignorance or doubt and imagines when it should only observe. It invents causes when it cannot discover them and not only distances us from truth but weakens our ability to discriminate. Out of this philosophy alone systems have been spun that are utterly lacking or false in their principles. Wishing to explain to man beyond what he can know and beyond what the wisdom of the ages has to tell us, these systems have disfigured or weakened the scope of the most useful and sacred moral truths, by mixing them with horrendous fables.

It is therefore not necessary to seek motives for being good outside of nature and always remote from it, as incomprehensible as they are independent of our direct and immediate concerns. By his moral constitution, then, man is neither a wicked or corrupt being, and he is not even indifferent to good because he bears in himself a general tendency to be good, and he has none to be malicious.

But is this motivation sufficient? This question, the most important in moral theory, deserves to be discussed all the more carefully because until now it has been treated only superficially and in a biased manner. There are two reasons for this: Either because those who have answered it resolved in advance to do so in the negative in order to substitute, for the natural arguments for morality, imaginary grounds favorable to their interests; or because this question has never been examined by distancing oneself from the present or recent state of civilization or by calculating what civilization could one day become. On the contrary, civilization has always been taken as an immutable given or as essentially incapable of being perfected.

To know if the fear of feeling the remorse of injustice sufficiently counterbalances one's interest in committing an injustice, we must examine this interest and the cause behind it. For, if one could prove that the immorality of man is less the work of nature than of social institutions and if the failure to abstain from injustice was almost entirely the result of those institutions, one would then have to seek to reform them and cease slandering human nature.

If a private interest to be just opposed the private interest to be unjust, and if the great preponderance of the latter could be attributed to corrupt institutions, such that, without them, the inclination to be just was in general nearly always equal or superior to the inclination to be unjust, then the proported inadequacy of our motives for doing good would be exclusively the effect of our errors and not of a naturally depraved disposition.

Finally, if it could be shown that the grounds for practicing virtue and following justice, grounds so easy fortified and spread by education, are, on the contrary, nearly always weakened and assailed by education and encounter insurmountable obstacles in the prejudices and anti-sympathetic sentiments to which we have become accustomed, it would then follow that for men formed and governed by reason the grounds for being just would be effective in nearly all circumstances and would not fail to produce results but in very rare circumstances or in actions of little importance. Now, it is hardly a matter here of proving that these grounds would always suffice or that all men, if no other motives were available to them, would infallibly be just, but only that they would be just more often. In essence, supernatural and bogus motives for doing good, on which morality is usually based, nearly always miss their mark and are even less capable than those under discussion here of acting with force, constancy, and in a manner sufficiently general to make them useful in all circumstances and palpable to all men. It is therefore sufficient to show that reason alone united with sentiment can still lead us to the good by more sure, pleasant, easy, and less complicated means that are liable to fewer errors and dangers. And these means, far from demanding sacrifice from us or silencing any of our faculties, on the contrary, open the door to our moral perfection flowing out of our intellectual perfection.

Let us stop here for a moment, my dear C***, to see how this single faculty of experiencing pleasure and pain at the idea of another's pleasures and pains, in perfecting itself through reason and magnifying itself by reflection and enthusiasm, becomes not only a rich source of delightful or angry feelings for us, but guarantees an always pleasant and peaceful existence to the person who, faithful to his reason and sensibility, bows to benevolence and justice, while it condemns to a perpetually painful and agitated existence someone who behaves in a contrary manner.

The former, faithful to reason and sensibility, lives amidst the good he has done or hopes to do, and always has an inner sense of peace and security. He can remain alone with himself experiencing neither emptiness nor indolence because one of his most active thoughts always centers on virtue. He is certainly liable to pain, but at least pain cannot penetrate the sanctuary of his conscience where an inexhaustible satisfaction dwells and where he can rest without loathing and find shelter from the storms of passion. Here, he can purge passion by means of delicate and philanthropic sentiments that bring happiness independent of their exercise. Life and all its disappointments and people and all their weaknesses cannot disturb or embitter him. He is easily contented with life because it offers him pleasures always within his grasp, pleasures which habit cannot blight and which even ingratitude cannot entirely debase. This contentment also comes because he considers men, not so much relative to what they could be or to what can be expected of them, than with regard to the happiness he can provide them. Thus, in his relations he is neither prickly nor anxious, and because he becomes happy in making others happy, he has a hard time believing anyone would wish him harm. He never fears being harmed, and he is more saddened than irritated when he is forced to recognize it. Excepting those to whom he is tied by a particular sympathy, what does he care about those among whom he finds himself since the unfortunate exist everywhere. Disinterested without effort and nearly without deserving to be so, rarely does he fail to touch those he loves and reciprocally to obtain happiness in return. But, if he does not succeed, bitter regret never tarnishes his distress, and the fervor of virtue distracts and comforts him.

How different is the fate of someone who resists his reason and sensibility! He loses even more happiness than he can wrest from others. His troubled existence constantly confronts an insurmountable obstacle to his tranquillity, and tormented by the need to escape from himself, the world seems empty to him and deserted because of the limited sphere of things that can distract him. Passion may momentarily trump his disquiet, but in vain. Its intoxication is insufficient to dull his conscience. His faculties no longer function, and the happiness he could draw from it evaporates before this secret turmoil tyrannically agitating and dominating his soul. If he seeks human company, he is soon brought back to the painful sentiment he wished to avoid because of his sense of own inferiority and by the mistrust he inspires in himself. Far from finding in his fellow men (as does the benevolent man) beings who, independently even of their will, can contribute to his happiness, he sees in them enemies if he reveals himself or if he is led to extremes of dissimulation and cunning. He cannot peacefully savor the satisfaction of being loved. Never will he possess this satisfaction because he always feels he is a usurper. Uncertain of the feelings he inspires in others, he does not expect the good he refuses to bestow on them except in proportion to his skill in deceiving them. Trusting only himself and rebelling against nature, he does not know how to dwell in the bosom of friendship and savor the tranquil letting-go that is trust because nature withholds this pleasure from him by denying him peace, the bedrock of all happy sentiments. Even more guilty and unfortunate is when, tired of loathing and self-hatred and too far removed from virtue to be touched or enlightened by it, he seeks to lose his reason and sensibility by becoming a brute so as to stifle the remorse that inevitably outlives the feelings and ideas that engendered it.

Letter **VII**

Continuing the Same Subject

The reasons leading people to be unjust all relate back to four primary interests.

The first is the passion of love, the only pleasure that cannot be bought, and therefore its appeal cannot be confused with the love of money. Here we are not equating love and sensuality because, sadly, the later term has been appropriated in the language and opinion of the depraved and is all too often the object of a most vulgar trafficking.

Second is the desire for money either to satisfy needs or to acquire riches as a vague route to pleasure.

Third is the appeal of ambition, to which the love of money is sometimes admixed.

And finally, there is self-love or vanity which is often the driving force and goal of the two preceding ones.

Let us examine first of all, my dear C***, the inclination to be unjust born of the desire for money or for something that can be bought. If it is to meet a real need, this interest can be pressing, and one gets the sense that someone lacking everything will have few scruples about being unjust, especially with respect to the rich man, if he can hope to get away with it. This pressing need in principle is strong enough to stifle the voice of conscience and to triumph over it, but is it common in a society governed by reasonable laws?

Suppose that the laws cease to favor the inequality of fortunes. Under this supposition, if humanity and justice are satisfied, cupidity, more difficult and slower to destroy than bad laws, would no doubt still have cause to hope. Natural inequality is born variously from different behaviors, different degrees of intelligence, and greater or lesser fertility of different families. But, would we be crediting the effects of such inequality enough to think that it would randomly redistribute three quarters of the land's productive wealth while the rest could be shared equally? For example, let us imagine some country with six million families and an agricultural base producing 1,200,000,000 pounds.[1] There would thus be 200 pounds of agricultural income for each family. Suppose the effects of natural inequality were to absorb three quarters of this sum and to constitute the share of the wealthy. Would not fifty pounds would remain for each family? Look at our peasants, my dear C***, and judge if, amongst those who have an income of fifty pounds, there are many reduced to poverty. On the contrary, everyone knows that as soon as they possess two or three acres of arable land, they become known among themselves as *possessing wealth*, and the average productive value of two or three acres, supposing these to be optimal for growing wheat, is about fifty pounds per annum.[2]

You will be convinced that this well-founded hypothesis is not exaggerated by observing that among those six million families a very large number will be involved in industry and commerce. They would have no interest in retaining their share of the nation's farmland and would even need to transform it to pursue their activities or investments profitably.

Grinding need nearly always triumphs over fear of retribution as well as remorse and can also arise for industrial workers, either from unemployment or from a temporary dislocation between wages and the cost of living, and indeed, such necessity is most common in these classes. Of all occupations

---

1. The *livre tournois* was the standard unit of currency in Old-Regime France, equaling very slightly more than an English pound.
2. The original text speaks of two or three "arpents." An arpent is a unit of area slightly less than an English acre.

agriculture is the richest in resources for individuals just as, for states, it is the unique source of real and lasting wealth.[3] But it has been proven in our day and the evidence shows that the lack of wages or their transitory insufficiency is caused almost entirely by restrictive laws that inhibit commerce and industry. These same laws further undermine the general welfare by allowing the slow accumulation of wealth in the hands of a few men who can freely use their riches as a means of oppression. Through the unrestricted interplay of competing interests these resources would otherwise have remained, if not equal, at least common to *all*. Unequal taxation ends up further overwhelming the lower classes that, without property or freedom and reduced to counting fraud as a resource, deceive without remorse because conscience soon fades when entangled by chains. The tendency to be unjust out of necessity is thus very rare in the absence of bad laws, because even when these are in effect, it manifests itself rarely and with the least extensive and least formidable effects.

You will next note, my dear C***, that pecuniary interests leading us to be unjust presuppose the possibility of success. Now in many respects this possibility is again the product of the laws. If they were transparent, everyone would be equally informed. If they were just, they would admit no exceptions. If they were precise, they would leave no opening for corruption and bad faith. If civil administration among nearly all peoples did not arrogate to itself a host of domains better left alone, no room would be left for arbitrary power, a power perhaps less sinister in its exercise than what its mere existence requires to bring it into being and to maintain it. Finally, if laws alone were to govern universally and if they alone were feared instead of men and classes, as is so often the case, then the only means of acquiring a surplus through injustice would be theft, taking this word in its proper sense. Thus, against the temptation to steal to acquire a gain, one must balance the force of the remorse of being unjust versus being guided by ingrained injustices favored by long-standing examples and almost authorized by silence or rather by the vices of the laws. Laws should supplement the citizen's conscience, yet all too often they are nothing more than oppressive chains or at most sometimes the last restraint

---

3. Here, Sophie de Grouchy shows her commitments to the French Physiocrats and the progressive economic views of Turgot and also, of course, of Adam Smith.

on iniquity. Now, given reasonable laws, the temptation of theft to attain more possessions would be so weakened by the costs of giving into it that theft would rarely be feared. In this case conscience would have to combat only petty theft, our interest in which is proportionately both less weighty and less powerful.

The inclination to be unjust that grows out of vanity and ambition is even more the product of social institutions. These alone make it so that man, rather than the law, dominates mankind. They make a great office something other than an onerous responsibility. They create posts that offer personal rewards beyond the honor of filling them well or beyond glory if they present opportunities for great talent. To obtain these posts qualifications other than public service and public esteem are necessary. Means are required other than being deemed worthy. Social institutions alone, in opening up fortune's gates to cunning, intrigue, cabal, and corruption for all classes, separate ambition from the love of glory that could ennoble it and purify its means. Social institutions, in consecrating hereditary rights (nearly always abusive from the first generation), have provided pompous mediocrity with an infallible means to promote itself and tyrannically at that. These means are or become tyrannical when not established for the general interest and not properly circumscribed. If in all posts one were bound by the laws and obligated to act only in accordance with them, and if all positions were conferred by a general choice and by a free election, conscience would rarely have to combat criminal intent and the injustices ambition can inspire. Morality would even cease needing to reproach the ambitious for their weakness of character, cowardice in opinions, base flattery, this art of toadying to vice and vanity, and lastly all those corrupting means too often required for success and that stubbornly undermine all the foundations of virtue.

Vanity, attached to non-personal things, is obviously the work of depraved social institutions because all these things owe their existence to these institutions that unreasonably adopt them by always preferring individual and local interests to the general interest. As for pride born of personal advantages, it becomes dangerous and can lead to crime only when general opinion, led astray by institutions, exaggerates the worth of frivolous qualities. The vanity of good looks and external charms is a passion spawning jealousies and intense hatreds only in countries where there are courts, great men, and ruinous fortunes, where favoritism rules and delineates ascent, and finally where these qualities can lead to anything and can sometimes even produce revolution. In which case, even men of the lower classes who cannot aspire to these brilliant successes contemplate them with admiration and envy and get excited by accounts of them, just as in Rome the sight of the honors of triumph left the lowest soldiers who could not hope for them drunk on the fury of conquest. The same is true for vanity based on intellect and talent. It is dangerous only when the enthralled multitude lavishes esteem and rewards upon charlatans and hypocrites that should belong only to true merit. But let all faulty institutions be abolished from one end of the earth to the other, let only necessary and reasonable laws remain, and let arbitrary power that sinks its victims into misery and servitude and reduces them to ignorance and credulity disappear forever, and human reason will reemerge healthy and vigorous from beneath its chains. It will predominate in all classes and will itself shape public opinion. False talent will no longer be able to seduce public opinion, and disguised vices will no longer dare appear before its tribunal. Besides, glory hardly has to contest with bad faith and base jealousy, the effects of which we hope conscience can forestall. True glory is indisputable and fought for only by means worthy of obtaining it. Only the outward signs of glory can be usurped and taken by injustice. The present social order amongst all peoples whose government is not based on the natural rights of man is thus the single cause of the obstacles that ambition and vanity oppose to the stirrings of conscience. And, in a well-ordered society conscience would nearly always suffice to block these obstacles because ambition and vanity, if they acquired any momentum, would then be in accord with reason and justice.

To these same faulty institutions one must impute immoral actions motivated by love.

Here, by love we do not understand this tender, profound, often generous and always delicate sentiment. The principle pleasure of this love derives from loving. Its primary aim is the delight of being loved, and its most constant concern is the happiness and tranquility of the loved. Love attaches greater weight to possession than to enjoyment; it knows neither usurpation nor deception; it wants to receive everything, grant everything, and deserve everything through the logic of the heart, and the only sensuality it knows it itself prescribes and endorses. This passion is hardly ordinary, for the sentiment of love presupposes a mutual sympathy that is hard to find and even harder to recognize. It requires a generous character and, lastly, a rare and potent sensibility that is nearly always accompanied by some other superior qualities. Nor does this passion often lead to injustice. The result and character of true love is the reciprocal commitment inspiring every sacrifice on both sides, yet allows none to be accepted that could be truly harmful to the other, and it entails the involuntary submerging of self in order to meld into the life and happiness of one's love. Besides, these sentiments, given their duration and delicacy, nearly always triumph easily over obstacles, and their generosity and disinterestedness usually make them into judges of themselves as severe as conscience. In general, therefore, the interest in being unjust in regard to love can only have as its motive the desire to possess a woman or of having possessed her.

Let us now separate this desire from what society can brutally superimpose by having faulty institutions stir up pride and vanity. We will find in the first instance that inequality produced by the laws—an inequality that will long outlast them—has by itself created this idle class for which gallantry is an occupation, an amusement, and a game. It alone brings about the capacity to sacrifice victims to the flames of this passion, turning this ability into an instrument and accomplice of ambition and cupidity. Let us then suppose that this same inequality and the laws envisaged to support it cease to reduce most marriages to nothing more than contracts and economic exchanges, the quick conclusion of which allows us to recognize only belatedly if individual consent enters into it and where the sale price of love, ordered more than obtained, is adjudged at the same time as the dowry and before one knows if one is capable of loving and especially of loving one another.

Let us suppose finally that man ceases to impose indisolvable ties upon his ever-changing heart and upon his even more variable will, ties that are then incompatible with his nature, the nobility and proud independence of which can only be domesticated by the habitual sentiment of liberty. Let us suppose that divorce were allowed among all peoples. Bowing to human weakness and the more persistent needs of one gender, let us even suppose that it were possible, as in Rome, to form transitory unions that the law defines rather than stigmatizes. From that point forward, one would see both that most of the unjust actions occasioned by love (or rather by the degradation of love) would lose their rationales and simultaneously that passion itself, through the ease in satisfying it, would lose the dangerous force it garners from these very obstacles. Thus it is society that for too long has placed impediments to unions which mutual predilections would have formed. Society has established barriers between the two sexes (under the pretext of maintaining virtue) that render almost impracticable the mutual understanding of hearts and minds that is nevertheless required for forming virtuous and enduring unions. Society excites and entices male vanity for the corruption of women. Society makes pleasure accompanied by true feeling more difficult. Society extends the realm of shame beyond what really deserves it, such as uncertainty regarding the welfare of children, breaking a formal promise, obsequious accommodations, or character flaws suggesting weakness or lack of self-control. I say these are all social abuses that have given birth to dangerous and corrupt passions that do not involve love and that have made love so rare.

Here I have considered these passions almost only in relation to men. But it would be easy to apply all that I have said about men on this subject to women and to justify the opinion of a philosopher even more wise than famous: *"The faults of women are the work of men, just as the vices of peoples are the crimes of their tyrants."*

You have just seen, my dear C***, how the vices of social institutions help stir up the various inclinations we have for being unjust. But it is not only by strengthening these interests that they debilitate the power of conscience. They also weaken this power by habitually resisting conscience. In essence, the motives we might have for committing injustice, having acquired greater import through the errors of the social system, lead men to do evil more often than conscience is able to keep them from it. Under these circumstances, the habit of disregarding the forewarnings of conscience in some people and in others that of having violated conscience have weakened its influence. Familiarity with evil or its frequent display indirectly diminishes remorse and the fear of being exposed to it, except in robust souls whose sense of justice and goodness has an incorruptible strength. I claim that familiarity with evil or the habitual sight of it diminishes remorse *indirectly* because we naturally seek to rid ourselves of any painful sensation, and someone tormented by remorse attempts to distance himself from ideas that foster remorse and to surround himself with the full panoply of reasons that can lighten this burden.

Here, depraved institutions complete what they started. They furnish the means for a lasting self-deception over one's own heart. They give us leave to consider as inevitable, necessary, politically neutral, or even useful the evil for which they are responsible and for which they then become the excuse. Besides, habit alone dulls every sentiment because pain, like pleasure (especially when neither is very strong), is always increased through juxtaposition with a different state and because the starting point for suffering and for pleasure is one of the elements behind the intensity of the feeling we experience.

The same is true for someone who is merely a habitual witness to injustice. Injustice becomes attenuated in his eyes if he is not endowed both with the strength of character to resist the excuses of vice and simultaneously with this strong, manly sensibility that cannot be derailed or corrupted and that can sustain prolonged assault without too great difficulty.

As vice becomes more common, its successes become more brilliant, more apparent, and greater in themselves, and the real advantage to doing evil is stimulated by the success and example of even more vast and audacious projects. The small-time speculator who pulls off a little scam to win fifty Louis has before his eyes the certified Cresus whose similar maneuverings bring millions. His cupidity does not stop at the advantages a few pistoles might bring.[4] The fanaticism of greed allows him to foresee the moment when he will possess heaps of gold, and it corrupts his conscience before the fact.

The authority of an ordinary conscience together with reasonable laws thus suffices for man to be just and good. But social institutions among so many peoples have degraded more often than perfected human nature. Man receives from society incomplete and false moral ideas and passions more dangerous than his natural passion, and on that account he has lost the rectitude and original vigor of his conscience. From that moment, in order to maintain itself on the path of virtue, mankind requires the potent force and insight nature so rarely gives and that, estranged from nature, can only be acquired by listening to her voice in deep and thoughtful meditation.

---

4. A gold Louis was pegged at 24 livres, 50 Louis being worth 1,200 livres. A silver pistole was worth 10 livres.

Letter VIII

You have seen, my dear C***, to what extent faulty institutions elevate and exacerbate one's interest in being unjust. Far from protecting man against his own weaknesses, they often do nothing but take advantage of them in order to lead him toward corruption by the most effective means that can entice the small number who benefit from corruption and that can impose it on the suffering multitude. In hindering the exercise of natural rights for whole centuries, these institutions have led man from simple misfortune to the trusting and idiotic blindness that makes one accept as a law of necessity the chains one has become incapable of judging and breaking. It will not be difficult to show how reasonable laws can both add to the personal stake in being just and cement the power of conscience even with respect to matters which it alone must govern and punish.

Actions contrary to justice can be divided into two classes. Some are genuine crimes that the law punishes. The others, either because they are unimportant or because they are difficult to prove, do not fall within the scope of the law. There are laws to punish crimes, but in all societies where established penalties seem at least strong enough to deter crimes but do so only to a very limited degree, one bemoans their inherent inadequacy. But has one examined with enough impartiality and attention what a too small number of philosophers have written about this subject in the last few years?[1] I do not fear reminding you of this situation here because one must repeat important truths, not only until they are adopted by all enlightened men but also until the vested defenders of abuses these truths proscribe are reduced to silence. It is less the intensity of penalties than their certainty that prevents crime, and their extreme severity always produces impunity. Indeed, a humane man does not denounce a servant who has stolen from him when the servant is subject to the death penalty. The same considerations of humanity almost always keep one from reporting minor thefts that actually entail a less serious penalty, but one that still does not fit the crime. On the other hand, if for lesser crimes we limit correctional penalties to public opinion and essentially punish by this means, and if for ordinary offenses as for the most heinous crimes we do not abruptly break all the links that tie him to society, that is to say, the last barriers between man and crime (either by taking the life of the guilty or by shaming him with indelible infamy), then out of the common interest everyone would make it a duty to denounce criminals. One would be even less lenient toward them if need and the degradation to which it leads were not almost always their excuse. Criminal laws by their severity and civil laws when they favor inequality thus license lesser crimes, and one can also regard these laws as the cause of bigger crimes, since the impunity of the former alone inspires the confidence to commit the latter.

For fear of punishment to be salutary and effective, the penalty must not be abhorrent. The justice behind it must be apparent to the most pedestrian reason, and most importantly it must awaken conscience while at the same time it punishes silence and lassitude. If, on the contrary, the penalties are too strong,…if, instead of inspiring the horror of crime, they themselves convey the idea of barbarism or of injustice,…if they do not at all punish the injustices the poor suffer at the hands of the rich,…if, when these injustices are not of a kind that makes them subject to punishment, the law does not prevent them in some other manner,…if the judge can arbitrarily stiffen or soften a penalty,…if there are personal privileges, hereditary

---

1. *Philosophes* in the original. The reference here and in what follows is to Cesare Beccaria (1738–1794) whose 1764 volume, *Dei delitti et della pene* [*On Crimes and Punishments*], framed debates, particularly among French intellectuals, on rationalizing the contemporary criminal justice system.

or local, that allow someone to legally avoid punishment or that provide indirect but reliable means of doing so,...then the people are tempted to consider the criminal laws as having been framed against them for the benefit of the rich and as the result of a coalition intended to oppress them. In which case the people hate even more than they fear laws that no longer sting their conscience because these laws sicken their reason. This hate conquers fear in resolute souls and in all those embittered by the conjoined sentiments of injustice and need.

Laws that favor the inequality of fortunes, beyond all the drawbacks I have pointed out to you, also multiply the number of people who have nothing to lose. The man who has some property not only feels more strongly that it is just to respect another's, but he is checked by the fear of losing his property, by fear of reprisal, and by the necessity of giving back at least the value of what he has stolen. The interest in pursuing him being increased by the hope of restitution, he fears even more being exposed to the slightest suspicion and of having to put up an always unpleasant and always expensive legal defense against accusations. Finally, if the vices of social institutions did not open the door to mischievousness that is difficult to overcome, impossible to seek reparations from, and sometimes even dangerous to complain about, there would also be fewer men reduced to committing overt theft. Thus, the social order, in preserving man his natural rights, would put men in the optimal position to lead them to mutually respect these rights, and then these rights would be guaranteed by the interest in each individual's happiness and tranquility even more than by the laws.

You see then, my dear C***, that social institutions are still very far from having reached the highest degree of usefulness one can draw from penal laws. And, for them to reach this degree the people must be able to consider those whose business it is to execute the laws, to arrest the guilty, and to condemn them, not as masters, but only as their defenders and their friends.[2]

It is thus in considering what criminal laws could be that philosophers [*philosophes*] have permitted themselves to attack laws that bring more abuses than advantages. This inquiry,

---

2. A possible reference to Louis Sébastien Mercier's *Memoirs of the Year Two Thousand Five Hundred* (1771) that portrays the execution of a criminal in the humane, 'philosophical' way.

solicited by all unbiased men and which too many injustices justify, nevertheless earned those who undertook it the label of innovators, in truth a name more honorable than injurious. To the extent that they called for laws that the guilty cannot escape and the innocent never have to fear, they called for just laws. If they sought laws less harsh, it is by demonstrating that their very severity is as dangerous as it is unjust. If they considered reason and public utility as the natural and immutable judges of social institutions, it is because these criteria provide the only general and infallible rules available. One must either cease to slander and attempt to silence these philosophers or claim that it is dangerous to make use of one's reason or that reason supports all that time has wrought. Another reproach leveled against these philosophers, one as apparently serious as it is obviously ridiculous, accuses them of wanting to substitute the wheel and the scaffold for the true foundation of morality and especially for supernatural reasons for being just. Those accused of wanting to govern men by these barbaric means (one wants to forget this?) are the very ones who sought a softening of the laws to make the laws more inescapable and efficacious. They are the ones who insisted that justice and reason balance crimes and punishments. Up until now, if cruel laws associated with supernatural thinking have not been able to keep people from turning to crime, then one can no longer accuse of slandering human nature those who said that gentler and better worked out laws, uniting their force to that of reason and conscience, could have more power to prevent crime. Do countries exist where a more felicitous and more common use of supernatural reasons make it unnecessary to establish a penal code? Does history reveal a people under the sway of these reasons who were neither barbaric nor corrupt? Let their defenders thus content themselves to offer heavenly rewards as a great hope and a sometimes useful and gentle consolation to the unfortunate individual for whom the sentiments of courage and virtue cannot suffice. But let them cease boasting that they elevate human nature the very moment they degrade it in offering up an imaginary and make-believe grandeur and in demeaning what is most grand and noble in human nature, *reason* and *conscience*. Let them further stop saying that conscience is insufficient, when they make it so themselves by establishing an extrinsic power on the ruins of reason that can only rule amidst their disunity.

Letter VIII

But, will you tell me here, my dear C***, what motive and interest would incline someone who has nothing to loose to respect another's property? This question is not perplexing when one thinks about it. In the first instance, if at issue is a craftsman or an established farmer who depends on his own labor for his subsistence, he has the greatest reason to respect another's property, either because without this respect he would soon be unemployed or because even when he has no predictable resources for his subsistence, yet possessing a few garments, some animals, some supplies, and a little furniture, the poorer he is, the more he must fear the loss of his last resources. If he lives in abundance, cupidity will exacerbate the fear of being robbed. If he is indigent, this fear must be commensurate with his needs. Besides, general utility leads one to respect the property of others and is palpable from the moment everyone can hope to possess something. (I have shown you that in a well-governed country nearly all the inhabitants will possess some little property.) From the instant he ceases to respect another's property, the worker who has nothing, but who in the prime of life can hope to amass the wherewithal for his old age loses this precious and necessary hope, the scope of which nonetheless cannot be appreciated unless one scrutinizes the existence of some of these unfortunate beings who, forced each day to weight their strength against their needs, never imagine a happiness beyond being able to live without work or at least without worry. Besides, supposing that theft were limited to what is absolutely necessary to preserve existence at the very moment an overriding need threatens it, morality would first of all look on this act with forbearance. But more, theft would still be the least useful option, as well as the most dangerous because from the moment bad laws cease multiplying needs and accidents, one will always gain more by attempting to obtain help through legitimate and peaceable means. Simply eliminate the extreme inequality that separates the poor too far from the rich for them to be seen or known or for the voice of humanity to touch the latter's hearts, and unforeseen misfortunes will become rarer and more definitively rectified. Take away the devastating specters from all the petty tyrants, and whisk away their heaps of gold, the smallest and least illegitimate of which will perhaps have secretly spawned a thousand victims, in order that man can no longer be so elevated above his fellow man to cease to see his duties alongside his interests, and thievery and fraud will become rare enough, and these threats will find their danger countered and their most fearsome punishments in publicity itself.

As to unjust actions that should not be the object of penal laws, one can observe that in general everyone is interested in obtaining the trust of others through a reputation for honesty and virtue. One likes one's tenant farmer to be an upright man and one's servant to be faithful. We prefer the craftsman whose probity is recognized to one whose honesty is suspect. If obtaining trust this way is weak in today's societies, it is because many social advantages are acquired independently of general trust. A host of institutions, apparently established for a useful purpose and preserved as prerogatives and sacred possessions, exempt civilized man from virtues that would be necessary even to savage man for living in peace with his fellow men. Nearly everywhere the preeminence of vanity trumps the rights of true merit and stifles its sentiment. The multiplicity and obscurity of laws, regulations, and so on and so forth, do not allow us to recognize whether or not probity exists, or they leave its reputation to be trampled on with impunity. Further, religious hypocrisy offers an almost certain means of doing so. By means of every abuse, prudence and artfulness can culpably obtain this reputation, even while hiding little and pretending nothing. And, the extreme inequality of fortunes and the great distance separating one class from another estrange men from one another. To be known and communicated, virtues have in some way to find themselves placed on the same level by fate. The powerful man and the worker he employs are too far apart to judge each other, and in this estrangement where their respective duties seem to evaporate, the one can oppress the other almost without compunction, and this one in turn can deceive that one with impunity and in so doing even believe he is doing right. Feelings of diffidence and greed that flow from the misery of a large group and that lead it to deceive make it all the more impossible to equivocate over the honesty of the man with whom it trades. Thus, in all social relations a host of nefarious social institutions, made so by the abuse of power on the one hand and on the other because they usurp natural rights, isolates man from his fellow man, makes probity and justice useless and foreign to him, and annihilates nearly all their advantages and reasons for being.

Thus these institutions, which should have perfected human happiness, have for long degraded and corrupted humanity, no doubt because until now humanity had sought to perfect nature by means of institutions and not by remembering nature.

The errors of social institutions make men almost indifferent to performing the most sacred duties. They restrict any robust interest in carrying out these duties to a small number of sensitive beings for whom the rewards of their exercise are necessary and who bear in themselves an indelible attraction for everything pertaining to virtue. But more, by means of the unnatural needs institutions have created, they have weakened a powerful motive that can lead to upright conduct, namely the lure of domestic tranquility. In one instance, through exaggerated rewards and by unfair and heady distinctions, they exalt self-love to the point of turning it into a dominant passion and making it capable of stifling the most powerful as well as the most delicate sentiments. In another, they derail, corrupt, and blind pride by associating laurels due great deeds and grand virtues with official positions and with contingencies of birth and fortune. In all classes and in all passions social institutions add to the principal and real existence of each individual an imaginary and mercurial existence, the needs of which are more diverse, more insatiable, and more fickle and whose pleasures are followed by an inevitable disgust. Thus, someone conditioned by these institutions is no longer in some respect *sui generis* happy nor unhappy because he lacks something, either through the good or bad use of his faculties or through the possession or deprivation of things institutional. No longer by means of his own thoughts and feelings does he judge, act, and take pleasure. He is hemmed in on nearly all sides by unjust laws, and he is blessed by fortune or enticed to it by the abuses spawned by these laws. Blinded and softened by his interests that are nearly always in opposition to the voices of reason and humanity, he is able to satisfy his most vainglorious pretensions without having to justify them by true merit, and he can gratify his most corrupt passions without universal contempt recalling him to his senses.

As soon as he is sufficiently provided for, he moves in the circle of the vain, a plaything of innumerable prejudices with which vanity entangles his steps. The opinion of others becomes the voice of his conscience, the always necessary justification of his pleasures and the first requirement for his happiness. This picture will doubtless seem exaggerated to you, my dear C***. Inevitably and effortlessly devoted to your works and personal attachments, and perhaps because of ingrained sentiments of reason and virtue, you are too distant from men to perceive all their errors, or at least, to discern the deep roots of these errors. Yet, who in society, in an honest self-examination, will not find that he bears within himself their principal traits? In the character of his home life, in the use of his time or his fortune, in his pleasures, tastes and even his affections, what man of the world (rare as he may be) is not still led (by the indirect, but nonetheless real effect of our institutions) to sacrifice to vanity what his true happiness requires?

Where is he who, faithful to reason and nature, prefers the true pleasures attached to peace and domestic virtues to the seductive pleasures of amour-propre, the habit for which makes one loose not only the need but also the taste and sentiment for others? Where is he who never allows himself to be carried away by all which idleness and corruption have contrived in order to insulate man from self-awareness?...an awareness that quickly becomes intrusive when the charm of virtue does not mix with the rapacious appeal of the passions and the dry pleasures of the mind. Where is he who still reserves a part of his soul for self-reflection and for enjoying nature's sentiments with this ease and self-consciousness that is the source of their delight and all their power? Surrounded by institutions, prejudices, and customs, the effect of which is to tightly bind sensitivity to self-esteem, where is the man who needs but simple and private pleasures in order to find around his own hearth the security of mutual esteem and the exquisite peace of reciprocal understanding, goodwill, and boundless indulgence? Where is that man who still feels some attraction for those gentle sentiments disdained by passion and vanity, but of which one can yet say that they are the warp and weft of happiness, the only fabric that time does not use up or cast away? Where is he who, instead of always seeking far from nature some new way of enjoying or abusing his blessings, each day discovers in his surroundings a new pleasure in transforming all the constraints of duty and servitude into relations of benevolence, good faith, and goodness and thereby making his house an asylum where his own happiness him forces him to relish his own existence? Intimate and consoling amusements attached to peace and private virtues! True and touching pleasures that never leave a heart they once melted! We are ceaselessly alienated from them by the tyrannical specter of vanity, whose seductive magic allows us to perceive ourselves only under the somber colors of duty, boredom, and monotony...woe unto him who disdains and abandons these domestic pleasures! If the female sex neglects or ignores them, woe especially unto woman, who for a day is blazoned with nature's most resplendent gifts and for whom nature is afterwards and for so long a cruel stepmother! For it is with domestic pleasures that she must spend half of her life and forget (if possible) this enchanted cup which the hand of time overturns for her in mid-life!

Bibliography

Editions of Sophie de Grouchy's translation of the Théorie des Sentiments moraux and her Lettres sur la sympathie

—*Théorie Des Sentimens* [sic] *Moraux, ou Essai Analytique Sur les Principes des Jugemens* [sic] *que portent naturellement les Hommes, d'abord sur les Actions des autres, et ensuite sur leurs propres Actions: Suivi d'une Dissertation sur l'Origine Des Langues; Par Adam Smith; Traduit de l'Anglais, sur la septième et dernière Édition, Par S. Grouchy V^e. Condorcet. Elle y a joint huit <u>Lettres sur la Sympathie</u>*. 2 vols. Paris: Chez F. Buisson, Imprim.-Lib., rue Hautefeuille, n° 20. An 6 de la République, (1798.). [The *Letters* are vol. 2, pp. 353–507.]

—*Théorie Des Sentimens* [sic] *Moraux, ou Essai Analytique Sur les Principes des Jugemens* [sic] *que portent naturellement les Hommes, d'abord sur les Actions des autres, et ensuite sur leurs propres Actions: Suivi d'une Dissertation sur l'Origine Des Langues; Par Adam Smith; Traduit de l'Anglais, sur la septième et dernière Édition, Par S. Grouchy V^e. Condorcet. Elle y a joint huit <u>Lettres sur la Sympathie</u>*. Second édition revue et corigée, 2 vols. Paris: Barrois l'Ainé, 1830. [The *Letters* are vol. 2, pp. 311–442.]

Théorie des sentiments moraux ou Essai analytique sur les principes des jugements que portent naturellement les hommes d'abord sur les actions des autres, et ensuite sur leurs propres actions par Adam Smith, traduit par Mme S. de Grouchy, M^{ise} de Condorcet; précédée d'une introduction et accompagnée de notes par H. Baudrillart, Professeur suppléant au Collége [sic] de France. Paris: Guillaumin et Cie, Libraires, 1860. [The *Letters* are vol. 2, pp. 434–514.]

Théorie des sentiments moraux ou Essai analytique sur les principes des jugements que portent naturellement les hommes d'abord sur les actions des autres, et ensuite sur leurs propres actions par Adam Smith, traduit par Mme S. de Grouchy, M^{ise} de Condorcet; précédée d'une introduction et accompagnée de notes par H. Baudrillart, Professeur suppléant au Collége [sic] de France. Plan de la Tour (Var): Éditions d'Aujourd'hui, 1982. [The *Letters* are not reprinted in this edition.]

Sophie de Grouchy, marquise de Condorcet: Lettres sur la sympathie: suivies des lettres d'amour. Jean-Paul de Lagrave, ed. Montréal-Paris: L'Étincelle Éditeur, 1994.

Other Sources

Ando, Takaho. "The Introduction of Adam Smith's Moral Philosophy to French Thought," in *Adam Smith: International Perspectives*, Hiroshi Mizuta and Chuhei Sugiyama, eds. New York: St. Martin's Press, 1993, pp. 199–223.

_____. "Mme de Condorcet et la philosophie de la sympathie," *Studies on Voltaire and the Eighteenth Century* 216 (1983), pp. 335–36.

Arnold-Tétard, Madeleine. *Sophie de Grouchy, marquise de Condorcet: Dame du coeur*. Paris: Éditions Christian, 2003.

Baker, Michael Keith. "Sketch for a Historical Picture of the Progress of the Human Mind: Tenth Epoch." *Daedalus* 133 (2004), pp. 65–83.

Baker, Keith Michael. *Condorcet: From Natural Philosophy to Social Mathematics*. Chicago and London: The University of Chicago Press, 1975.

Badinter, Elisabeth and Danielle Muzerelle, eds. *Madame du Châtelet: La femme des Lumières*. Paris: Bibliothèque nationale de France, 2006.

Badinter, Elisabeth and Robert Badinter. *Concorcet: Un Intellectuel en Politique*. Paris: Fayard, 1988.

Barth, Else M., ed. *Women Philosophers, A Bibliography of Books through 1990*. Bowling Green, Ohio: Philosophy Documentation Center, Bowling Green State University, 1992.

Boissel, Thierry. *Sophie de Condorcet: Femme des Lumières*. Paris: Presses de la Renaissance, 1988.

Brookes, Barbara. "The Feminism of Condorcet and Sophie de Grouchy," in *Studies on Voltaire and the Eighteenth Century* 184 (1980), pp. 297–361.

Brown, Karin. *Sophie Grouchy de Condorcet On Moral Sympathy and Social Progress*. Ph.D., The Graduate Center, City University of New York, 1997.

_____. "Madame de Condorcet's Letters on Sympathy," in *Presenting Women Philosophers*, Cecile Tougas and Sara Ebenreck, eds. (Philadelphia: Temple University Press, 2000), pp. 225–37.

Brown, Vivienne, ed. *The Adam Smith Review*. London and New York: Routledge, 2004.

Cabanis, Pierre-Jean-Georges. *On the Relations Between the Physical and Moral Aspects of Man*, 2 vols, George Mora, ed., Margaret Duggan Saidi, trans. Baltimore and London: The Johns Hopkins University Press, 1981. Translated from the French, *Rapport du physique et du moral de l'homme*, 2 vols. 2nd. ed; Paris: Crapart, Caille, et Ravier, 1805.

Calhoun, Cheshire, ed. *Setting the Moral Compass: Essays by Women Philosophers*. Oxford: Oxford University Press, 2004.

Campbell, T.D. *Adam Smith's Science of Morals*. London: George Allen & Unwin Ltd., 1971.

Condorcet, Antoine-Nicolas. *A Sketch for a Historical Picture of the Progress of the Human Mind*, June Barraclough, trans. New York: The Noonday Press, 1955.

Dawson, Deidre. "From Moral Philosophy to Public Policy: Sophie de Grouchy's Translation and Critique of Smith's *Theory of Moral Sentiments*," in *Scotland and France in the Enlightenment*, Deidre Dawson and Pierre Morère, eds. (Lewisburg, PA: Bucknell University Press; London: Associated University Presses, 2004), pp. 264–83.

_____. "Is Sympathy so Surprising? Adam Smith and French Fiction of Sympathy," *Eighteenth Century Life* 15 (1991), pp. 147–62.

Dykeman, Therese Boos, ed. *The Neglected Canon: Nine Women Philosophers, First to the Twentieth Century*. Dordrecht/Boston/London: Kluwer Academic Publishers, 1999.

Eltis, Walter. "Emma Rothschild on Economic Sentiments: and the True Adam Smith," *European Journal of the History of Economic Thought* 11 (2004), pp. 147–159.

Evensky, Jerry. *Adam Smith's Moral Philosophy: A Historical and Contemporary Perspective on Markets, Law, Ethics and Culture.* Cambridge and New York: Cambridge University Press, 2005.

Fitzgibbbons, Athol. *Adam Smith's System of Liberty, Wealth and Virtue: The Moral and Political Foundation of The Wealth of Nations.* Oxford: Clarendon Press, 1995.

Fleischacker, Samuel. *On Adam Smith's Wealth of Nations.* Princeton and Oxford: Princeton University Press, 2004.

Forget, Evelyn L. "Evocations of Sympathy: Sympathetic Imagery in Eighteenth-Century Social Theory and Physiology," *History of Political Economy* 35 (2003b), pp. 287–308.

———. "Cultivating Sympathy: Sophie Condorcet's Letters on Sympathy," *Journal of the History of Economic Thought* 23 (2001), pp. 319–337.

———. "Cultivating Sympathy: Sophie Condorcet's Letters on Sympathy," *The Status of Women in Classical Economic Thought*, Robert Dimand and Chris Nyland, eds. (Cheltenham, UK; Northampton, MA: Edward Elgar, 2003a), pp. 142–64.

Gay, Peter. *The Enlightenment: An Interpretation. Vol. 2: The Science of Freedom.* New York, London: W.W. Norton & Company, 1977; reissued 1996.

Gardner, Catherine Villanueva. *Women Philosophers: Genre and the Boundaries of Philosophy.* Boulder, Colorado: Westview Press, 2004.

Gatens, Moira, ed. *Feminist Ethics.* Brookfield, VT: Aldershot, 1998.

Gilligan, Carol. *In A Different Voice: Psychological Theory and Women's Development.* Cambridge, Massachusetts, and London, England: Harvard University Press, 1982.

Gottschalk, Louis. *Understanding History: A Primer of Historical Method.* New York: Alfred A. Knopf, 1963.

Griswold, Charles L., Jr., *Adam Smith and the Virtues of the Enlightenment.* Cambridge: Cambridge University Press, 1999.

Guillois, Antoine. *La Marquise de Condorcet: Sa Fammile, Son Salon, Ses Amis, 1764–1822.* Paris: Paul Ollendorff, 1897.

Haakonssen, Knud. *The Science of A Legislator: The Natural Jurisprudence of David Hume and Adam Smith.* Cambridge and London: Cambridge University Press, 1981.

Held, Virginia. "The Ethics of Care," *Oxford Handbook for Ethical Theory*, David Copp, ed. (New York: Oxford University Press, 2006), pp. 537–66.

Held, Virginia. *The Ethics of Care: Personal, Political and Global.* Oxford & New York: Oxford University Press, 2006.

Held, Virginia. "Taking Care: Care as Practice and Value," in *Setting the Moral Compass: Essays by Women Philosophers,* Cheshire Calhoun, ed. (Oxford: Oxford University Press: 2004), pp. 59–71.

Held Virginia. "Care and the Extension of Markets." *Hypatia: A Journal of Feminist Philosophy 17* (2002), pp. 19–33.

Held, Virginia. *Feminist Morality: Transforming Culture, Society, and Politics.* Chicago and London: The University of Chicago Press, 1993.

Held, Virginia. "Feminist Transformations of Moral Theory," in *Feminist Ethics,* Moira Gatens, ed. (Brookfield, VT: Aldershot, 1998), pp. 3–26.

Held, Virginia. "Feminism and Moral Theory," in *Women and Moral Theory,* Eva Feder Kittay and Diana T. Meyers, eds. (Totowa, NJ: Rowman & Litterfield Publishers, Inc., 1987), pp. 111–28.

Held, Virginia. "Non Contractual Society," in *Science, Morality & Feminist Theory,* Marsha P. Hanen and Kai Nielsen, eds. (Calgary: The University of Calgary Press, 1987), 111–37.

Held, Virginia. *Rights and Goods: Justifying Social Action.* Chicago and London: The University of Chicago Press, 1984.

Hill, John E. *Democracy, Equality, and Justice: John Adams, Adam Smith and Political Economy.* Lanham and Boulder: Lexington Books, 2007.

Hume, David. *A Treatise of Human Nature*, Selby-Bigge, ed. Oxford: Clarendon Press, 1968.

Hume, David. *Inquiry Concerning the Principles of Morals.* La Salle, Illinois: Open Court, 1966; reprinted from 1777 edition.

Hutchings, Noël and William D. Rumsey, eds. *The Collaborative Bibliography of Women in Philosophy.* Bowling Green, Ohio: Philosophy Documentation Center, Bowling Green State University, 1997.

Jaggar, Alison M. "Love and Knowledge: Emotion in Feminist Epistemology," in *Women, Knowledge and Reality: Explorations In Feminist Philosophy,* Ann Garry and Marilyn Pearsall, eds. (Unwin Hyman, Inc. 1989; New York and London: Routledge, 1992), pp. 166–90.

Jaggar, Alison M. *Feminist Politics and Human Nature.* Sussex: Rowman & Allanheld Publishers, 1983.

Jones, Gareth Stedman. "An End to Poverty: the French Revolution and the Promise of a World Beyond Want." *Historical Research* 78 (2005), pp. 193–207.

Kersey, Ethel M. *Woman Philosophers: A Bio-Critical Source Book*, Calvin O. Schrag, Consulting Editor. New York: Greenwood Press, 1989.

Lagrave, Jean-Paul de. "A propos de Sophie de Grouchy," in Béatrice Didier and Jacques Neefs, editors, *Chantiers Révolutionnaires: Science; Musique, Architecture: manuscrits de la Révolution II* (Saint-Denis: Presses Universitaires de Vincennes, 1992), pp. 47–49.

_____. "L'influence de Sophie de Grouchy sur la pensée de Condorcet," in *Condorcet, mathématicien, économiste, philosophe, homme politique* (Paris: Minerve, 1989), pp. 434–42.

Lefebvre, Georges. *Napoleon From 18 Brumaire to Tilsit, 1799–1807*, Henry F. Stockhold, trans. New York: Columbia University Press, 1969.

Locke John. *An Essay Concerning Human Understanding*, Peter H. Nidditch, ed. Oxford: Clarendon Press, 1988.

Lyons, Nona Plessner. "Two Perspectives: On Self, Relationships, and Morality," *Harvard Educational Review* 53 (1983), pp. 125–45.

Manning, Rita C. *Speaking From the Heart: A Feminist Perspective on Ethics*. USA: Rowman & Littlefield Publishers, Inc., 1992.

McAlister, Linda Lopez, ed. *Hypathia's Daughters: Fifteen Hundred Years of Woman Philosophers*. Bloomington and Indianapolis: Indiana University Press, 1996.

McDonald Lynn. ed., *Women Theorists on Society and Politics*. Waterloo, ON: Wilfrid Laurier University Press, 1998.

Montes, Leonidas and Eric Schliesser, eds. *New Voices on Adam Smith*. London and New York: Routledge, 2006.

Montes, Leonidas. *Adam Smith in Context: A Critical Assessment of Some Central Components of His Thought*. New-York: Palgrave Macmillan, 2004.

_____. "Das Adam Smith Problem: Its Origins, the Stages of the Current Debate, and One Implication for Our Understanding of Sympathy," *Journal of the History of Economic Thought* 25 (2003), pp. 65–90.

Mossner, Ernest Campbell and Ian Simpson Ross eds. *The Correspondence of Adam Smith*. Indianapolis: Liberty Classics, 1987.

Noddings, Nel. *Caring: A Feminine Approach to Ethics & Moral Education*. Berkeley, Los Angeles and London: University of California Press, 1984.

Poirier, Jean-Pierre. *Histoire des femmes de science en France: Du Moyen Age à la Révolution*. Paris: Pygmalion, 2002.

Raphael, D. D. *The Impartial Spectator: Adam Smith's Moral Philosophy.* Oxford and New York: Clarendon Press, Oxford University Press, 2007.

_____. *Moral Philosophy.* Oxford, New York: Oxford University Press, 1987.

_____. *The Moral Sense.* London: Oxford University Press, 1947.

Reeder John. *On Moral Sentiments: Contemporary Responses to Adam Smith.* England: Thoemmes Press, 1997.

Riskin, Jessica. *Science in the Age of Sensibility: The Sentimental Empiricism of the French Enlightenment.* Chicago and London: The University of Chicago Press, 2002.

Ross, Ian Simpson. *The Life of Adam Smith.* Oxford: Clarendon Press, 1995.

Rothschild, Emma. *Economic Sentiments: Adam Smith, Condorcet, and the Enlightenment.* Harvard University Press, 2001.

Ruddick, Sara. *Maternal Thinking: Toward a Politics of Peace.* New York: Ballantine Books, 1989.

Schattschneider, Laura. "Propriety *and* Convenance: Smith and de Grouchy," *Center & Clark Newsletter* 41 (Spring, 2003), pp. 4–5.

Schapiro, Salwyn J. *Condorcet and the Rise of Liberalism.* New York: Octagon Books, 1963.

Skousen, Mark. *The Big Three in Economics: Adam Smith, Karl Marx and John Maynard Keynes.* Armonk, New York: M.E. Sharpe, 2007.

Smith, Adam. *An Inquiry into the Nature and Causes of the Wealth of Nations*, 2 vols. Indianapolis: Liberty Fund, 1981.

Smith, Adam. *Theory of Moral Sentiments.* Indianapolis: Liberty Fund, 1982.

Smith, Adam. *Théorie des sentiments moraux d'Adam Smith,* Michaël Biziou, Claude Gautier, Jean-François Pradeau, eds. and trans. Paris: Presses Universitaires de France, 1999.

Smith, Adam. *Théorie des sentiments moraux,* texte traduit, introduit et annoté par Michaël Biziou, Claude Gautier, Jean-François Pradeau, Édition révisée. Paris: Quadrige/PUF, 2003.

Spelman, Elisabeth. "The Virtue of Feeling and the Feeling of Virtue," in *Feminist Ethics,* Moira Gatens ed. (Brookfield, VT: Aldershot, 1998), pp. 205–24.

Staum, Martin S. *Cabanis: Enlightenment and Medical Philosophy in the French Revolution.* Princeton, New Jersey: Princeton University Press, 1980.

Stephen, Leslie Sir. *History of English Thought In the Eighteenth Century*, 2 vols. New York and Burlingame: Harcourt, Brace & World, Inc., 1962; first published 1876.

Sutton, Geoffrey V. *Science for a Polite Society: Gender, Culture, and the Demonstration of Enlightenment*. Boulder, CO: Westview Press, 1995.

Terrel, Mary. "Emilie du Châtelet and the Gendering of Science," *History of Science* 33 (1995a), pp. 283–310.

_____. "Gendered Spaces, Gendered Audiences: Inside and Outside the Paris Academy of Sciences," *Configurations* 2 (1995b), pp. 207–32.

Tong, Rosmarie. *Feminine and Feminist Ethics*. Belmont, California: Wadsworth Publishing Company, 1993.

Tong, Rosmarie. "Feminist Ethics." *Stanford Encyclopedia of Philosophy*. http://plato.stanford.edu/

Tronto, Joan C. *Moral Boundaries: A Political Argument for and Ethics of Care*. New York and London: Routledge, 1993.

Voltaire. *Philosophical Dictionary*, Theodore Besterman, trans. England: Penguin Classics, 1972.

Voltaire. *Letters Concerning the English Nation*, Nicholas Cronk, ed. Oxford, New York: Oxford University Press, 1994.

Warnock, Mary, ed. *Woman Philosophers*. London, Vermont: Everyman Library, 1996.

Waithe, Mary Ellen. *A History of Woman Philosophers*, 4 vols. Dordrecht/Boston/London: Kluwer Academic Publishers, 1991.

Werhane Patricia H. *Adam Smith and His Legacy for Modern Capitalism.*, New York and Oxford: Oxford University Press 1991.

Zinsser, Judith P. *La Dame d'Esprit: A Biography of the Marquise Du Châtelet, From a Life of Frivolity to a Life of the Mind*. New York: Viking, 2006.

Index

Abstract idea of pain, see pain
Abstraction, power of, 9, 32, 33
Actions, 23, 26-27, 30, 33, 57, 63, 65, 77, 81, 86, 77
Adversity, 9
Affections, 7, 14, 23, 36, 60-61
Altruism, 36, 38
Ambition, 53-54
Anxiety, 10, 40, 45, 59
Approval, 23, 24, 41, 61, 80
Arnold-Tétard, Madeleine, xiii, xiv, xix, xxxiii
Aversion, 9, 23

Bacon, Francis, xxii
Badinter, Elisabeth and Robert, xiv, xxi, xxii, xxix, xxxvi
Baker, Keith Michael, xxi
Behavior, xxiii, 21, 36, 49, 53, 55, 69, 74, 78, 85, 89
Belleguic, Thierry, xvii
Beloved, 60
Beneficence, 17, 41, 47
Benevolence, 39, 41, 44, 47, 48, 51, 52, 58; universal, 40, 42, 46; particular, general 45
Benevolent, 36, 40, 64
Bernier, Marc-André, xvii

Blame, 23, 25
Boissel, Thierry, xiv, xvii, xxi, 64-65
Bonaparte, Napoleon, xxviii-xxix, xxxiv, xxxvi-xxxvii
Brookes, Barbara, xxi

Cabanis, Pierre-Jean-Georges, xiii, xxix, xxx-xxxii, xxxvi, xxxviii, 7-8, 11, 66
Chabot, François, xxvii
Calhoun, Cheshire, 94
Campbell, Thomas D., 14
Capitalism, 58
Care, 6, 11, 22, 23, 36-37, 41-43, 45-46, 52, 56, 66, 68, 71-73, 76-77, 80, 83-85, 88, 91-93, 95-96; capacity for 70; ethics of, see ethics of care
Cared for, 69, 73
Caretakers, 11, 68, 92; and justice, 22, 76, 79
Caring, 37, 40, 42, 45, 68, 69-70, 73, 77-78, 84-85, 88, 91-92, 95-96
Character, 5-6, 23, 25, 62
Childhood, 55, 72
Commerce, 50-51

193

Community, 52, 73
Compassion, 13, 44, 54
Compassionate, 9
Competition, 40, 49
Condillac, Étienne Bonnot de, xxiv
Condorcet, Antoine-Nicolas, xiii, xx, xxi, xxii, xxiv, xxv, xxvii-xxxviii, xxix, xxxii-xxxvii, xxxix, 5-6, 50-51, 56, 74
Conduct, 23, 28, 32, 39, 40, 46, 50, 63, 69, 81, 83
Connected, 16, 37, 46, 64, 72, 80, 86
Connection, 37-38, 40, 42, 44-45, 62, 70, 81-83, 85-86, 93
Conscience, 27, 32-33, 39, 54, 55, 63
Conscientious, 53-54
Contempt, 25
Contextual, 83-84
Contract, 71, 91; social, see social contact theory
Contractarianism, 76 , 68
Contractual, 89, 90, 91
Conveniences, 50, 54, 59, 72
Cooperation, 41, 49, 71, 73
Corruption, xxiv, 53
Crime, 23, 29, 37, 53, 92
Cruelty, 15, 77
Culture, 87-89

d'Alembert, Jean le Rond, xx, xxviii
David, Jacques-Louis, xxxvi
Dawson, Deidre, viii, xiii, xiv, xvii, xvii-xviii, 50, 52-53, 57
Deceive, 54-55; self, see self-deception
Dependency, 11, 45, 72, 76
Dependent, 11, 71-72, 76
Depression, xx, 64-65; see also ennui
Descartes, René, xxii
Deterrence, 25-26
Development, moral, xvi, 17, 32, 68, 72
Discrimination, xxiv, 56
Distance, 40, 43, 54-56, 81-83, 85
Distant, 37-40, 45, 54-55, 78, 80, 83
Distribute, 50, 52
Distribution, 49, 51
Divorce, xxviii, 54
Dread, 20, 23, 25, 60

Duties, 28, 54
Duty, 37-38, 40, 42, 44, 46
Economics, 42, 44, 49, 50, 53-54, 56-58, 90, 91
Economy, 51-52
Education, xxii, xxiv, xxxv, xxxix, 17, 33, 45, 56, 69, 70, 79, 91-92, 96
Egalitarian, xix, xxxix, 52, 57
Egoism, 73, 82, 84, 96
Eltis, Walter, 50
Emotional, 7, 10, 18, 25, 31-32, 34, 44, 48, 63-64, 77, 79, 90, 94-95
Emotions, xxxi, 14-16, 22, 24, 28, 32, 65, 68, 77-78, 81, 83, 86-88, 95; moral, 22, 25, 62, 83, 94
Empathy, 77-78, 84, 91
Empirical, 4, 5, 9, 25, 32, 68, 79, 85-86
Empiricism, xxiv, 5, 33, 86
Emptiness, 63-64
Enlightenment, xiii
Ennui, 64-65; see also depression
Enthusiasm, 17-18, 65, 78, 83
Epistemology, 3; moral, 22; feminist, 76-77
Equal, xxiv, 48-49, 51, 71, 74, 80
Equality, xxi, xxiv, xxxiv, 30, 32, 53, 56, 57, 58, 74-75, 91-92
Ethical, 4, 24, 31, 38, 61, 69, 85; response, 69; see also unethical
Ethics of care, xvi, 67-68, 72-74, 76, 84, 91-92, 94
Evensky, Jerry, 35, 51
Evil, 5, 14, 23, 26-27, 29-30, 55; bodily, 10; and good, see good and evil
Experience, xxiii, 4-6, 9, 11, 14-17, 27, 33-34, 43, 62, 65, 67-69, 79, 82, 85, 86-88, 90-91, 95-96

Famine, 10, 37, 85
Fear, 15, 24-25, 27, 32, 60, 76
Feeling/s, 5, 6- 9, 12-14, 16, 21-30, 32, 37, 39, 43-46, 50, 56, 60-62, 64-65, 69, 77-79, 85-86, 92-93, 95
Feminist, xiii, xxi, xxviii
Fitzgibbons, Athol, 41-42, 58

Fleischacker, Samuel, 35, 44, 48-49, 52, 56-57
Forget, Evelyn, xi, xiii, xvii-xviii, 17, 48
Franklin, Benjamin, xxii, xxxvi
Freedom, xxxiv, 56, 71, 74, 91
Freteau, Marie-Gilberte-Henriette, xix

Garat, Maillia, xxxv
Gay, Peter, xxx, xxxii
Gender, 64, 87-88, 91, 94-96
Generosity, 24, 57
Gilligan, Carol, 68
Giving, 61, 64
Global, 42, 46, 84-85, 91
God, 20, 41, 60
Good, 5, 15, 20, 24-27, 29-39, 31, 40-41, 55, 59, 61, 63, 65, 70, 77, 82, 89, 96; and evil, 5, 29-30, 33, 76, 82
Goodness, 20, 23, 93
Gottschalk, Louis, 67
Government, 88, 92
Gratitude, 24, 28, 62
Greed, 54
Griswold, Charles, 35, 44, 52
Grouchy, Charlotte de, xix, xxix
Grouchy, Henri-Francois de, xix
Guillois, Antoine, xiv, xix, xx, xxxviii, 6

Haakonssen, Knud, 44
Habit, 55, 59, 78, 82, 95
Habitual, 17, 27, 45, 65
Habituated, 36
Happiness, xxx, 4, 11, 16, 25, 40, 41, 44-45, 59-66, 69, 74, 92, 96
Harm, 14-15, 27, 30, 48, 95
Harmful, 75
Harming, 9, 25, 27
Hatred, 23, 25, 60, 81, 83; self, see self-hatred
Heart, 23, 28, 32, 39, 54-56, 59, 60-61, 65, 75, 89
Held, Virginia, 67-68, 72, 74, 76-77, 84-93, 95
Helevtius, Claude-Adrien, xxiv
Help, 9, 11, 12, 14-16, 25, 37, 39, 45-46, 83, 85
Helping, 27, 35, 61, 64
Helpless, 71, 90
Hill, John, 52, 58

Household, 87-88
Human being, 11, 14, 23, 45, 72-73
Human morality, 5, 20, 25, 42, 68, 70, 76
Human nature, xxx, xxxii, 20, 32, 36, 38, 42, 53-54, 59, 66, 71-74
Human relations, 11, 48, 60, 70, 89, 90
Humane, 38, 57
Humanitarian 57
Humanity, 11, 32, 37, 39, 43-45, 48, 55, 57, 60-61, 75, 78, 89, 92
Hume, David, xxiii, 5, 20-22, 29, 70, 94
Hutchings, Noel, xvi

Ideas, general and abstract, 9, 26, 32-33, 43-44, 79, 85
Ideas, moral, 4-5, 31-33
Ideologues, xiii, xxviii, xxxiv
Illegal, 56
Imagination, 10-13, 15-17, 62
Impartial spectator, 16-17, 24-25, 27, 29, 37, 39, 42-44, 46, 57, 81, 83-84
Impartial, 80, 83-84
Impartiality, 79, 81-85, see also partiality
Impressionable, 6, 30
Impressions, 5-7, 9, 26, 43-44, 65
Impropriety, 14
Independent, 71, 73-75, 80, 90
Individualism, 37, 41, 42, 46, 52, 70-72, 74-75, 80, 91
Individualistic, 36, 73-74
Industry, 51
Inequality, xxiv, 48, 52-56, 94
Infants, 68, 79, 92
Injury, 6, 25, 31, 47, 51
Injustice, xv, 24, 30-31, 42, 47, 53, 55, 75, 92
Instinct, 8, 17, 27, 89
Intention, 14, 76; see also unintentional
Interdependent, 72, 75, 80
Interests, 25, 37-41, 43, 51, 55, 61, 71, 81-82, 84-85, 90-91
Invisible hand, 35, 48-51

Jaggar, Alison, 71, 73, 76-77, 79
Jefferson, Thomas, xxii
Jones, Gareth Stedman, 50

Judgment, 12, 14, 21, 22, 23, 29, 32, 77, 80-81, 83; self and others, 37, 81, 83
Judgment, moral, 12, 24, 39, 44-45, 93
Just, 30-32, 53, 62, 64, 75, 78, 80; see also unjust
Justice, 20, 22, 30-31, 41, 44, 46-49, 51-58, 74, 76, 79-80, 88, 93; see also care and justice

Kant, Immanuel, xxiii
Kirwan, Richard, xxxvi
Kuiper, Edith, xvii

Lagrave, Jean-Paul de, ix, xiii, xiv, xxi, xxxv, xxxviii, xxxix
Lavoisier, Antoine-Laurent, pp. xxix, xxxvi
Lavoisier, Marie-Anne Paulze, Madame, xxxv-xxxvi, xxxix
Laws, xxxiv, 8, 32, 50-54, 56, 63, 88 92, 94
Legal system, 53, 55, 94
Legislation, xxviii, xxxiv, 43, 51- 56, 58, 75
Legislator, 44, 50, 75
Liberal, xxiv, 52, 67, 71, 73-76, 89, 91
Liberalism, xix, 47, 70, 72, 73-74
Liberty, xxxiv, 49, 56
Locke, John, xxii-xxiv, xxx-xxxi, xxviii, 3-5, 9, 33, 86
Love, 10, 23, 25, 31, 37, 42, 47, 50, 53-54, 59-64, 68-69, 76
Lyons, Nona Plessner, 79-81, 83

Manning, Rita, 70, 72-73, 78, 84-85, 94-95
Market, 49-53, 57, 90, 91
Marriage, 53-54
McDonald, Lynn, xvii
Memory, 6, 14, 26-27, 69; painful, 6 26
Merit, 14-15, 23, 53, 60; demerit, 14
Michelet, Jules, xiv
Miserable, 13, 63
Misery, 23, 38, 40, 45, 60, 65, 89
Misfortune, 14, 39, 40, 55, 64
Money, 53, 59
Montes, Leonidas, 12, 35, 42, 50, 58
Montesquieu, Charles de Secondat, baron de, xxiii

Moral, theory, 3, 5, 9-10, 20, 29, 33, 35, 37, 41, 46, 57, 67, 69, 74-75, 84, 86-90, 94-95; motivation, 14, 22, 26, 45, 46, 80; ideas, 4-5, 31-33; development, 17, 32, 68, 72; agent, 32, 63, 71; experience, 85-87; epistemology, 22; understanding, 77; presence, 9-10; tendency, 68; judgment, see judgment moral; emotions, see emotions moral.
Mother, 69, 90-91, 96
Mothering, 89-91, 95-96
Murder, 20, 23-24, 28-29, 47

Napoleon, see Bonaparte
Natural liberty, see liberty
Necessities, 49, 52, 72
Necker, Jacques, xxxvi
Need, 11, 45, 47, 53, 56, 65, 71, 80, 90-93
Nervous system, 7
Network, 44, 74, 84
Newton, Isaac, xxii
Noddings, Nel, 69-70, 74, 78
Non rational, 18, 32, 76

Obligation, 17, 39, 42, 43, 45, 46, 70, 85, 95
Oppression, 37, 51, 54, 75, 82, 88, 93
Organs, xxxi, 6-7, 9, 43-44

Pain, 6-7, 9-11, 14-17, 25-26, 28, 30-31, 36, 43-44, 48, 63, 69, 82; abstract idea of, 9, 26, 43; and pleasure, see pleasure and pain
Paine, Thomas, xxii, xxv, xxii, xxvii, xxxix
Parsimony, 41, 46
Partiality, 38-39, 81, 83-84, see also impartiality
Particular others, 84-85
Passion/s, xxiv, 7, 10, 13, 14-16, 18, 23, 33, 36, 40, 42, 54, 62, 74-75, 79, 83, 96
Paulze, Marie-Anne, see Lavoisier, Madame
Peace, 63-4, 91-92
Perfection, xxv, 36, 60
Persons, 37, 48, 71-73, 75, 86, 90-91, 93

Physiology, 6
Pleasure, 4-6, 14, 17, 25-27, 30, 36, 38, 55, 60-63, 65; and pain, 4-5, 7, 8, 11, 25, 27, 33, 65, 77, 86
Poor, 13, 48-49, 50-52, 54, 55, 76, 89
Poverty, 43, 48, 50, 84-85, 89
Praise, 23, 25, 60
Prejudice, xxiv, 33, 56, 63, 82, 92
Principles, 28, 32, 52, 57, 69, 87
Private, 52
Privilege, 74
Progress, xxiv, xxxii, xxxiv, 16, 31, 52, 54, 57, 93, 97
Property, 54, 74, 94
Propriety, 14, 16, 24-25, 57, 81
Prudence, 15, 41, 46
Public spirit, 50, 57
Public/private, 88, 93

Racism, 77, 86
Radical, xix
Raphael, David Daiches, 17, 21, 31
Rational, xxii, 8, 20-21, 27-28, 30-32, 41, 46, 57, 68, 71, 76-77, 87; see also non-rational
Rationalism, 21, 22, 28-29, 31, 34, 68, 94
Reason, xxiii, 19-34, 39, 46, 63-65, 75-79, 88
Reciprocal, 42, 79
Reciprocity, 80
Recollection, 6, 26-28, 30, 43
Redistribution, 48, 51-52, 65-57
Reeder, John, xv
Reflection, xxiii, 4-5, 23, 30-33, 44, 48, 52, 65, 78, 83
Reform, xxi, xxiv, xxv, 51, 54, 94
Regret, 22-23, 26-27, 32
Relation/s, 11, 14, 37, 45, 48, 57, 60, 62-64, 70, 74, 76, 80, 82, 85, 89-93
Relational, 36, 42, 71-73, 76, 91
Relationship/s, 28, 36, 45-46, 54, 60-61, 63, 69, 70, 72-73, 75, 77, 79-81, 83-84, 86, 89, 90, 96
Religion, xxiii, 20, 59
Remorse, 15, 22-27, 31, 54-55, 64
Remote, 40, 42-43, 45, 47, 60, 69; see also strangers
Resentment, 31, 29, 62

Resources, 51
Response, 10, 16, 69, 73, 76, 78, 80
Rich, 48, 50-51, 53-56, 60, 65
Right and wrong, 22, 27, 30, 33, 46, 75, 77
Rights, xxi, xxiv, xxxix, 27, 30, 32, 51, 53, 56, 71, 74-76, 85, 88, 91-93
Riskin, Jessica, xvi, 19
Robespierre, Maximilien, xxvii-xxviii
Ross, Ian Simpson, xv
Rothschild, Emma, 19, 35, 49, 52, 57
Rousseau, Jean-Jacques, xxiii
Ruddick, Sara, 91, 95
Rules, 28-32, 42-43, 46-47, 77, 83, 85
Rumsey, William, xvi

Satisfaction, 14, 24, 26,-27, 30, 64
Schattschneider, Laura, xvii
Scorn, 23, 25, 60
Scottish philosophers, 8
Self, separate/connected, 72, 80
Self-command, 46, 57
Self-control, 57, 83
Self-correction, 24
Self-deceit, 24, 55,
Self-denial, 57
Self-hatred, 64
Self-interest, 35, 38, 41-43, 51, 53, 73-74, 79, 82, 84, 90-91
Selfish, 4, 24, 35-36, 39-40, 42-43, 64, 82
Selfishness, 35-38, 41-43, 48, 73-75, 81-82, 85
Self-judgment, 37, 81, 83
Self-love, 39, 41-42, 53, 74
Self-neglect, 42
Self-restraint, 49
Self-sufficient, 71, 72, 90
Sensationalism, xxiv, xxv, xxviii, 3, 8, 11, 16, 33, 65
Sensations, xxiii, xxix, xxxi, 4-8, 10-12, 15, 16, 26, 28, 33, 36, 43, 61, 65, 86
Sensibility, xxxi, xxxii, 7-8, 17, 19, 30, 64, 78, 96
Sensible, 4, 15, 41
Sensitive, 7, 15, 69, 90
Sensitivity, 6, 9, 14, 17, 33, 44, 52, 91

Sentient beings, 5, 41, 44
Sentiment/s, xvi, 7-34, 38, 40-41, 44, 46, 48, 55-57, 59, 61-62, 69-70, 75-83, 92, 95
Sentimentalism, 11, 28, 21, 22, 31, 34
Sexism, xv, 77, 96
Sketch for a Historical Picture of the Progress of the Human Mind, xxvii, 5, 50
Skousen, Mark, 49
Slavery, xxi
Social action, 31, 96
Social beings, 37, 41 see also unsocial
Social bonds, 48, 90
Social classes, 54
Social consciousness, 94
Social context, 22, 71
Social contract theory, 20, 71, 75-76
Social institutions, 42, 43, 53-54, 70-71, 74, 88
Social justice, 54, 74, 76, 88; injustice, 92
Social progress, 54, 93
Social reform, 45-46, 56, 58, 93, 97
Social relations, 48, 63, 74, 90-91
Social scorn, see scorn
Social status, 53
Social structure, 55, 70, 92
Socially constructed, 43, 76
Solipsism, 71
Sorrow, 3-4, 8
Spelman, Elisabeth, 95
Staël, Germaine de, xxxvi, xxxvii-xxxix
Staum, Martin, xxxiv
Stephen, Leslie, Sir, 19-20
Strangers, 37, 43-44; see also remote
Subsistence, 53, 57
Suffer, 6, 9, 26, 62, 65, 69-70

Sufferer, 10, 12, 15-16, 44, 48
Suffering, 5-6, 8-10, 13, 15-16, 18, 37, 40, 43-44, 55, 60, 75, 77-78, 80, 89; bodily, 10, 18

Taxes, 51-52
Thomson, Benjamin (Count Rumford), xxxvi
Tong, Rosemarie, 72, 94
Torture, 12, 27, 55
Trade, free, 50
Tronto, Joan, 92
Trust, 63, 91

Unethical, 63
Unintentional, 49
Unjust, 29-30, 32, 51, 53-55, 78
Unsocial, 36, 83

Values, 71, 73-77, 79, 91, 94
Vanity, 53-54, 96
Vices, 22, 54
Victim, 23, 25, 31, 78
Vigée-Lebrun, Marie-Anne-Élisabeth, xix
Violence, 15, 95
Virtues, 25, 41-42, 46-47, 51-54, 57, 63
Voltaire (François-Marie Arouet), xxiii, 17

Wages, 50-51
Waithe, Mary Ellen, xvi
War, 86, 91, 95
Wealth, 48, 50-53, 56-57, 59, 92
Welfare, 11, 40, 48, 50, 52
Well-being, 63, 66, 69-70, 72, 74, 80, 91
Werhane, Patricia H., 41, 49, 50, 52
Wollstonecraft, Mary, xxxviii-xxxix
Women, xv, xvi, xxi, xxviii, xxxiv, 54, 57, 67, 72, 74, 87-88, 91, 94-96